FREE VIDEO   FREE   FREE VIDEO

Essential Test Tips Video from Trivium Test Prep

Dear Customer,

Thank you for purchasing from Trivium Test Prep! We're honored to help you prepare for your PECT exam.

To show our appreciation, we're offering a **FREE *PECT Special Education Essential Test Tips* Video by Trivium Test Prep.*** Our video includes 35 test preparation strategies that will make you successful on the PECT exam. All we ask is that you email us your feedback and describe your experience with our product. Amazing, awful, or just so-so: we want to hear what you have to say!

To receive your **FREE *PECT Special Education Essential Test Tips* Video**, please email us at 5star@triviumtestprep.com. Include "Free 5 Star" in the subject line and the following information in your email:

1. The title of the product you purchased.
2. Your rating from 1 – 5 (with 5 being the best).
3. Your feedback about the product, including how our materials helped you meet your goals and ways in which we can improve our products.
4. Your full name and shipping address so we can send your **FREE *PECT Special Education Essential Test Tips* Video**.

If you have any questions or concerns please feel free to contact us directly at 5star@triviumtestprep.com.

Thank you!

– Trivium Test Prep Team

*To get access to the free video please email us at 5star@triviumtestprep.com, and please follow the instructions above.

PECT Special Education PreK–8 and 7–12 Study Guide:

Comprehensive Review with Practice Exam Questions for the Pennsylvania Educator Certification Tests

J.G. Cox

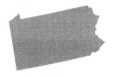

Table of Contents

Online Resources i

Introduction iii

ONE: Student Growth and Development...1

    DEVELOPMENTAL STAGES AND MILESTONES...1

    SOCIO-EMOTIONAL DEVELOPMENT...2

    COGNITIVE DEVELOPMENT 7

    LANGUAGE DEVELOPMENT 11

    PHYSICAL DEVELOPMENT 15

    STUDENT LEARNING 18

    MOTIVATION 22

TWO: Disability Categories 31

    DIAGNOSING DISABILITIES..31

    SPECIFIC LEARNING DISABILITIES 32

    SPEECH OR LANGUAGE IMPAIRMENT 38

    OTHER HEALTH IMPAIRMENTS 44

    AUTISM SPECTRUM DISORDER 53

    DEVELOPMENTAL DELAY...63

    INTELLECTUAL DISABILITIES..65

    EMOTIONAL DISTURBANCE 72

    MULTIPLE DISABILITIES 79

    DEAFNESS AND HEARING LOSS 83

    ORTHOPEDIC IMPAIRMENT 90

    BLINDNESS AND VISUAL IMPAIRMENT..95

    DEAF-BLINDNESS 101

    TRAUMATIC BRAIN INJURY 106

THREE: Planning and the Learning Environment 119

LESSON PLANNING 119

ORGANIZING THE LEARNING ENVIRONMENT 125

MANAGING STUDENT BEHAVIOR 128

CLASSROOM MANAGEMENT 138

FOUR: Instruction 149

INSTRUCTIONAL MODELS AND STRATEGIES 149

UNIVERSAL DESIGN FOR LEARNING 161

CO-TEACHING STRATEGIES 163

FIVE: Assessment

MEASUREMENT CONCEPTS 171

STANDARDIZED ASSESSMENTS 172

TYPES OF ASSESSMENTS 179

INTERPRETING AND USING ASSESSMENT RESULTS 187

SIX: Reading Instruction 197

LANGUAGE AND READING DEVELOPMENT 197

SPECIALIZED INSTRUCTIONAL STRATEGIES 207

SEVEN: Transition 225

TRANSITION PLANNING 225

RESOURCES FOR STUDENTS WITH DISABILITIES 230

EIGHT: Professional Responsibilities 237

ROLES AND RESPONSIBILITIES 237

FEDERAL LEGISLATION AND REQUIREMENTS 238

DETERMINATION OF ELIGIBILITY 245

INDIVIDUALIZED EDUCATION PROGRAM 248

SPECIAL EDUCATION IN PRIVATE SCHOOLS 252

COLLABORATION 253

BIAS ISSUES 259

IMPACT OF FAMILY SYSTEMS OF INDIVIDUALS WITH DISABILITIES 261

ENVIRONMENTAL AND SOCIAL INFLUENCES ON INDIVIDUALS
WITH DISABILITIES 263

NINE: Practice Test 271

ANSWER KEY 291

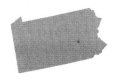

Online Resources

To help you fully prepare for your PECT Special Education exam, Cirrus includes online resources with the purchase of this study guide.

To access these materials, please enter the following URL into your browser: **www.cirrustestprep.com/pect-special-education-online-resources**.

PRACTICE TEST

In addition to the practice test included in this book, we also offer an online exam. Since many exams today are computer-based, getting to practice your test-taking skills on the computer is a great way to prepare.

FLASH CARDS

A convenient supplement to this study guide, Cirrus's e-flash cards enable you to review important terms easily on your computer or smartphone.

FROM STRESS TO SUCCESS

Watch *From Stress to Success*, a brief but insightful YouTube video that offers the tips, tricks, and secrets experts use to score higher on the exam.

REVIEWS

Leave a review, send us helpful feedback, or sign up for Cirrus's promotions—including free books!

Introduction

Congratulations on choosing to take the Pennsylvania Educator Certification Tests (PECT) Special Education PreK–8 exam! By purchasing this book, you've taken the first step toward becoming a special education teacher.

This guide will provide you with a detailed overview of the PECT, so you know exactly what to expect on test day. We'll take you through all the concepts covered on the test and give you the opportunity to test your knowledge with practice questions. Even if it's been a while since you last took a major test, don't worry; we'll make sure you're more than ready!

WHAT IS THE PECT?

The PECT Special Education exam is a part of teaching licensure in Pennsylvania. PECT scores are used to complete a state application for teacher certification. The assessment ensures that the examinee has the skills and knowledge necessary to become a special education teacher in Pennsylvania public schools.

WHAT'S ON THE PECT?

The PECT is a multiple-choice test designed to assess whether you possess the knowledge and skills necessary to become a special education teacher in Pennsylvania. The PECT Special Education PreK–8 exam is a computer-based assessment with two modules. Each of the modules has forty-one multiple-choice questions and a sixty-minute time limit. If you choose to take both of the modules in one testing session, you will have a fifteen-minute break between modules. The questions are single-select multiple-choice with a single correct answer and contain both scenario-based and general-knowledge questions.

MODULE 1

What's on the PECT Module 1?			
Subject	**Subtopics**	**Number of Questions***	**Percentage**
Foundations and Professional Practice	▶ Historical, philosophical, and legal foundations, and professional/ethical roles of special education teachers ▶ Collaboration with team members, students, and families	13 – 14	33%
Understanding Students with Disabilities	▶ Atypical/typical human growth and development and characteristics of students with disabilities ▶ Factors affecting learning development and daily living in students with disabilities	13 – 14	33%
Assessment and Program Planning and Implementation	▶ Characteristics, selection, use of, and results of assessments ▶ IFSPs/IEPs, behavior plans, and designing specially designed curricula and instruction	13 – 14	33%
Total		**41**	**60 minutes**

*Numbers are approximate.

The Foundations and Professional Practice subarea focuses on legislation such as FERPA, IDEA, ESEA, and HIPAA; recent trends and issues in special education; and various other foundations of providing special education services such as RtII, SDI, UDL, and LRE, among others. This subarea also focuses on professionalism, ethics, advocacy, and professional growth. Additionally, it focuses on working with other team members, families, and the community. This might include co-teaching, referral to outside agencies, and forming and maintaining myriad relationships with various members of the school, community, students' families, and outside agencies in support of students with disabilities.

The Understanding Students with Disabilities subarea focuses on the various domains of human development and the characteristics and identification criteria of children with disabilities. It also assesses knowledge of the educational and medical implications of different disabilities and how families and teachers impact students with disabilities. This subarea also focuses on school readiness and lifelong implications without early interventions.

The Assessment and Program Planning and Implementation subarea focuses on all matters related to the use of both formal and informal assessments with students with disabilities as well as interpreting and using assessment data. It also focuses on creation and use of IFSPs, IEPs, behavioral intervention plans, and many other types of specialized planning and instruction. This might include SDI, modifications and accommodations, use of Alternate Academic Standards, and many other types of specialized instruction appropriate for students with disabilities.

MODULE 2

What's on the PECT Module 2?			
Subject	**Subtopics**	**Number of Questions***	**Percentage**
Inclusive Learning Environments	▶ Planning, managing, and modifying learning environments and strategies for positive behavioral interventions and supports ▶ Fostering receptive/expressive communication and social skills ▶ Teaching independent and functional living skills and promoting successful transitions	20 – 21	50%
Delivery of Specially Designed Instruction	▶ Foundations of reading instruction for students with disabilities ▶ Literacy instruction for students with disabilities ▶ Specially designed instruction (SDI) to promote content-area learning	20 – 21	50%
Total		**41**	**60 minutes**

Numbers are approximate.

The Inclusive Learning Environments subarea assesses knowledge of optimal learning environments including LRE, addressing barriers to accessibility and acceptance, classroom management and tiered behavioral interventions, and use of FBAs as well as positive behavioral interventions. It also focuses on developing communication skills in students through various instructional strategies, use of AAC systems and devices, and overall language development. This subarea further assesses knowledge of vocational and career-focused instruction and functional living skills as well as transitions between learning environments.

The Delivery of Specially Designed Instruction subarea covers various topics pertaining to reading and literacy instruction and intervention as well as the use of SDI across the content areas, including mathematics and generalization skills.

How is the PECT Scored?

Each multiple-choice question is worth one raw point. The total number of questions you answer correctly is added up to obtain your raw score. This raw score is then used to create a scaled score from 100 to 300. The minimum passing score for each module is a scaled score of 220.

Keep in mind that a small number of selected-response questions are experimental and will not count toward your overall score. ETS uses these to test out new questions for future exams. However, as those questions are not indicated on the test, you must respond to every question.

There is no penalty for guessing on the test, so be sure to eliminate answer choices and answer every question. If you still don't know the answer, guess; you may get it right!

Your preliminary results are available after your test session ends. Formal score reports are available in your account within ten days after testing. Scores are automatically reported to the Pennsylvania Department of Education and to the program where you will complete your certification as indicated upon registration.

How is the PECT Administered?

The PECT is a computer-based test offered continuously at a range of universities and testing centers throughout Pennsylvania and the nation. It may be taken in its individual modules, or both modules can be taken together with a fifteen-minute break in between. Check https://home.pearsonvue.com/ for more information. You will need to print your registration ticket from your online account and bring it, along with your identification, to the testing site on test day. No pens, pencils, erasers, or calculators are allowed. However, a list of PECT acronyms will be made available to you during the testing. You may take the test once every twenty-one days.

About Cirrus Test Prep

Cirrus Test Prep study guides are designed by current and former educators and are tailored to meet your needs as an incoming educator. Our guides offer all of the resources necessary to help you pass teacher certification tests across the nation.

Cirrus clouds are graceful, wispy clouds characterized by their high altitude. Just like cirrus clouds, Cirrus Test Prep's goal is to help educators "aim high" when it comes to obtaining their teacher certification and entering the classroom.

ABOUT THIS GUIDE

This guide will help you master the most important test topics and also develop critical test-taking skills. We have built features into our books to prepare you for your tests and increase your score. Along with a detailed summary of the test's format, content, and scoring, we offer an in-depth overview of the content knowledge required to pass the test. Our sidebars provide interesting information, highlight key concepts, and review content so that you can solidify your understanding of the exam's concepts. Test your knowledge with sample questions and detailed answer explanations in the text that help you think through the problems on the exam, and practice questions that reflect the content and format of the PECT. We're pleased you've chosen Cirrus to be a part of your professional journey!

Student Growth and Development

DEVELOPMENTAL STAGES AND MILESTONES

Children are constantly growing and changing. This growth and change happens at different rates depending on the individual child. However, there are some established time frames within which most children will be able to complete certain tasks or exhibit certain behaviors. These tasks or behaviors that occur within a certain age range are called **developmental milestones**. It is important for educators to be familiar with common developmental milestones so that they can provide appropriate referrals and interventions when milestones are not met.

Developmental delays and disabilities are most properly diagnosed by trained professionals. However, one of the most frequent indications of atypical development is the loss of skills the child once had. Because of this, it is essential that teachers, particularly those who work with very young children, track student development over the course of time. Checklists are vital tools and can be helpful as teachers observe students and determine which skills each child has mastered. However, this should not be the only tool used to track development across domains. Ongoing portfolios, observational records, and frequent informal assessments should be used to ensure that students are continuing to develop throughout the year. Each developmental domain—socio-emotional, cognitive, language, and physical—should be observed and recorded for each student at the prekindergarten level and per the individual school and district guidelines for other grade levels as appropriate.

DID YOU KNOW?

More than 2 percent of children ages six to eleven were previously diagnosed with a developmental delay but are no longer classified with a specific disability. Many children make tremendous gains through early identification and intervention.

The developmental milestones discussed in this chapter reflect typical child development; however, many students may already have individualized education programs (IEPs) in place that specify different milestones. Students who have atypical development or a diagnosed disability or delay may need a variety of interventions from many providers to address different developmental domains.

It is important to not have expectations for children in one domain of development that are based on another. A five-year-old child receiving speech therapy for a language delay, for example, may or may not experience problems in socio-emotional and cognitive development. Conversely, a fifth grader with a diagnosed emotional disturbance may still excel cognitively. One must make every effort to see the nuanced way in which each domain is both interconnected and distinct for each individual child.

Socio–Emotional Development

A child's socio-emotional development will be dependent upon many factors. These include the child's overall environment (school/childcare, community, availability of resources), family risk factors (low socio-economic status, chemical dependency, abuse, and so forth), and factors internal to the child, such as overall temperament and health. Teachers will encounter students with a variety of past educational experiences which may or may not have helped them develop appropriate social interactions and emotional regulation. In spite of these variables, there are some general **developmental milestones** in the domain of socio-emotional growth that can help determine where a child fits on the spectrum of typical development. It should be kept in mind that even if socio-emotional development happens on a continuum, different children will progress at different rates. This is not always indicative of a behavioral or developmental disability.

Age Three

At age three, most children who are developing at a typical rate will show an increasing degree of **independence**. This is generally exhibited by easy separation from parents when dropped off at familiar places, such as school or the home of a close relative, and the ability to dress, undress, and feed oneself appropriately. Some three-year-olds also have an increasing desire to complete many tasks on their own and might begin to refuse the help of parents or teachers while they are trying new things. While they are more adaptable to changes in schedule and routine than their younger counterparts, three-year-olds will still need reliable, consistent routines as deviations from such routines are likely to cause an emotional response.

Three-year-olds will also show an increasing desire to participate in social interactions, both with peers and adults. They may copy the actions or speech of adults and friends whom they admire and will enjoy entertaining others and receiving attention. Three-year-olds will also begin to take turns while participating in games or activities with others. However, they often have a very clear understanding of possession in "mine," "hers," and so on, and sharing might be an issue in certain situations.

Additionally, they will often and spontaneously show affection toward peers and adults and may also seek to comfort a friend who is crying. They will, themselves, likely express a wide range of emotions, from anger, fear, and frustration to excitement and joy. While three-year-olds will express a wide range of emotions, they may not always be aware of the emotions they are experiencing or the best means of expression. This still-developing **emotional competence,** or the ability to recognize and express emotions appropriately, will need to be continually nurtured by adults.

AGE FOUR

By age four, the typically developing child will become increasingly independent in relation to parents and will crave more social interaction. By this age, most pre-kindergartners will prefer playing with others as opposed to playing alone. These students will also be more cooperative when they play and will often enjoy dramatic play and make-believe scenarios. While participation in make-believe play is a very important part of the development of more mature play for the typically developing child, four-year-old students are not always aware of, nor should they be expected to be aware of, the line between reality and fantasy. Though prekindergartners may not always fully understand the full scope and implications of classroom rules, they

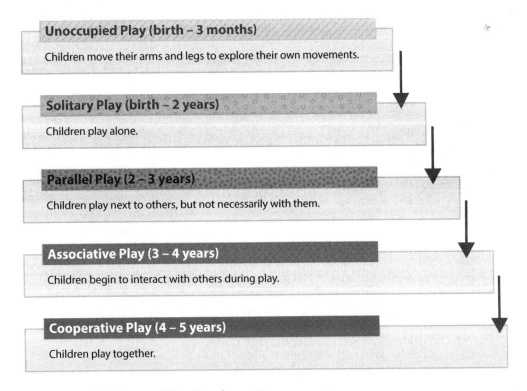

Figure 1.1. Typical Stages of Play Development

should be able to recognize situations and behaviors that are unsafe or dangerous, such as being left outside alone on the playground or walking out into a busy street.

KINDERGARTEN

By kindergarten or age five, the typically developing child will now understand with much more accuracy what is real and what is make-believe. He or she will also generally strive for even more social interaction and acceptance from a peer group and will often initiate play and conversation with peers. This will involve attempts to be included and well-liked. Typically developing five-year-olds are also increasingly independent, often seeking out new and varied environments, such as a friend's house or a new park or playground. Children of this age are also increasingly likely to understand and follow classroom rules and procedures. However, students of this age may vacillate between being highly cooperative and highly uncooperative, and this is expected.

FIRST GRADE

By first grade, most children developing at a typical rate will continue to become more independent while simultaneously seeking attention from both adults and peers. At this age, their circle of friends may expand, contract, or change with some frequency. This will likely be part of a growing awareness and understanding of their own feelings and positive and negative emotions and a growing ability to recognize and react to the hurt feelings of others. They will continue to work at developing positive relationships with peers and will generally continue to increase their ability to solve conflicts with friends and classmates without adult intervention. Building upon the appreciation for rules and procedures established earlier, first graders generally understand rules and norms but may seek out particular "gray areas" in which they might evade a particular regulation in order to get what they want.

> **QUICK REVIEW**
>
> What type of social interaction with a peer group would you expect to see in a prekindergarten classroom? A kindergarten classroom? A first-grade lunchroom?

SECOND AND THIRD GRADES

By the second and third grades, most typically developing children will continue to seek out social interactions and may desire to join formal sports teams, clubs, or informal friend groups. While they will likely spend the bulk of their time with peers, they will need significant encouragement from parents, particularly when insecurities and feelings of lack of belonging become issues. Like younger children, second and third graders generally vacillate between being highly cooperative and agreeable to being somewhat selfish. By this age, most students will cease to be entirely egocentric and be able to appreciate the viewpoints of others. This ability to understand and share in the feelings of others is known as **empathy**. The development of empathy in early elementary school is critical to a student's future ability to build and maintain positive social relationships with adults and peers.

FOURTH AND FIFTH GRADES

By fourth or fifth grade, most typically developing children will have learned many of the skills they need to be successful in the classroom, but they may still try to find ways to test boundaries. They will usually form very strong friendships but may still struggle with acceptance into a peer group and overall self-esteem. Some children will also develop a first crush at this age, though this certainly varies from child to child.

Table 1.1. Milestones in Socio-Emotional Development

Age/Grade	Milestones
Three years old	able to separate from parents in familiar situations
	able to take turns
	shows affection
	able to dress, undress, and feed self
	increasing independence—may refuse help
Four years old	prefers play with peers to playing alone
	will enjoy make-believe
	able to recognize unsafe behaviors
Kindergarten	knows the difference between real and make-believe (most of the time)
	initiates play and conversation
	wants to visit a friend's house
	can understand classroom rules
First grade	changing circle of friends
	ability to recognize feelings in others
	can solve some conflicts with peers without adult help
	understands the rules and norms of most situations
Second and third grades	development of empathy
	seeks out social interaction
	spends the bulk of their social time with peers
	may feel insecure at times and need reassurance
Fourth and fifth grades	may develop a first crush (or pretend to have one)
	may have very strong friendships, such as a "best friend"
	has most social skills needed to be successful in the classroom

It is important to note that even though the typically developing child will go through milestones of socio-emotional development in a somewhat linear fashion, there is no single course. Furthermore, all children, whether they are developing typically or atypically in this domain, need very frequent modeling, support, and reinforcement from teachers to develop these skills. It should also be noted that some children have more opportunities for social interaction with peers than others, and expectations should be adjusted accordingly. A five-year-old kindergarten student, for example, who has never before attended school or been in a similar social environment with other children, will likely need more scaffolding and teacher support to engage in appropriate social interactions. Additionally, a child's home environment may be markedly different from that of the school, and a period of adjustment may cause some disruption across the developmental continuum. A child from a very permissive household who enrolls in a school with very specific rules and procedures may struggle initially.

> **DID YOU KNOW?**
>
> Even though screening rates are roughly equal, boys are more likely to have an identified developmental delay than girls.

Students who do show consistent atypical development in the socio-emotional domain should be referred to a professional for appropriate interventions. Sometimes, these signs may be indicative of a delay in another domain, or they may be related to an environmental situation. For example, a student with atypical speech and language development may not initiate play with peers due to challenges in communication. As another example, a student who has been in foster care in many homes may cry when dropped off at school longer than is typical. It is important that the entirety of a child's situation be considered but that professionals be consulted when appropriate since early intervention can often make a tremendous impact on the future course of a child's life.

SAMPLE QUESTIONS

1) Which of the following describes atypical development for a first-grade student?

   A. frequent changes in the friend group

   B. recurring fear and crying when dropped off at school by a parent

   C. challenging rules, such as the established bedtime

   D. a desire to do many things independently

2) By what grade do most typically developing children form an understanding of the difference between reality and make-believe?

   A. preschool (age three)

   B. prekindergarten (age four)

   C. kindergarten

   D. first grade

COGNITIVE DEVELOPMENT

Students in any classroom, be it a classroom designed for specific needs or simply a general education classroom, will develop different cognitive abilities at different rates. However, there are some milestones of cognitive development that can be used as baselines for the typically developing child. As with socio-emotional development, the whole child should be considered when determining the need for interventions, and educators should be weary of labeling developmental delays based on a single or finite number of criteria.

AGE THREE

At three years old, most typically developing children should have the cognitive capacity to play with toys that have moving parts, such as buttons, levers, and components that move or fit together. However, they may only be able to complete puzzles with few pieces (perhaps three or four). They may not quite yet understand the concept of *three* or *four* but should have some understanding of the idea of *two* in that it is more than *one*. They will typically enjoy playing make-believe with a wide variety of toys, from dolls to trucks and animals. Though they may not fully understand all concepts of print, they will generally be able to turn the pages of an appropriately designed book one at a time. They will also usually be able to copy some shapes or forms with a crayon or large pencil, but this will be limited to very basic shapes, such as a circle or square. Three-year-old children can also typically figure out most simple mechanisms, such as how to remove the lid from a container or jar and how to turn the handle to open a door.

AGE FOUR

By age four, children will be able to name and identify some colors, shapes, and numbers though they may not be able to count all the way to ten. They will generally understand the concepts of same and different and be able to sort some objects by shape or color or class (animals versus cars, for example) but might not yet understand that an upside-down triangle is the same as a triangle that is right-side up.

Many prekindergartners will begin to understand some concepts of time, such as before and after. However, they may still struggle with more advanced concepts of time. Prekindergarten classrooms often employ daily calendar activities to help students understand and mark off the passing of time. Visual schedules assist students in developing this somewhat abstract concept.

Students this age will generally become interested in more advanced creative projects and should be able to use scissors with some dexterity. Typically

QUICK REVIEW

The Common Core State Standards begin in kindergarten, so each state has its own standards or guidelines for prekindergarten. What are they called in your state? What guidelines are included?

developing prekindergartners should also be able to participate in basic board and card games with scaffolding from adults as needed. They should also be able to copy many capital letters and generally master copying the letters of their first name.

Beyond merely being able to turn the pages of a book, most four-year-olds who have had appropriate exposure to books and other materials designed to aid in the development of literacy have a better understanding of the overall structure of a story. They will generally remember parts of short stories when asked to recall basic events and be able to make predictions about what they think will happen next. They will also often begin to understand many concepts of print, such as the structure of a book (cover, title, beginning, middle, end, and so forth), as well as have an understanding that words are made up of letters and that these are what are read on a page.

KINDERGARTEN

By the end of kindergarten, typically developing children should be able to count to at least twenty and identify most colors and shapes. They should also be able to write most numbers up to twenty, though they may still be developing the fine motor skills that enable these numbers to be formed quickly and skillfully. Beyond the basic concepts of *same* and *different*, kindergartners should be able to understand basic attributes of things, such as size, position, color, shape, and so forth, and place them into categories based on these attributes. They should also be able to determine things that are largest and smallest and compare objects based on many attributes, like size, length, weight, and more. At this age, most students will also have a relatively firm understanding of basic shapes, like a square, triangle, circle, and rectangle.

Most kindergartners should be able to print their names as well as begin their journey to full literacy by gradually developing skills that allow them to read and write more words and sentences. Of course, this will happen over the year, and most kindergartners will not begin the year with these skills. They should also be able to focus on a single activity for around fifteen minutes and be able to complete short, developmentally appropriate projects assigned to them.

FIRST GRADE

By first grade, most typically developing students will begin reading a variety of words both by sounding out and through sight word recognition. This is generally accompanied by an increased ability to write and spell more words and sentences. Students of this age will also have a far better understanding of the passing of time, including days, weeks, and months. In addition, their logical reasoning skills will increase as they begin to learn from a variety of inputs: auditory, visual, and print. They will also build on the basic numeracy skills developed in kindergarten as they learn to add, subtract, and solve a variety of math problems through logical reasoning.

SECOND AND THIRD GRADES

By the second and third grades, typically developing children will often develop specific interests that lead them to ask more in-depth questions about things. They may also desire to start their own collections of items in which they have an interest, like rocks, fossils, and stuffed animals. Children of this age will begin to plan ahead more by making predictions before an experiment or drawing out a design before building an engineering project. They will also start to make greater overall and in-depth connections and begin to understand cause and effect in social studies, science, and mathematical concepts, such as the commutative property of addition.

> QUICK REVIEW
>
> What are some other examples of "deeper meanings of texts" that can only be gleaned once a child has fully mastered the mechanics of decoding?

Generally, typically developing children of this age will have also developed literacy skills sufficient to make the transition from learning to read to reading to learn. This shift, which usually happens during the third-grade year, marks the time during which a child's mental energy ceases to be so exerted on simply decoding the words on the page that he or she can begin to focus on a deeper understanding of texts. This allows students to go beyond the most basic, literal meaning of words and enables them to make inferences based on what they have read.

FOURTH AND FIFTH GRADES

By the fourth and fifth grades, the ability to make in-depth connections will only continue to grow in the typically developing child. He or she will usually be able to fully glean broader cause and effect relationships, such as the interconnectedness among all living things or the way that acid rain impacts the entirety of the water cycle. Fourth and fifth graders will also generally seek out various sources of information, such as that which they obtain through friends and digital media. Students at this age should be firmly in the reading-to-learn phase of literacy development, though they may still encounter complex texts, vocabulary, and subjects which they may find challenging.

Table 1.2. Milestones in Cognitive Development	
Age/Grade	**Milestones**
Three years old	plays with toys with moving parts (buttons, levers, puzzles)
	understands two is more than one
	can turn pages of a book
	can copy simple shapes on paper with crayon or large pencil
	can remove jar lids and open doors

Age/Grade	Milestones
	Table 1.2. Milestones in Cognitive Development (continued)
Four years old	can identify some colors, shapes, and numbers
	can sort items that are the same and those that are different
	understands concepts of *before* and *after*
	can use scissors
	can copy letters of first name
	is developing concepts of print
	understands basic story events
Kindergarten	can count to twenty and identify most shapes and colors
	can write numbers to twenty
	can categorize shapes
	understands the concepts of largest and smallest
	can print name
	can focus on a single activity for around fifteen minutes
	is in beginning stages of literacy
First grade	can begin decoding and sight word recognition
	is able to write many words and basic sentences
	understands the passing of time (days, weeks, months)
	can use logical reasoning
	can add and subtract basic numbers
Second and third grades	asks many in-depth questions
	often develops collections
	can plan ahead and make predictions
	understands cause and effect
	makes transition from learning to read to reading to learn
Fourth and fifth grades	makes in-depth connections
	understands broad or complicated cause/effect relationships
	seeks out new information from many sources

Like development in the socio-emotional domain, cognitive development will be different for each child. Educators at each grade level should aim to develop an individual student's cognitive abilities and plan appropriate interventions to help typically developing children meet cognitive milestones. Students who show consistent atypical development should be referred to the appropriate specialist to screen for developmental delays and plan appropriate interventions and accommodations.

3) **Tristan is a third grader who is struggling with identification of sight words and letter-sound correspondence. What can be said about Tristan?**

   A. His cognitive development is typical of his age and grade.

   B. He is ready to begin the transition from learning to read to reading to learn.

   C. He could benefit from further practice on distinguishing cause-and-effect relationships.

   D. He should be targeted for intervention as his development is atypical.

4) **Mrs. Howard gives a math activity to her prekindergarten class in which she asks them to write the different addition equations that lead to an answer of ten (for example: 9 + 1, 8 + 2, 7 + 3, and so forth). What will be the likely result?**

   A. Most typically developing children in her class will be able to complete this activity independently and with ease.

   B. Most typically developing children in her class will be able to complete this activity with some scaffolding.

   C. This activity will be a great assessment tool to enable Mrs. Howard to screen for developmental delays.

   D. Most students in the class will not be able to complete this activity as it is not developmentally appropriate.

LANGUAGE DEVELOPMENT

While there are a variety of theories on whether language is innate or learned, it is essential that its ongoing development be nurtured in children. Because speech and language delays are also somewhat common in early childhood, it is also important that attention be paid to typical language and communication milestones to ensure that appropriate interventions are being undertaken in cases where they are warranted.

Even at age two, children can usually use around 300 words but understand up to 1,000. These numbers only continue to grow through a child's **receptive language**—what he or she can understand—which typically exceeds the number of words that fall into a child's **expressive language** bank of words, which they can speak or use to communicate.

AGE THREE

At this age, most typically developing children should be able to follow simple two- or three-step instructions. They should also know the word for—and be able to pronounce the name of—most everyday objects. Children of this age are expected to know and say their own name and age and understand basic prepositions such as *in, on,* or *under.* They should use many basic pronouns such as *me, mine, we, you,* and *I,* and form the plural of some simple nouns, such as *cars.* They will also typically be able to speak at least two or three sentences and hold a simple conversation with a few exchanges. Their speech should be clear enough for someone who does not know them to understand the bulk of what they are saying.

AGE FOUR

By age four, a typically developing child's speech will often become more complex and he or she will know more basic grammatical conventions, such as the correct use of most pronouns and many verbs and nouns. Prekindergartners can also typically recite a familiar song or rhyme from memory and tell simple stories as well as state their first and last name. They will also generally understand more of what is being said and will be able to talk about their favorite stories and the characters in them. They will usually be able to answer many *who, what,* and *where* questions and follow directions with four steps. Like younger children, most typically developing four-year-olds will understand far more words than they are able to use in their own speech, though many estimates put their expressive vocabulary near 900 words.

KINDERGARTEN

By age five, or kindergarten, most typically developing children will be able to speak with clarity and from a variety of verb tenses, including the future and past tenses (though some challenging irregular constructions may still be misused). They will begin speaking in more complex sentences and tell more intricate stories using several complete sentences. Kindergartners should also generally be able to state their address and phone number in addition to their full name. By kindergarten, language use should be purposeful and may often argue a point of view, often with heavy use of the word *because.*

FIRST GRADE

By first grade, most typically developing students will have both a receptive and expressive vocabulary that numbers in the thousands. They should be able to communicate with some oral skill about events of the past and present and events that are anticipated to occur in the future. They will also have an increasing knowledge of the connection between written and spoken language, particularly if they have received thorough phonics instruction. They should begin to communicate both orally and in writing (aligned with developmentally appropriate expectations) and should understand the various ways that people communicate.

SECOND AND THIRD GRADES

By second or third grade, children will have an increasingly growing vocabulary and will try using many new words, including those that might be considered "bad."

They will also begin to understand more language that is not being used literally, including jokes that are plays on words and riddles. Generally, they will have the ability to skillfully communicate through language that goes beyond speaking, such as writing notes or letters to friends and using writing to express their feelings in a journal or to tell a story.

FOURTH AND FIFTH GRADE

By fourth or fifth grade, most typically developing children should be quite proficient in using language to communicate both orally and in writing. While vocabulary and the conventions of written language are still developing, most oral language skills should be quite proficient.

Table 1.3. Milestones in Language Development

Age/Grade	Milestones
Three years old	follows 2 – 3-step instructions
	can say the name of most everyday objects
	can say name
	can speak 2 – 3 sentences
	can hold a simple conversation
Four years old	can use most pronouns and many verbs and nouns correctly (in speech)
	can recite a familiar song or rhyme
	can say first and last name
	can answer *who, what, when, where* questions
Kindergarten .	can form future and past tenses (in speech)
	can tell a story using several sentences
	can say name, address, and phone number
	can use language purposefully
First grade	can clearly communicate past and present events (in speech)
	can express themselves orally and in writing
	understands connection between written and spoken language
Second and third grades	can understand language use that it not literal
	can communicate purposefully in writing
	tries out many new words
Fourth and fifth grades	proficient oral language skills
	more advanced skills with written language

Certain particulars may influence a child's language development. Many children might speak or hear English only in the school setting, and this may impact their rate of development of vocabulary and certain oral proficiencies. However, most research suggests that **dual language learners**, or children who are developing skills in two languages simultaneously, have many lifelong advantages over monolingual children. For this reason, it is important to nurture a child's development in both languages and to expect many parts of this development, such as **code-switching**—the switching between both languages—as natural parts of this process. It is also important to be aware that some students who are placed in an immersive environment in which they do not yet speak the dominant language will go through a silent period in which they simply listen and avoid most oral communication. This is a natural part of learning a new language and should not be misinterpreted for atypical development.

> **DID YOU KNOW?**
>
> The most common form of code-switching is beginning a sentence in one language and then switching to another. For example, a student learning both English and Spanish might say "I want *una manzana.*"

Students who display consistent atypical development in language development should be referred to professionals for early intervention. Many schools and programs have audiologists and speech-language pathologists on staff to help plan and provide appropriate interventions.

SAMPLE QUESTIONS

5)   Marcus is a first grader in Mrs. Hyatt's class who very rarely speaks. She notices that he is unable to answer the following question: "When is your birthday?" What would her most likely reaction be?

 A.   She would not be concerned since a first grader wouldn't be expected to know this answer.

 B.   She would likely be concerned about a possible speech or language problem.

 C.   She would assume that his family simply does not celebrate birthdays.

 D.   She would likely have concerns about a possible emotional disturbance.

6)   Zakk, a second grader, is overheard by his teacher using a mildly profane word. What would be her best response?

 A.   to call his parents to express concern that he likely had an emotional disturbance

 B.   to meet with his parents to discuss his television and internet use habits

 C.   to speak with Zakk about the word and explain how it is not a nice word to use

 D.   to provide immediate punitive consequences

PHYSICAL DEVELOPMENT

Though a child's physical development is also linked to a variety of factors, it is somewhat more predictable than other domains of development and is often being tracked by physicians and parents alongside observations made in educational environments. Nevertheless, teachers should make observations regarding the physical development of children—especially very young children—part of their overall observations, particularly during outside time or recess. Since childhood is a time of rapid growth, teachers should be prepared for significant physical changes in their students over the course of the year.

> **DID YOU KNOW?**
>
> The age of potty training has been significantly increasing in the United States. In 1947, sixty percent of children were potty-trained by eighteen months.

AGE THREE

By age three, most typically developing children should be able to feed themselves with appropriately sized bites with some skill, though they may still use their fingers either alongside or in lieu of utensils. Children this age are generally able to run, walk up and down stairs one foot at a time, climb on playground equipment, and pedal a tricycle. They are also usually able to build a tower with at least six blocks and hold a crayon using the appropriate pressure (most of the time) to scribble and draw. While the age for completed toilet training averages thirty-nine months for boys and thirty-five months for girls, this may vary considerably based on the individual child. Nevertheless, most typically developing children should be able to use the bathroom on their own by age four and prekindergarten, though accidents are still to be expected.

> **STUDY TIP**
>
> Think of a "fine-tipped pen" when you think of fine motor skills to help remember that this describes small muscles, such as those needed to grip a pen.

Prekindergarten teachers should make the development of both gross and fine motor skills a part of their overall goals for their students. **Gross motor skills** focus on the large muscle groups of the body, while **fine motor skills** focus on dexterity with the hands and fingers.

AGE FOUR

At age four, most children should be able to use utensils to pick up and mash food, though they should only use a knife when supervised. They should have the ability to pour liquids with some proficiency as long as the size and weight of the containers are appropriate. They should also be able to dress themselves and drink from a cup and straw without dribbling. Children at this age can usually catch a ball bounced toward them (at an appropriate speed) as well as hop and stand on one foot for up to two seconds. While fine motor skills will still be developing in prekindergarten, more interest and attempts at writing are expected at this age, and precision should gradually increase.

KINDERGARTEN

By kindergarten or age five, most children can tiptoe, walk on a balance beam, jump rope, swing without the aid of someone pushing, catch a ball the size of a softball, and begin to explore new physical activities. Examples of these include soccer, basketball, swimming, or other physical activities, such as an interest in dance or gymnastics. Students of this age should be able to use the bathroom with proficiency and wash their hands afterwards. They should have the ability to use all eating utensils easily and proficiently and can also usually grip a pencil correctly. They may also begin to show hand dominance as they undertake more and more activities related to the development of fine motor skills. While kindergartners should become somewhat proficient at writing both numbers and letters over the course of the year, their fine motor skills stamina may still be low. Students this age may tire quickly when given writing assignments.

FIRST GRADE

By first grade, students will develop more proficiency with gross motor tasks—like kicking and catching a ball—and fine motor tasks, such as tying shoelaces. Their handwriting will also generally become smaller and more readable. They should be able to write for longer stretches and with increased speed.

SECOND AND THIRD GRADES

By second or third grade, the typically developing child will have more refined fine motor skills and should be able to handle many more complicated fine motor tasks, such as fastening buttons, zippers, and snaps. They also typically have more stamina for physical activity and can run and play longer without needing a rest. They can usually jump rope and ride a bike. Students at this age may also lose their first teeth.

FOURTH AND FIFTH GRADES

By fourth or fifth grade, most children will have a significant growth spurt and fully set hand dominance. They may begin to have muscle pains or cramps associated with rapid growth, and some children may begin to enter puberty at this age.

Table 1.4. Milestones in Physical Development

Age/Grade	Milestones
Three years old	takes appropriately sized bites of food can run fairly easily can walk up stairs, climb, and pedal can build a tower of six blocks can draw and scribble begins potty training
Four years old	can use spoon and fork can pour liquids can drink from a cup and straw can catch a ball bounced at them has completed potty training
Kindergarten	can tiptoe, walk on a balance beam, jump rope can catch a ball can use the bathroom and wash hands independently shows hand dominance can use all eating utensils
First grade	can kick and catch easily can tie shoelaces handwriting becomes more readable has more stamina when writing
Second and third grades	can fasten buttons, zippers, and snaps can run and play longer without resting can ride a bike begins to lose baby teeth
Fourth and fifth grades	growth spurt hand dominance is fully formed may begin to enter puberty

In order to get the fullest picture of a child's physical development, he or she must be observed participating in physical activity. Regrettably, physical education and even recess have been severely limited or removed from certain grade levels at schools across the country. When it is present, teachers should use the opportunity to observe children as they play and provide as many opportunities as possible for children to develop their full physical capabilities in a controlled and safe way.

A child's rate of physical development will depend on many factors, such as nutrition, genetics, and overall health. As in other domains, a problem in physical development may impact other facets of a student's schooling. For example, a child whose fine motor skills are lagging behind others may take a long time to complete assignments. Most atypical physical development is initially diagnosed and addressed by a physician; however, the classroom may be one of the first places the problem becomes apparent, so teachers should be mindful of the types of physical development expected in students at various ages.

SAMPLE QUESTIONS

7) Fauzia's parents come to her first-grade teacher to ask if they should be concerned that Fauzia is unable to dress herself or use the bathroom without help. What should the teacher's response be?

   A. She should tell Fauzia's parents that she has an intellectual disability.

   B. She should suggest screening for autism spectrum disorder.

   C. She should advise Fauzia's parents to consult her pediatrician about her physical development.

   D. She should tell Fauzia's parents that her development is on course with set milestones.

8) A prekindergarten teacher is using observational notes to track the physical development of her students. She is concerned about one student who seems to lack interest in drawing and coloring. What activities would be most useful for her to observe in order to collect more data along this same line?

   A. the child's interactions with other students at the dramatic play center

   B. how the child feeds herself at lunch and snack time

   C. which centers the child is most drawn toward

   D. how fast the child runs during outside time

STUDENT LEARNING

Developmental theories pertaining to childhood and development abound. While teachers will not need to know the details of every theory described below, it's important for them to have a general understanding of the many competing and complementary theories about how children learn.

The **maturational theory**, first proposed by **Arnold Gesell**, posits that all children go through the same sequential stages of development but at different rates. This theory helps underscore the need for developmentally appropriate practices in education, yet it focuses primarily on the idea of "natural" maturation and gives little consideration to learning or environment.

In contrast, the **cognitive theory** of development, proposed by **Jean Piaget**, proposes that both biological maturation and a child's own interaction with the environment, through which he or she constructs knowledge, determine overall development. While Piaget's theory also occurs in predictable and sequential stages, the emphasis is on the way in which the child interacts with the learning environment during each stage. The major stages of development in Piaget's framework are outlined below:

1. **Sensorimotor stage** (birth to age two): In this stage, a child learns **object permanence**, or that objects continue to exist even if they are unseen by the child.

2. **Preoperational stage** (two to seven years): This is when children learn symbolic thought and that a word or object can symbolize something beyond itself. For example, *fear* can mean the general idea of fear, not just one person's feeling.

3. **Concrete operational stage** (seven to eleven years): This stage marks the true beginning of logical (operational) thinking during which children can make deductions based on thought rather than actual physical realities. They also learn the concept of **conservation**, during which the core of a thing remains the same even if its appearance is transformed. This involves the conservation of numbers— where three hot dogs are still three hot dogs even if they are cut in half, for example—and the conservation of mass, where eight ounces of milk is the same amount whether it is in a tall glass or a short glass.

4. **Formal operational stage** (eleven years old and up): This stage lasts until adulthood and involves the ability to think abstractly and test predictions.

Piaget is known as a disciple of **constructivist theory** because he theorized that part of a child's development is determined by interaction with the environment. Constructivists believe that children learn by "constructing" knowledge from their environment. Other notable theorists in this camp include:

▶ **John Dewey**, who was essential in reforming American education in the early twentieth century;

▶ **Maria Montessori**, whose methods and learning materials are still used in countless early childhood programs across the world; and

▶ **Lev Vygotsky**, whose theories regarding the development of language and learning through the zone of proximal development are still widely studied.

While only Vygotsky is formally considered a constructivist theorist in the strictest interpretation of the word, both Dewey and Montessori were important contributors to this

QUICK REVIEW

What are examples of activities across each of Bruner's stages that might lead a child to learn the concept of friendship?

movement which now dominates all other educational theories at most institutions. It was John Dewey who first proposed the idea of hands-on learning, or learning by doing. This idea, which can be seen in action in classrooms across America, is seminal to understanding the framework of most modern education, which is more focused on the application of knowledge than listening to lectures. Maria Montessori believed that children have a natural desire to explore their environment and learn. Therefore, the learning environment must be structured in such a way as to support this. Even in schools that do not fully embrace the Montessori philosophy, this underlying principle can be seen in the design of classrooms and outdoor spaces for children, especially at the early childhood level.

Another notable constructivist who followed Piaget is **Jerome Bruner**. His theory, similarly to Piaget's, is based on the stages of cognitive development of children. And, like those of Piaget, these stages are sequential, but they are not linked to a particular age range. In the first stage, known as the **enactive or concrete stage**, children learn by manipulating concrete objects. This may range from counting out three of something to learn the number *three*, or touching an ice cube to glean the meaning of *cold*. In the **iconic or pictorial stage**, children learn through images. These images represent the hands-on experiences of the enactive stage. For example, a page with three butterflies could represent the number *three* just as a picture of an ice cube could represent *cold*. In the **symbolic or abstract stage**, the images used to learn in the iconic stage are now represented by abstract ideas. For example, the student would now have the idea of *three* or *cold* without needing either a tactile or visual representation.

Table 1.5. Developmental Theories

Theorist	Theory
Arnold Gesell	maturational theory—children go through the same sequential stages at different rates
Jean Piaget	cognitive theory (cognitive constructivism)—children mature both biologically and through interaction with their environment
John Dewey	progressive education—children learn by doing and need a hands-on approach
Maria Montessori	Montessori method—children have an innate desire to learn from their environment
Lev Vygotsky	zone of proximal development—children learn in part through the assistance of more capable peers or adults
Jerome Bruner	stage of cognitive development—children construct knowledge and move from a concrete stage to an abstract stage
Albert Bandura	social learning theory—children learn through observing and imitating the behavior of others that is rewarded
Benjamin Bloom	mastery learning—students must master one skill before they can learn the next
	Bloom's taxonomy—classification of learning objectives

In somewhat stark contrast to constructivism are **behaviorist learning theories**. Popular theorists in this school include B.F. Skinner and John Watson. These theories bypass higher-order cognitive development in favor of the view that human behavior is the result of a response to an environmental stimulus. In other words, it is not really about thinking per se; all human behavior is the result of conditioning. In the mind of a behaviorist, a child will learn to count, add, throw a ball, or sit still as the result of the praises and punishments bestowed upon him or her by the surrounding environment. Those behaviors for which a child is rewarded, which may include desirable learning or social behaviors, will be repeated by the child until they are mastered. Those behaviors that are punished will be avoided.

Although many behaviorist theories are backed by results of carefully conducted experiments, they are widely criticized for their reduction of humans to nearly the same state as other animals: merely trainable. Hoping to strike somewhat of a balance, **Albert Bandura** developed what he called the **social learning theory**. Like Skinner and Watson, Bandura believes that learning happens as the result of a stimulus and a response; however, he believes there is a cognitive process involved in between.

Bandura also believes in **observational learning**, which describes the idea of children learning from those around them. In his eyes, the process involves children first observing the behavior of those around them. For example, a child may observe a peer throwing his or her paper plate away after lunch. The child may then imitate this behavior the next day. If the teacher then sees this and praises the child, he or she is highly likely to repeat the behavior. On the other hand, if the child sees a friend throw his or her banana peel across the room at lunch and copies this behavior, resulting in a scolding by the teacher, the child will be unlikely to repeat this behavior. In this way, both positive and negative behaviors are being reinforced, but the child is engaging in thinking (versus pure response) prior to making the decision of whether or not to imitate behaviors.

Another theorist of note is **Benjamin Bloom**. One of his contributions is the theory of **mastery learning**. This theory states that a student must master each requisite skill before learning new information. This means that if mastery is not obtained after initial teaching, the student must be retaught and then re-assessed until the material is mastered. Only then will new material be introduced. The underlying principle is that all students can master material; they simply need different amounts of exposure for this to happen.

In addition to his theory of mastery learning, Benjamin Bloom is perhaps most remembered for **Bloom's taxonomy**, or the system of classification of levels of learning objectives. Although named after him, the system was actually developed as part of a larger series of meetings aimed at better matching curriculum and assessment with learning goals. The system provides for three core domains of learning: cognitive, affective, and sensory.

▶ The **cognitive domain** focuses on learning that is strictly knowledge based, such as recall, comprehension, and the application of knowledge.

▶ The **affective domain** is based on emotions and deals primarily with the socio-emotional growth of an individual.

▶ The **psychomotor domain** is action-based and covers the use of physical tools or machinery.

Bloom's taxonomy, alongside a more recent theory known as *depths of knowledge*, created by **Norman Webb**, is a very popular framework for curriculum and assessment development.

SAMPLE QUESTIONS

9) **Which of the following theorists would NOT be considered a constructivist?**

   A.   Jean Piaget

   B.   Lev Vygotsky

   C.   John Dewey

   D.   John Watson

10) **A kindergarten teacher notices that after one of the students in the class begins wearing the macaroni necklace she made in art class on her head, several other students also put their necklaces on their heads. Which learning theory might she be observing in action?**

   A.   social learning theory

   B.   the sensorimotor stage

   C.   operant conditioning

   D.   the cognitive theory of development

11) **One of the criticisms of behaviorism is that**

   A.   it lacks any empirical evidence.

   B.   it fails to account for both positive and negative behaviors.

   C.   it does not explain change over time.

   D.   it does not make any distinction between humans and animals.

MOTIVATION

While developmental theories explain part of a child's learning situation, they do not always give the fullest picture. This can only be gleaned from also considering a student's motivation. As with learning, there are a number of different theories that attempt to describe mechanisms for motivation in children.

Some theories of motivation rely on theoretical foundations from previously mentioned developmental theorists. One such example is the idea of **extrinsic motivation**, or providing motivation to students with the promise of a reward or the avoidance of a consequence. This relies heavily on the behaviorist developmental theory, in which children are thought to respond and adjust their behavior based solely on their desire to be rewarded or avoid a negative consequence. Extrinsic motivation is not always tied directly to interactions between students and teachers. A child might study hard for a spelling test, for example, to earn a high-five from a parent or avoid having his or her television time cut. High schoolers might begin to focus more heavily on their studies in the hopes of improving their SAT scores, thus bettering their chances to gain admittance into the college of their choice.

Extrinsic motivation—particularly the use of rewards—is being used in many schools in programs such as **positive behavior interventions and supports (PBIS)**, which is usually implemented as a school-wide program of behavior management. The underlying belief is that positive behaviors must be taught, like any other subject. Schools that implement PBIS use a host of strategies and tiered behavioral interventions to encourage positive behaviors and reduce undesirable ones. Many schools that have implemented the PBIS model use carefully planned reward systems that often involve the use of tickets or slips that denote good behavior or the successful completion of tasks. The idea behind the use of extrinsic reward systems is backed by research studies that show that students (and many times faculty) who are recognized and rewarded for positive behaviors will repeat them. (PBIS is discussed in depth in chpater 4.)

There is some debate over the widespread use of extrinsic motivation in education, both as part of the broader goals of PBIS and in other isolated settings. While research thoroughly backs up successful outcomes when students are rewarded for certain desirable behaviors, it is often difficult to ensure that students are consistently being rewarded in nuanced and appropriate ways that will sustain their desirable behaviors. There is other research that indicates that once the reward is removed, the motivation ceases. Critics also say that consistent use of extrinsic motivation might lead to a decrease in intrinsic motivation.

In contrast to extrinsic motivation is **intrinsic motivation**, or that which exists inside the individual and needs no outside encouragement. Students might have intrinsic motivation to learn certain subjects because they find them interesting, or they might feel good about themselves after certain academic achievements. Some research suggests that individuals have varying levels of intrinsic motivation, so this is often a harder motivator for teachers to tap into to encourage students. Theories and research surrounding the intrinsic motivation of students generally link the desire of students to feel in control of their learning and overall interest in the subject matter to higher rates of intrinsic motivation.

Unlike extrinsic motivation, there is less teachers can do to impact students' intrinsic desire to meet learning objectives. However, allowing students greater autonomy in regard to their learning by giving choices and tailoring lessons to student interest can help. Teachers might, for example, allow elementary students to

STUDY TIPS

Use the prefixes to help remember these two types of motivation: **ex**trinsic motivation is **ex**ternal to a person; **in**trinsic motivation is **in**ternal to a person.

select their own book for silent reading time or allow high school students to select their own topic for a research project.

A more recent theory on human motivation is **self-determination theory**, which posits that while all humans have an intrinsic motivation to learn and grow, this does not happen in isolation. Ongoing social interactions will either help or inhibit this natural tendency. In order for an individual to remain motivated toward a task or goal, three psychological needs must be met:

▶ **competence**: the feeling of mastering something

▶ **relatedness:** the desire to connect knowledge or experiences

▶ **autonomy**: the desire to control one's learning and growth

When these needs are met, an individual's natural, intrinsic motivation will be heightened. When these needs are not met, intrinsic motivation toward a task decreases as does overall well-being.

Typically, self-determination theory is used in education to ensure these psychological needs are being met for all students in all learning situations so as to optimize motivation. In particular, teachers of certain subjects that might be thought by students to be "useless," or to have little practical application, can use strategies to meet students' need for relatedness by helping students see the connection between knowledge and its application. Teachers can also promote the need for autonomy by allowing students ample ownership over their learning. One example of meeting this need might be to allow students "free choice" learning time during which they can choose from multiple learning activities.

Another theory related to student motivation is **attribution theory**. On its most basic level, this theory seeks to understand how people explain events through cause and effect relationships. As it pertains to education and student learning, this theory is concerned with helping students understand how their choices or actions cause certain other events or consequences. Some students may have a belief that causality is outside of themselves: "it's not my fault; he is too loud; it's too hard," and so forth. This is the attribution of events to an **external locus of causality**. Other students however may assume that most events are the result of their own actions: "I messed up; I'm bad at math; I should have tried harder," and so on. This is known as **internal locus of causality**.

Another part of attribution theory is stable versus unstable attribution. Those with a **stable attribution** believe that events are the result of consistent factors. Those with **unstable attribution** believe that events are the result of constantly shifting factors. For example, a student with stable attribution (with an external locus of causality) might believe that a poor grade is the result of the notion that "teachers never like me." A student with an unstable attribution might believe "this particular teacher was having a bad day and gave me a bad grade."

It is often far more common in the classroom for students to ascribe causality to outside forces and fail to see their own role in certain outcomes. In these cases, teachers can help students see the clear connection between their choices and actions and the outcomes. A teacher might, for example, help a kindergarten student link the consequence of having to clean up art materials that he threw across the room as being the direct result of his choice to throw the materials.

Attribution theory can also help teachers encourage students to think about the results of their efforts. Did the student study for the test? What was the result? Helping students make a clear link between their own actions and their results can help students increase actions that lead to positive results and decrease or eliminate those that lead to negative results. Some students have a natural inclination toward a particular attribution style, and they will need support from teachers to ensure they make appropriate connections between their actions, those of others, and the resulting events.

Another theory regarding human motivation is that proposed by David McClelland. It is often called the three needs theory, or simply **needs theory**. This framework states that all people, independent of any culture or setting, have three types of motivation: the need for achievement, the need for affiliation, and the need for power. Individuals will vary in their levels of each need, and some will be particularly disposed to a particular need. Those with a high **need for achievement** will often seek out challenging tasks and display high levels of independence. Because recognition for their achievements is their ultimate goal, these individuals want to ensure that their accomplishments are of sufficient rigor and independence to merit praise. Students who have a high need for achievement may work very hard to get good grades, make the honor roll, win awards, and generate frequent praise from school staff.

Those with a **need for affiliation** value belonging above all else, and this motivates their actions. A student with a high need for affiliation may begin to make certain choices in hopes of fitting in with a peer group, and his or her highest motivation will come from the approval of that group and being well-liked by others. Those with a **need for power** are typically motivated by a desire to control people or situations. They draw motivation from having others follow them or comply with their wishes. These students might be motivated by being given the opportunity to lead other students as line leader or head of a group project.

Although numerous theories and practices regarding student motivation exist, it must be reiterated that all students are individuals and that what motivates one student may be of no interest at all to another. Most current research suggests that students need both intrinsic and extrinsic motivation to tackle the many social and academic challenges they will face in school. It is up to educators to offer a variety of motivators to help students put forth their best effort. Sometimes, particularly for students with diagnosed learning or cognitive exceptionalities who may experience feelings of inferiority, motivation can be a challenge. Some students may subscribe to the fallacious belief that they simply cannot learn something and may therefore lack the motivation to try. In these cases, teachers must often use several different motivational strategies drawing from a broad theoretical base to encourage students to reach their fullest potential.

SAMPLE QUESTIONS

12) Mrs. Reyes gives a piece of candy to each student who scores 100 percent on the weekly spelling test. What is this an example of?

   A.   intrinsic motivation

   B.   extrinsic motivation

   C.   attribution theory

   D.   self-determination theory

13) Rebecca is a sixth grader who has historically worked very hard in school and maintained good conduct grades. Recently, she has begun to socialize with a new group of friends and joins in as they throw food in the lunchroom causing them to receive detention. What can be said about Rebecca?

   A.   She needs retraining to attribute her behavior to an external locus of causality.

   B.   She has lost intrinsic motivation to follow school rules.

   C.   She might be responding to a high need for affiliation with this peer group.

   D.   She would benefit from more choice and autonomy to increase her intrinsic motivation.

14) Which of the following is an example of an intrinsic motivation to read for enjoyment?

   A.   the desire to improve reading skills in order to get good grades

   B.   the feeling of pleasure gleaned from the act of reading

   C.   the craving for praise from those who see one in the act of reading

   D.   the desire to be "well-read" in order to garner envy from classmates

ANSWER KEY

1) A. Incorrect. This is very typical development of a first-grade student; the friend group may change with great frequency.

   B. Correct. Most typically developing first graders will be able to separate easily from a parent at a familiar place, such as school.

   C. Incorrect. It is normal for children of this age to challenge some rules to see which rules are flexible and which are not.

   D. Incorrect. First-grade students may delight in being able to complete many tasks independently.

2) A. Incorrect. Preschool-aged children typically have trouble understanding the difference between reality and make-believe.

   B. Incorrect. While prekindergartners generally enjoy playing make-believe, they may not clearly understand what is real and what is pretend.

   C. Correct. Typically developing kindergartners generally develop an understanding of the difference between reality and make-believe.

   D. Incorrect. Most typically developing children should have this mastered prior to first grade.

3) A. Incorrect. By third grade, Tristan should be reading with some fluency.

   B. Incorrect. Tristan is still learning to read.

   C. Incorrect. Tristan might need to work on distinguishing cause-and-effect relationships, but this is not the problem described here.

   D. Correct. By third grade, Tristan should definitely have mastered letter-sound-correspondence and recognition of most sight words.

4) A. Incorrect. This activity is often introduced in first grade per the Common Core State Standards, but it is not necessarily "typical" until second or third grade and is certainly not appropriate for prekindergarten.

   B. Incorrect. This is not a developmentally appropriate activity for prekindergarten.

   C. Incorrect. This is neither an appropriate activity to screen for developmental delays nor is it appropriate for this age group in general.

   D. Correct. This is more appropriate for an elementary school class, not a prekindergarten class.

5) A. Incorrect. A first grader should be able to explain when his or her birthday is.

   B. Correct. Marcus's inability to respond to a simple "when" question and his uncommunicativeness are concerning and might indicate a speech or language problem.

C.   Incorrect. His family might not celebrate birthdays, but Marcus's overall uncommunicativeness is a problem here.

D.   Incorrect. An emotional disturbance could be an additional concern, but Marcus's atypical development is more indicative of a possible speech or language delay.

6)   A.   Incorrect. Experimenting with language is part of Zakk's typical development.

B.   Incorrect. Zakk may have heard the word on TV or the internet, but it is an overreaction to call a meeting with his parents about it. His experimentation with the word is not unusual at his stage of development.

C.   Correct. Zakk is likely experimenting with "bad" words and needs to understand that the word he used is not appropriate.

D.   Incorrect. Zakk is likely just experimenting with language; he is not necessarily trying to behave badly.

7)   A.   Incorrect. The teacher is not qualified to diagnose this.

B.   Incorrect. This is also outside the scope of the teacher's role and does not relate to the issues of physical development.

C.   Correct. Fauzia is behind most physical development milestones and needs to be seen by a pediatrician.

D.   Incorrect. Fauzia should be able to dress herself and use the bathroom on her own by first grade, so her development is atypical.

8)   A.   Incorrect. Interacting with other children pertains to socio-emotional development, not fine motor skills.

B.   Correct. Using utensils also pertains to the development of fine motor skills with which the child seems to be struggling.

C.   Incorrect. This might help determine the child's overall interests but is not directly related to fine motor skills development.

D.   Incorrect. Running is related to gross motor skills development.

9)   A.   Incorrect. Piaget is often considered the father of the constructivist movement.

B.   Incorrect. Lev Vygotsky was a constructivist who is best known for his theory regarding the zone of proximal development.

C.   Incorrect. John Dewey was both a constructivist and a pioneering educational reformer.

D.   Correct. John Watson was a behaviorist. He is often considered to be the one who coined the term *behaviorism*.

10) **A.   Correct.** Bandura's social learning theory suggests that children learn by observing and imitating the behavior of those around them.

B.   Incorrect. The sensorimotor stage is one of the stages of Piaget's theory of cognitive development.

C.   Incorrect. Operant conditioning is a behaviorist theory that says that humans can be trained to respond in a certain way.

D.   Incorrect. Piaget's theory of cognitive development involves learners going through sequential stages.

11) A.   Incorrect. Many empirical studies support the perspective of behaviorism.

B.   Incorrect. This theory accounts for both positive and negative behaviors; whichever behavior is reinforced will continue.

C.   Incorrect. Change over time is the result of certain behaviors being more consistently reinforced, leading to their replication.

D.   Correct. True behaviorists are often criticized for lumping humans and animals together as having identical responses to stimuli.

12) A.   Incorrect. Intrinsic motivation would come from each student's desire to do well on the test without any promise or hope of reward.

B.   Correct. Giving students rewards, like candy, is an example of extrinsic motivation.

C.   Incorrect. Attribution theory explains how people ascribe causality to events.

D.   Incorrect. Self-determination theory outlines psychological needs that must be met for optimal motivation.

13) A.   Incorrect. There is no indication that Rebecca does not know or understand the cause and effect relationship between her actions and the consequences.

B.   Incorrect. One cannot necessarily know this from the example.

C.   Correct. It would appear that Rebecca is being motivated by a need to be accepted by her peer group.

D.   Incorrect. This situation is not the result of lack of choice and autonomy since Rebecca freely made the choice to join in with the behavior.

14) A.   Incorrect. Grades are examples of extrinsic motivation.

B.   Correct. Learning for the joy of learning very much describes intrinsic motivation.

C.   Incorrect. Praise from others is an example of extrinsic motivation.

D.   Incorrect. Having someone else express envy is an example of extrinsic motivation.

2

Disability Categories

DIAGNOSING DISABILITIES

The **diagnosis** of disabilities is done by qualified medical professionals (for example, medical doctors or psychologists). Students may enter the school environment with an existing diagnosis since many conditions are diagnosed when children are very young. The following disability categories require medical diagnoses in order to qualify for special education services:

- other health impairments (OHI)
- traumatic brain injury (TBI)
- multiple disabilities
- hearing impairment (hard of hearing or deaf)
- visual impairment
- deaf-blindness

However, students do not need a medical diagnosis of a disability to receive special education services under some IDEA categories. Qualified professionals in the school setting may identify students who qualify for services under the following categories:

- speech or language impairment
- specific learning disability
- developmental delay
- intellectual disability

A medically diagnosed disability alone does not guarantee a student qualifies for special services within the school setting. In order for students to be **eligible** for special education services under IDEA or Section 504, they must have a disability that directly impacts their educational outcomes. A **multidisciplinary evaluation team** determines the student's eligibility through a multifactored evaluation.

Educational team members include the school psychologist, district representative, general education teacher, and special education teachers. Other professionals, such as physical or occupational therapists, behavioral specialists, or a **speech-language pathologist (SLP)** may be on the evaluation team depending on the specific needs of the student. Parents are also an important part of the multidisciplinary team. They provide information about a student's developmental history and functioning outside the school setting.

Evaluations almost always include a developmental history and background, observations within the school setting, and reports of progress in the general education curriculum. Most evaluations of students also include cognitive (IQ) testing and standardized assessments of academic achievement. Assessments in other areas, such as gross motor ability, fine motor ability, language, speech, and behavior may be completed depending on the suspected disability of the student.

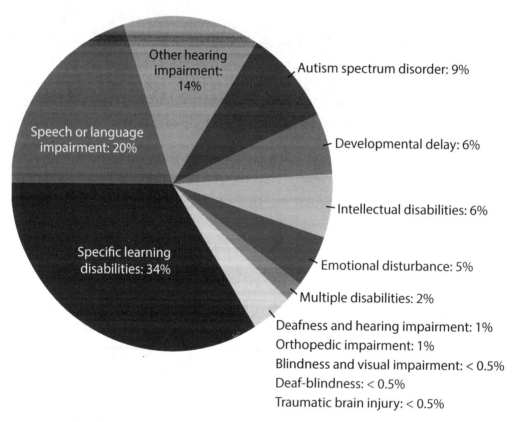

Figure 2.1. Disability Categories under IDEA (Children Aged 3 – 21, 2015 – 2016)

SPECIFIC LEARNING DISABILITIES

CHARACTERISTICS OF SPECIFIC LEARNING DISABILITIES

The largest percentage of students receiving special education services are accommodated under the category of a specific learning disability. IDEA defines a **specific**

learning disability (SLD) as a disorder of at least one psychological process affecting spoken and written language. An impairment in psychological processes may affect a student's ability to listen, think, speak, read, write, spell, or solve mathematical problems. A child with a learning disability may experience delays in a single area or in several areas. The IDEA definition includes perceptual disabilities, brain injury, minimal brain dysfunction, dyslexia, and developmental aphasia. The IDEA definition excludes disabilities resulting from hearing, visual, motor, or cognitive impairments, emotional disturbance, or environmental and economic factors.

The most common area of difficulty for students with learning disabilities is reading. Students with learning disabilities in reading often have difficulty with **phonological awareness**, or the understanding of how sounds combine to create words. A student who has low phonological awareness is not able to separate sounds within a word or blend sounds to decode an unknown word. Students with learning disabilities in the area of reading struggle with decoding at the word level, lacking sight word automaticity paired with difficulty using sound or syntax strategies to decode unknown words. As a result, students with learning disabilities often have poor **oral reading fluency**, reading word-by-word instead of in phrases.

> **DID YOU KNOW?**
>
> It is estimated that up to 90 percent of students with learning disabilities have difficulties with reading.

Dyslexia is a learning disability in basic reading skills. It is characterized by difficulties with single-word decoding and comprehension and is accompanied by some of the following common symptoms:

- having a difficult time memorizing the alphabet and word sequences (e.g., days of the week)
- having a small written vocabulary compared to spoken vocabulary
- inserting or deleting letters when spelling
- confusing similarly shaped letters
- misspelling common words
- reading words in the wrong order
- losing place when reading
- having poor handwriting

Other specific learning disabilities may affect reading comprehension (among other educational outcomes). **Reading comprehension** is the ability of a person to understand what they have read. In some cases, reading comprehension difficulties are caused by disfluencies in reading coding which impair ability to comprehend. Other students can read a passage fluently but cannot apply meaning to what they have read. Students with reading comprehension impairments may struggle with **literal comprehension**, or understanding and relaying back information that is explicitly available in the text. More often, students have difficulty with **inferential**

comprehension, or the ability to make interpretations and draw conclusions about information read.

Students may also have learning disabilities in the area of math. **Dyscalculia** describes a specific learning impairment in mathematical reasoning or calculation. Students with difficulties in **mathematical reasoning** struggle to understand basic principles of mathematics and how those principles are applied to increasingly complex math concepts. Students who find mathematical reasoning challenging may lack basic number sense, struggle with sequencing, and/or have difficulty understanding place value and/or mathematical vocabulary. Students with deficits in mathematical calculation struggle to understand basic mathematical operations such as addition, subtraction, multiplication, and division.

Many students with learning disabilities struggle with written language. **Dysgraphia** is a learning disability in which a person's ability to use written expression is impaired. Students with written language impairments may struggle with **composition**, or the ability to create grammatically correct writing. Legible handwriting and correct spelling are also often extremely difficult for students with written language disabilities.

Some students with a specific learning disability may struggle in the area of **oral expression**. These students experience difficulty using language to communicate their thoughts. Learners with deficits in oral expression may have difficulty with word retrieval, requiring extended response time to answer questions. A student with an oral expression deficit may use more simplistic vocabulary or sentence structures than a typically developing peer might.

HELPFUL HINT

Use word roots to remember the names of specific learning disorders: *dys* (impaired, abnormal); *lexi* (word or saying); *calculia* (to calculate); *graphia* (written); *dys* + *lexia* = impaired ability to read words; *dys* + *calculia* = impaired ability to calculate; *dys* + *graphia* = impaired ability to write.

Students may also exhibit specific learning disabilities in the area of **listening comprehension**—the ability to understand and act upon auditory information. Students who struggle with listening comprehension are able to hear speech correctly; however, they have difficulty applying meaning to what they have heard. A student with a specific learning disability in the area of listening comprehension may find it challenging to follow spoken directions or may frequently ask others to repeat what they have said.

Students with learning disabilities often exhibit delays in other areas of development. Because learning disabilities occur as a result of psychological impairments in the understanding of language, impairments in speech or language are common among students with learning disabilities. Students with learning disabilities may also experience difficulty maintaining attention. Many students with learning disabilities have poor fine motor skills which impact functioning in other areas of delay, such as the impact of poor handwriting in reading and production of written expression. Students with learning disabilities are also at a greater risk for social-emotional problems than nondisabled peers.

ELIGIBILITY AND IDENTIFYING SLDs

Students qualify for services in the area of specific learning disabilities based on an evaluation completed by an interdisciplinary school team. Evaluations of students who may qualify as having a learning disability must include information about types of instruction and intervention which the student has received to address learning concerns. Furthermore, the evaluation must include assessments of a student's performance according to age-level expectations in language, writing, math, reading, and overall cognitive ability. Academic achievement information should be presented through both school-based and standardized assessments, such as an IQ test to evaluate cognitive ability. Evaluations must also include at least one observation of the student in the regular classroom setting. Depending on the needs of the student, evaluations in socio-emotional development, behavior, language, speech articulation, fine motor skills, sensory processing, gross motor skills, or medical reports may also be included.

Students can qualify as having a specific learning disability by meeting either of two eligibility criteria. Historically, students have qualified as having a specific learning disability based on the presence of a severe discrepancy between achievement and intellectual ability. A severe discrepancy occurs when intelligence scores (verbal, nonverbal, or combined IQ) are significantly higher than scores in one or more area of achievement, including listening comprehension, oral expression, written expression, basic reading skills, reading comprehension, and mathematics calculation or reasoning.

When IDEA was reauthorized in 2004, the law changed to require that schools also consider student response to research-based intervention when determining the presence of a specific learning disability. Most schools use a response-to-intervention (RTI) process of instruction and intervention to address diverse learning needs. (Chapter 4 contains a more detailed discussion of RTI.) Even if no significant discrepancy exists between intellectual ability and achievement scores, schools may determine a child has a specific learning disability if the student continues to perform below peers in any of the previously stated areas after receiving targeted intervention through an RTI (or similar) process.

It is the responsibility of the school to show that a student's low achievement is not the result of lack of appropriate instruction. Therefore, as part of the evaluative process the school is required to provide documentation that the student has received research-based intervention to address areas of concern prior to evaluation for special education services. The evaluative team must also determine that achievement deficits do not result from other factors, including visual, hearing, or motor impairments, and/or intellectual disabilities, emotional disturbances, or environmental or socio-economic disadvantages.

EDUCATIONAL PRACTICES FOR STUDENTS WITH SLDS

Educational practices for students with specific learning disabilities begin with specialized instruction in areas of deficit. The most common area of impairment for students with specific learning disabilities is reading. Students with reading deficits must be provided with research-based interventions to improve reading skills. The Every Student Succeeds Act (ESSA) requires reading instruction to include five essential components: phonemic awareness, phonics, vocabulary development, reading fluency, and reading comprehension. All students should be provided with instruction in these areas as a part of their core reading program. However, a student with a learning disability may require direct instruction in any or all of the five essential reading areas (depending on individual student characteristics) in order to make educational progress.

Many specific learning disabilities in the area of reading, such as dyslexia, occur because of deficits in phonological awareness and decoding at the word level. Therefore, many students with learning disabilities in reading benefit from intensive, direct instruction in phonological awareness, phonics, and word decoding. Students who are able to read fluently but struggle with comprehension may benefit from direct instruction in vocabulary development and reading comprehension strategies (for example, compare/contrast, sequencing, summarizing, retelling, inferring, visualizing).

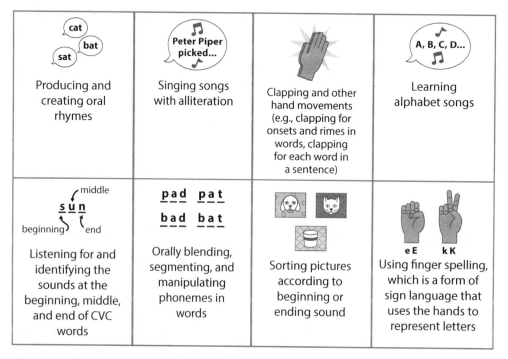

Figure 2.2. Phonological Awareness and Phonics Strategies

Students with learning disabilities in the area of math may require explicit, systematic instruction in order to address this deficit. Many students who struggle in math benefit from the use of hands-on materials, such as math manipulatives, to aid understanding of math concepts. In many cases, students need explicit instruction in mathematical vocabulary in order to understand the language used in this subject. Students may also need practice with explicit problem-solving strategies to understand and correctly solve word problems.

One instructional framework used to improve understanding of mathematical concepts for students with learning disabilities is a **concrete-semiconcrete-abstract (CSA)** instructional sequence. In a CSA sequence, introduction of a mathematical concept begins at a concrete level through the use of manipulatives or other hands-on materials (e.g., *Students combine blocks to demonstrate addition*). Once students demonstrate concrete understanding, the same concept is practiced with drawings or pictures at a semi-concrete, or representational, level (e.g., *Students draw pictures to solve addition problems*). Finally, students practice solving mathematical problems at the abstract level using numerals and mathematical symbols (e.g., *Students use a numeral to write the answer to 2 + 4*).

Learning disabilities in writing may occur because of difficulties with letter identification, spelling, motor ability, or understanding of grammar. Students with learning disabilities may require more direct and intensive practice in handwriting and letter formation than typically developing students in order to support writing fluency.

Students may also need additional intervention in spelling. One spelling intervention which is effective for students with learning disabilities is cover-copy-compare. Using the cover-copy-compare method, a student studies the word, covers the word, writes the word from memory, and then compares his or her spelling to the original. The student should repeat the process for a word which is misspelled and move on to a new word if the spelling is correct. Other spelling interventions are similar in process to cover-copy-compare but require the student to spell the word out loud. Students with difficulties understanding grammar may need explicit instruction in sentence formation, sentence combining, and improving sentence complexity.

Students with learning disabilities should be provided with accommodations to limit the impact of their disability in all settings. As much as possible, accommodations should minimize a disability's interference and allow a student with a learning disability to demonstrate an understanding of learning objectives. The following are examples of common accommodations:

STUDY TIP

Accommodations for students with any disability can be separated into the following four main categories:

- presentation accommodations (braille, auditory, large print)
- response accommodations (oral presentations, scribes)
- setting accommodations (learning in a quiet setting)
- timing and scheduling accommodations (allowing frequent breaks)

- ▶ allowing students with reading disabilities to have test questions read aloud or listen to an audio recording of text

- ▶ having a teacher differentiate the ways students demonstrate what they know, such as allowing an oral presentation instead of a written paper

- ▶ allowing students extended time for an assignment or having a task broken down into smaller steps

- ▶ offering students with handwriting or fine motor difficulties the use of graph (or specially lined) paper to improve writing organization and legibility

- ▶ having students use guided notes or recorded lectures if they have difficulty keeping up when trying to write down information

- ▶ letting students use graphic organizers to support reading comprehension or plan expressive writing assignments

- ▶ allowing a student who struggles with math to use a calculator to perform basic calculations

SAMPLE QUESTIONS

1) **Which type of learning disability is characterized by difficulty with the motor movements required for written expression?**

   A. dyslexia

   B. dysgraphia

   C. dyscalculia

   D. dysrhythmia

2) **Which best describes an instructional model which helps students with learning disabilities master complex mathematical concepts by beginning with hands-on introduction before progressing to representation and application of the concept?**

   A. concrete/semi-concrete/abstract instruction

   B. scaffolding

   C. problem-solving strategies

   D. mnemonic techniques

SPEECH OR LANGUAGE IMPAIRMENT

CHARACTERISTICS OF SPEECH OR LANGUAGE IMPAIRMENT

A **speech or language impairment** is a communication disorder characterized by impairments in voice, speech fluency, articulation, or language. Such an impairment may occur in any one of the listed areas or may appear as a combination of impairments in multiple areas. Speech and language impairments may be congenital or adventitious in nature.

Voice disorders occur when a vocal quality such as pitch, loudness, or tone significantly differs from age or social expectations. Voice disorders may occur as a result of structural changes in voice mechanisms (e.g., vocal nodules or larynx structure). Other voice disorders are due to problems with the central or peripheral nervous system affecting the ability to use voice mechanisms. Voice disorders may also occur as a result of misuse of vocal mechanisms.

Dysphonia is a term used to describe most voice disorders and includes hoarseness, roughness, breathiness, or strangled quality of tone; it can also include abnormal pitch, volume, or resonance. Frequent coughing or throat clearing is common for a person with a voice disorder. Individuals with voice disorders might experience vocal fatigue following prolonged speaking and may require increased vocal effort to speak.

Speech fluency impairments occur when the flow of speech is regularly interrupted. While most individuals occasionally demonstrate some type of disfluency, stuttering or other fluency impairments are characterized by excessive disfluency which interrupts daily functioning. Furthermore, students with fluency impairments often have secondary characteristics, such as ritualistic behaviors (avoiding certain sounds) or movements (facial grimaces, head nodding, leg tapping, fist clenching).

The most common fluency impairment is **stuttering**, which usually begins before a child turns five. Stuttering is characterized by repetitions, prolongations, blocks, interjections, and revisions.

- A **repetition** is when a single sound within a word is repeated ("b-b-b-ball") but may also occur at the syllable, word, or phrase level.
- A sound **prolongation** occurs when a sound within a word is held out for a longer than typical amount of time. ("*Sssssssoon* we will go.")
- **Interjections** are word fillers ("That is *like* a great idea.") or nonword fillers ("I want *um* chocolate.") that interrupt speech.
- **Blocks** are characterized by an inability to initiate a sound or an inaudible utterance during a pause in speech.
- **Revisions** occur when the speaker pauses to revise their speech. ("We has—*we have*—to leave early.")

A second type of fluency impairment is cluttering. **Cluttering** is characterized by speech that is rapid or has an irregular rate. Cluttering also includes the deletion of syllables as well as the dropping of word endings, making it difficult to understand speech.

Speech sound production impairments (articulation impairments) occur when an individual has difficulty with the motor production and/or phonological representation of speech sounds. Atypical speech sounds may include sound substitutions, omissions, additions, or distortions which decrease intelligibility of speech. Articulation impairments happen for many reasons.

▶ **Apraxia of speech** occurs when an individual's brain has difficulty processing the motor plan to initiate and carry out speech movements.

▶ **Dysarthria** is a speech disorder in which muscle weakness impairs ability to speak, often resulting in slurred or slow speech.

▶ Other speech sound disorders are caused as a result of structural abnormalities. For example, children who have a **cleft palate**, or opening in the roof of the mouth, may have difficulty articulating all speech sounds.

▶ Sensory conditions, like hearing loss, or other genetic conditions, such as Down syndrome, may also cause speech sound disorders.

Language impairments occur when a child has difficulty comprehending and/or using spoken language. Deficits may occur in form (phonology, morphology, and syntax), function (semantics), and/or use (pragmatics) of language. **Phonology** is the pattern of sounds in languages. Phonological language deficits may include a delay in phonological awareness (such as rhyming, sound segmentation, and sound blending) and the use of simplistic or repetitive syllable structures. **Morphology** refers to word structure while **syntax** refers to the structure of sentences. Students with deficits in morphology and syntax may exhibit a restricted **mean length of utterance** (average number of morphemes per utterance), speaking in short phrases rather than full sentences. They may also have difficulty identifying grammatical errors or using correct forms of verbs, function words (articles and prepositions), and pronouns.

Semantics is the understanding of the meaning of words and combinations of words in language. Deficits in semantics include delayed vocabulary development, difficulty responding to questions or directions, problems understanding relationships between words (e.g., synonyms and antonyms), and a lack of understanding of figurative language like idioms and metaphors. **Pragmatics** is the use of language in natural settings. Students with deficits in pragmatics may have difficulty initiating play with others, expressing ideas or feelings, contributing to class discussions, or participating in multiple-turn conversations.

Speech and language impairments are closely linked with many other forms of disability. Language deficits (especially in pragmatic language) are part of the criteria used to identify students with autism spectrum disorders. Individuals with learning disabilities and cognitive impairments often also have language deficits. Students with emotional disturbances and/or attention deficit/hyperactivity disorder (ADHD) are

STUDY TIP

Speech refers to the actual sound of spoken language (talking). Therefore, speech impairments are characterized by trouble producing spoken language. Language refers to how a person uses words and body movements to communicate meaning. Language impairments are characterized by an inability to express one's own thoughts and/or understand the meaning of others' speech.

at a higher risk for fluency and language impairments. Many genetically related disabilities, such as Down syndrome, also impact speech and/or language development. Students with sensory impairments (e.g., hard of hearing or low vision) may experience speech and/or language delays as a result of the impact of the impairment on development.

ELIGIBILITY AND IDENTIFYING SPEECH OR LANGUAGE IMPAIRMENT

IDEA defines speech and language impairments as communication disorders that affect a child's articulation, speech fluency, language, or voice/resonance. Students may qualify for services under the category of speech and language impairments based on the presence of deficits in one or more of these subcategories. A multidisciplinary evaluation team must assess each area of speech or language concern to determine if a student qualifies for services. Students may receive special instruction in speech or language under the category of speech-language impairment.

For students who have a speech-language impairment secondary to another disability, the student receives special education services under the other disability category and speech instruction is provided as a related service.

To qualify for special education services for a speech and language impairment, the evaluation team must provide documentation that the student received research-based instruction and intervention prior to evaluation. As part of the evaluation, the speech-language pathologist conducts a comprehensive assessment of the student's speech and language ability. The evaluation should include documentation of how the impairment affects learning in the general education classroom. In the case of a potential voice/resonance impairment, a medical examination may be necessary to rule out a medical condition causing the impairment (which cannot be addressed through speech therapy). Usually, assessments in articulation, language, fluency, voice, and oral motor competency are also done. In many cases, assessments of intelligence, academic achievement, and functional behavior are done to provide further information of the nature and impact of a child's disability.

EDUCATIONAL PRACTICES FOR SPEECH OR LANGUAGE IMPAIRMENT

Interventions for speech or language impairments are almost always planned and directed by an SLP. For example, interventions for students with voice disorders are largely driven by SLPs in collaboration with medical professionals like otolaryngologists, pulmonologists, neurologists, and psychologists, who treat the underlying issues that may be causing the voice disorder. Especially in the case of voice disorders, direct therapies for speech and language impairments may be outside a special education teacher's area of expertise. However, it is the responsibility of all team members, including parents, general education teachers, special education teachers, and paraprofessionals to ensure that prescribed supports for students with speech or language impairments are implemented throughout a child's day and not just during direct therapy times.

When implementing interventions for students with fluency impairments, it is key that all professionals working with the student try to minimize negative emotional reactions related to stuttering or other issues. Parents and teachers should always give the student time to communicate, without interrupting or trying to finish the thought for the child. Teachers should help students accept that disfluencies happen and work to build self-confidence in the student.

Students with fluency difficulties are at a higher risk of being bullied than other students. A teacher with a student who stutters may want to do class-wide instruction in understanding what stuttering is and why it occurs (without singling out or embarrassing the student). The teacher should also work directly with the student who has speech disfluencies on strategies to address anxiety (which results in an increase in disfluent behavior) and how to respond if another person has a negative reaction.

Finally, teachers working with students should follow through on speech modification strategies implemented by the SLP. Some speech and stuttering modification strategies used to improve speech fluency include:

▶ rate control

▶ prolonged syllables

▶ light articulatory contact

▶ using appropriate pausing

▶ reducing physical tension

Several strategies help students hear and produce speech sounds. An SLP may bombard a student with varied exemplars of the target sound to train the student's ear to hear the sound correctly. A student may also be asked to practice non-speech oral motor exercises to improve motor control or strength. SLPs may have students practice producing word pairs that are either very similar or very dissimilar in manner of production. Similar pairs help train a student's ear to hear the contrast between similar sounds while very dissimilar pairs help students contrast motor movements required to make sounds. A mirror may be used to provide a student with visual feedback of his or her oral motor movements.

Treatment of speech sound disorders usually begins with targeted practice of the sound error(s). Once the sound is mastered in isolation, practice is generalized to the correct use of the sound at various locations within a word and phrase. The last step in articulation interventions is practicing automaticity of sound production and teaching self-monitoring of speech, including self-correction of errors.

Interventions for students with language impairments vary widely based on the specific need of the student. Often, speech-language pathologists work closely with classroom and special education teachers to support language development for students. Learners with phonological deficits benefit from the same interventions used to promote early literacy skills, such as practice with letter-sound correspondence, sound blending (e.g., *b-e-d* to *bed*), sound segmenting (e.g., *bed* to *b-e-d*), and rhyming.

Students with difficulties in morphology and syntax benefit from interventions with a targeted use of more complex words and sentences in oral and written language. Students challenged by semantics may need extra practice with curricular vocabulary. Teachers may help students improve semantics through rich discussion of the vocabulary encountered in reading as well as by providing multi-modal opportunities to learn new vocabulary. Students who have difficulty in the area of pragmatics may benefit from direct social skill instruction to help learn appropriate language uses in social and academic situations. Teachers should also provide ongoing opportunities for guided practice and role playing within the classroom environment to allow students the chance to practice pragmatic language in more naturally occurring situations.

SAMPLE QUESTIONS

3)   **Apraxia is which type of disability?**

   A.   voice disorder

   B.   speech fluency impairment

   C.   speech sound production impairment

   D.   language impairment

4)   **Mr. White's ninth-grade English class is giving oral presentations following a literature study. Billy is a student in Mr. White's class who stutters and has extreme anxiety about speaking in front of people, which causes increased disfluency. Which would be the best accommodation to help Billy give his oral presentation?**

   A.   allowing Billy to read off cue cards

   B.   allowing Billy to pre-record his presentation and play the video for the class

   C.   excusing Billy from the assignment

   D.   having Billy do a deep breathing exercise prior to the presentation

Other Health Impairments

Characteristics of Other Health Impairments

Students with health impairments have limitations in strength, vitality, or alertness which adversely impact educational progress. The category of **other health impairments (OHI)** covers a multitude of chronic and acute health conditions. Each condition has a varying effect on a student's health and subsequent educational progress. Examples of health conditions which may be covered under this category include (but are not limited to) attention deficit/hyperactivity disorder (ADHD), epilepsy, Tourette syndrome, asthma, diabetes, heart disease, blood disorders, and pediatric cancer.

Students with **attention deficit/hyperactivity disorder (ADHD)** make up by far the largest percentage of learners served under OHI. The three primary characteristics of students with ADHD include inattention, hyperactivity, and impulsivity. Students may be diagnosed with ADHD based on symptoms in some or all areas that impact daily functioning.

▶ **Inattention** refers to difficulty maintaining focus on a task which is not of high interest. Inattention related symptoms in children include difficulty staying organized, frequent loss of items, not listening when spoken to, frequent change of conversational topic, and being easily distracted from an activity.

▶ **Hyperactivity** refers the tendency of children with ADHD to be in constant motion. Hyperactivity is often the most easily recognized symptom of ADHD. Hyperactivity-related symptoms include constant fidgeting, excessive talking, bouncing from one activity to the next, running or climbing in inappropriate situations, and overall difficulty sitting still.

▶ **Impulsivity** refers to difficulties with self-control, which are common for children with ADHD. Symptoms of impulsivity include frequent interruption, invasion of others' space, guessing rather than taking the time to problem solve, difficulty waiting, making comments that are considered rude, and emotional outbursts/tantrums.

ADHD often interferes with a student's ability to make progress in school. Students with ADHD have difficulty following the behavioral expectations of a typical classroom—sitting quietly, following directions, and focusing on instruction. A student with ADHD may frequently miss out on important instruction because of inattentive, hyperactive, and/or impulsive behaviors. Consequently, students with ADHD may have difficulty making educational progress at the same rate as their peers. Students with ADHD may require social-emotional supports to learn and maintain socially expected

QUICK REVIEW

Does a person have to display all major symptoms to receive an ADHD diagnosis?

behavior in the classroom. They may also require academic supports to ensure adequate educational progress.

Epilepsy is a neurological condition characterized by the presence of seizures which can vary in frequency and intensity. Some seizures are momentary while others last several minutes. Anti-seizure medication may be able to decrease the frequency and/or intensity of seizures. In some cases, surgery, special diets, nerve stimulation, or other treatments are used to treat epilepsy.

Seizures may be generalized or focal.

▶ **Generalized seizures** affect both sides of the brain and may be absence or tonic-clonic.

▶ When having an **absence seizure** (petit mal), a person may rapidly blink or stare into space and be unresponsive.

▶ When having a **tonic-clonic seizure** (grand mal), a person may lose consciousness, fall to the ground, or have muscle jerks and spasms.

▶ **Focal seizures** (partial seizures) affect just one area of the brain and may be simple or complex.

▶ **Simple focal seizures** may cause twitching or a strange sensory sensation (unusual taste or smell).

▶ A person experiencing a **complex focal seizure** may be dazed, confused, or unresponsive to verbal stimuli.

▶ **Secondary generalized seizures** begin as focal seizures but then spread to both sides of the brain, becoming generalized seizures.

Epilepsy in children is associated with developmental difficulties in multiple areas. The effect of seizures on development varies by the frequency and intensity of the seizure as well as the area of the brain affected by the seizure. Epileptic seizures may cause damage to or abnormalities in specific areas of the brain, affecting learning. Furthermore, after having a seizure, students may be confused or fatigued for up to several hours, disrupting learning. Many students with epilepsy struggle with attention, organizational skills, and short-term memory problems, impacting their ability to make academic progress. Emotional and behavioral difficulties such as anxiety, depression, and hyperactivity are also common for students with epilepsy. For some students with epilepsy, seizures cause extensive damage to the brain, resulting in global learning difficulties.

Tourette syndrome is a neurological disorder often characterized by **tics**—repetitive, stereotyped involuntary movements or vocalizations. Tics may be either simple or complex. Simple tics, such as eye blinking, head jerking, or throat-clearing, are brief and involve a small number of muscle groups. Complex tics are patterns of movement which involve several muscle groups. Complex motor tics may be a combination of simple motor tics or movements such as sniffing objects or jumping. Complex vocal tics include repeating or uttering words and phrases.

While some tics cause minimal interruption, others can be disruptive or even dangerous. For example, a small percentage of individuals with Tourette syndrome experience **coprolalia**, the utterance of socially inappropriate words, or **echolalia**, the repetition of words said by another person. Others may have self-harming tics, such as biting oneself or hitting oneself in the face. Tourette syndrome is also associated with other neurobehavioral difficulties, including ADHD, obsessive-compulsive disorder (OCD), and learning difficulties.

Students with chronic diseases requiring daily management, such as asthma and diabetes, may receive services under the category of OHI if the disease negatively impacts education. For most students with asthma and diabetes, daily supports can be managed under a 504 or student health plan. However, if the disease impacts learning as a result of missed instruction or other disability-related factors (for example, a student struggles to pay attention when their blood sugar level is off), the student should receive special education services under the category of OHI.

Asthma is a condition characterized by the swelling or narrowing of airways in combination with excess mucus production. Symptoms of asthma include shortness of breath, chest tightness, coughing, wheezing, and difficulty breathing. When airway swelling causes extreme difficulty breathing, an asthma attack results. Severe asthma attacks may be fatal and require emergency medical treatment. Treatments for asthma include daily medications and inhalers to address symptoms, and emergency inhalers or medications to provide immediate relief in the event of an asthma attack. Asthma-related issues may cause students who have the condition to regularly miss school days, instructional time, and school activities.

Type 1 diabetes (formerly juvenile diabetes) occurs when the pancreas fails to produce insulin, creating sugar build-up in the bloodstream. **Type 2 diabetes** occurs when insulin does not work properly, leading the body to produce less of it. Most students with diabetes follow treatment plans that include glucose monitoring, individualized diet plans, and daily insulin shots.

Complications related to diabetes, including **hypoglycemia** (low blood glucose) and **hyperglycemia** (high blood glucose) may impact learning or result in medical emergencies at school. Hypoglycemia can affect cognitive ability, attention, behavior, and mood and may result in loss of consciousness or seizure if left untreated. Hypoglycemia is treated with glucose tablets, snacks, or emergency glucose injections. Hyperglycemia does not immediately result in a medical emergency but may result in diabetic ketoacidosis—a build-up of ketones in the bloodstream—which can cause serious health problems or be fatal if untreated. Hyperglycemia may be treated with a supplemental insulin dose, extra water, or by checking pump functioning for students who use an insulin pump.

Heart conditions in children are often congenital and caused by multiple factors. Congenital heart conditions, which occur when genetic anomalies or environmental factors cause abnormal development of the heart in utero, include the following:

- ▶ holes in the heart
- ▶ obstructed blood flow
- ▶ abnormal blood vessels
- ▶ heart valve abnormalities
- ▶ an underdeveloped heart
- ▶ a combination of defects

Treatment for heart conditions can involve surgical intervention with ongoing cardiac monitoring, which may include medication, dietary restrictions, or physical activity restrictions.

Congenital heart conditions may have different impacts on a student's development depending on the nature and severity of the heart defect. Babies with heart disease sometimes undergo early surgery, requiring hospitalization and time in intensive care. As a result, infants may have restricted movement and sensory input, which can delay their reaching developmental milestones. For older children, illnesses, surgeries, or hospitalizations related to heart disease may cause the child to miss out on learning opportunities. Many children with heart disease tire more easily than their peers, meaning decreased opportunities for learning. Further, genetic problems that cause heart defects could also impact cognitive and motor development.

Child development may also be affected by **blood disorders**. As with other complex medical issues, medical needs associated with blood disorders could result in developmental or learning delays because of medical complications or missed instructional time. Two genetic blood disorders that may impact student learning are hemophilia and sickle cell disease.

In **hemophilia**, the body lacks blood-clotting proteins. Students with hemophilia bleed much longer than normal because the blood is unable to clot to stop the bleeding. Deep bleeding around joints and internal bleeding which does not clot can cause organ damage and may be life threatening for students with hemophilia.

Sickle cell disease is a blood disorder in which red blood cells cannot adequately carry oxygen throughout the body. In students with sickle cell disease, red blood cells become rigid and are shaped like crescent moons (rather than round and flexible), causing them to become stuck in small blood vessels, blocking blood flow. Individuals with sickle cell disease may experience periods of significant pain due to blocked blood flow, which may last days or weeks. Sickle cell disease can also cause frequent infection, delayed growth, and vision problems. In the United States, sickle cell disease is most common among people of African descent.

Cancer occurs when cells in the body grow out of control. **Pediatric (childhood) cancer** refers to cancers that occur in children under fourteen years old. There are many types of pediatric cancer; those that most commonly impact learning in children include brain tumors, tumors affecting the eye or ear, leukemia, and non-Hodgkin lymphoma. Treatment for cancer includes chemotherapy, surgery, or radiation. Once cancer treatment is completed, survivors have regular follow-up care to ensure the disease has not returned. Students who are survivors of, or who are currently being treated for, pediatric cancer may miss extended periods of school. Both the treatments for cancer and the disease itself may affect motor ability, hearing, vision, memory, energy levels, or cognitive ability.

Table 2.1. Conditions That May Qualify as Other Health Impairments Under IDEA

Attention deficit/hyperactivity disorder (ADHD)	characterized by inattention, hyperactivity, and impulsivity that affects a student's ability to progress in school
Epilepsy	a nervous disorder characterized by frequent seizures
Tourette syndrome	a nervous disorder characterized by repetitive, involuntary words or actions
Asthma	a respiratory disorder characterized by narrowing of the airways that restricts breathing
Diabetes	an endocrine disorder in which the body cannot produce and/or respond appropriately to insulin
Heart conditions	an abnormal development of the heart that negatively affects cardiovascular performance
Hemophilia	inability of the blood to clot properly, caused by lack of clotting proteins
Sickle cell disease	characterized by sickle (crescent)-shaped red blood cells that cannot adequately carry oxygen
Cancer	uncontrolled cell growth

Many conditions that may qualify a student as having a health impairment affect multiple body systems. Students with serious health conditions may have social-emotional issues, such as depression or anxiety, which may also need to be addressed. Other illnesses affect students' mobility and may result in an orthopedic condition. Students with serious health conditions are also at a higher risk for hearing loss, visual impairment, and cognitive impairment.

ELIGIBILITY AND IDENTIFYING OTHER HEALTH IMPAIRMENTS

For a child to qualify as a student with a health impairment, a multidisciplinary evaluation team must determine that a child has an acute or chronic health problem which impacts strength, vitality, or alertness (including heightened alertness to extraneous stimuli) that results in limited engagement toward instruction. The school team must also determine that symptoms related to the health impairment negatively impact educational performance. Health conditions may affect educational performance due to the following:

► a long period of absence from school

- ▸ the inability to maintain attention for the same length of time as peers as a result of a health condition or as a side effect of medication taken for a health problem
- ▸ the inability to attend to school for the duration of the day as a result of limited strength or vitality

Evaluations for learners who may qualify as students with OHI should include medical, developmental, cognitive, academic, and behavioral information. An evaluation of a student with a health impairment should include details of developmental and medical history related to the impairment. In addition to information supplied by a student's family, medical and developmental information should be provided by a medical professional. Evaluations must also include assessments of a student's cognitive ability, academic achievement, and adaptive behavior, including social-emotional development. Assessments of language, communication, and fine and gross motor development are often included, especially if a health condition impacts a student's strength and vitality.

Based on results of the evaluation, school teams must determine that the student has a qualifying health condition and that the health condition impacts education. If cognitive, academic, behavioral, communication, or motor assessments indicate a need, a student qualifies for special education services. If a student requires special accommodations as part of their health condition but does not require additional interventions to support learning, that student may receive accommodations through a 504 plan or individual health plan instead of an IEP.

EDUCATIONAL PRACTICES FOR STUDENTS WITH OTHER HEALTH IMPAIRMENTS

Because the OHI category includes students with a range of health conditions and unique learning challenges, there are no set educational practices for this category. Instead, educational interventions for students with OHI should specifically address ways in which the health condition impacts learning.

Teachers should use several behavioral and instructional strategies to support students with ADHD in the classroom. Students with ADHD perform best in highly structured classroom environments with limited distractions. Since work that is fine-motor intensive or involves many steps (such as large writing assignments) can often be difficult for students with ADHD, teachers of these students should ensure that classroom rules are clearly and positively stated and that classroom routines are consistently maintained. Learners with ADHD respond best to directions that are brief, specific, and positively stated; directions involving multiple steps may need to be modeled or written down. Teachers may ease workload by allowing frequent breaks within the work task, allowing extra time to complete the work, reducing the length of the assignment, or providing the student with choices within the assignment (such as only completing the odd numbers or choice of topic).

As much as possible, teachers should establish a predictable environment with consistent routines and expectations. Teachers can support the need for movement of students with ADHD by embedding opportunities for mobility within daily activities. Flexibility in seating and grouping may also be beneficial. For example, some students with ADHD may do best while standing in a group to work; others may work best in a quiet desk space. Often, students with ADHD benefit from having a seat near instruction with limited distractions surrounding the student. Classroom materials should be well organized, and teachers should support students with ADHD in personal organization. Potential organizational supports for students with ADHD include assignment notebooks, color-coded work systems, embedded time for re-organization of materials, and checklists.

Many behavioral interventions effective for students with emotional disabilities also benefit students with ADHD, who profit from positive supports for appropriate behavior. When working with a student with ADHD, teachers should ensure that positive directions are given five times more frequently than correction. Students with ADHD often respond best to visual prompts of expected behavior, such as cue cards, video modeling, or even teacher proximity. Opportunities to earn reinforcement through behavioral contracts or check-in/check-out systems benefit students with ADHD.

Self-monitoring is an effective behavioral intervention strategy for students with ADHD. Self-monitoring interventions teach students to independently evaluate and record their own performance toward behavioral objectives. Self-monitoring reinforces on-task behavior or task completion. Students may be cued to self-monitor on-task behavior by an auditory cue, such as a tone, or a visual prompt.

Table 2.2. Summary of Educational Practices for Students with ADHD

Intervention	Description
Flexible seating	standing option or adapted seating, such as exercise balls or wiggle cushions
Frequent breaks	allowing students a break, such as a walk or drink, in the middle of the work period
Graphic organizers	visual map or diagram used to organize information
Highly structured environment	classroom contains limited distractions; rules and routines are explicitly taught
Movement	opportunities for movement are embedded into the school day through alternative seating options or scheduled movement breaks
One-step directions	using brief, direct instructions rather than instructions that contain multiple steps
Self-monitoring	behavioral intervention in which a student is in charge of monitoring their own behavior and reinforcement
Visual behavior supports	cue cards, video models

Many students with health impairments require an **individual health plan** as part of (or in addition to) their IEP. Health plans are developed by educational support professionals in collaboration with school nurses or other medical professionals within the school setting. Individual health plans should outline a daily strategy of care to meet a student's medical needs while limiting impact on education. For example, a plan should be in place for daily medications (including inhalers), dietary needs, or glucose checks.

The plan should also address situations where symptoms arise that could indicate a medical emergency for the student. For example, a blow to the head or chest might result in a medical emergency for a student with hemophilia, while teachers of students with diabetes should be aware of signs of hypoglycemia. Every person who works with a student with a health condition should have a working knowledge of emergency warning signs for that student.

Finally, the health plan should specify steps school personnel must take in the event of a medical emergency. For example, an emergency plan should indicate which medication should be given in an emergency and under what circumstances the school should send a student for emergency treatment at a hospital.

Students with epilepsy often have a **seizure action plan** as part of or in place of an individual health plan. The seizure action plan should include the following information:

- the symptoms, type, frequency, and duration of seizures
- list of current medications, dosages, and potential side effects
- a plan of action if a student has a seizure at school or on the bus, including when parents should be contacted
- general first aid for the person having a seizure
- definitions of when a seizure episode constitutes a medical emergency for the student
- steps to be taken in the event of a medical emergency

Students with health impairments may need specialized training to independently monitor and care for their individual health condition. For instance, a student with diabetes may receive training on managing glucose testing and insulin, self-monitoring for symptoms of hypoglycemia and hyperglycemia, and addressing social-emotional difficulties (mood swings, irritability, anxiety) that can result from fluctuations in blood sugar. Students with health impairments also may benefit from training in self-advocating for needs related to their impairment. For example, a student with asthma needs

DID YOU KNOW?

First aid for students having a seizure includes staying with the student, timing the duration of the seizure, easing the student to the floor, turning them onto one side, and clearing the area to ensure safety and privacy. Teachers should never restrict movements or put anything into the mouth of a person having a seizure.

to self-advocate when they need an emergency inhaler. Through training in self-advocacy and self-care, students with health impairments are able to participate more fully and independently in their educational setting.

Teachers should establish an environment that supports the health care needs of the student. A schedule gives students the opportunity to access any needed medical care including inhalers, medications, and glucose testing. Students who fatigue easily may need a quiet place in the classroom where they are able to rest; other students may benefit from specialized seating arrangements because of physical, attention, or sensory needs. Many students with health impairments follow specific dietary and physical activity regimens. It is often the responsibility of the teacher to ensure that all dietary and movement needs (or restrictions) are met throughout the school day.

In many cases, other students in the classroom may have difficulty understanding the needs of a student with a health impairment. For example, some students may feel jealous of a student with diabetes who receives a "special snack" or frightened if a friend has a seizure. Other times, classmates may worry when a student is frequently absent from school. It may be beneficial for a teacher to educate the entire class about a student's health needs in order to build understanding; however, teachers should never share information about a student's condition with classmates without specific permission from parents to do so. In fact, partnering with families to share information and experiences with the class is often the best way to provide class-wide education about a health condition.

Students with health impairments may also need specialized instruction to address developmental and educational delays resulting from their condition. Students with health conditions who are behind their peers academically may need direct intervention in reading, math, or writing in order to make progress at the same rate as their peers. Students who miss large periods of instruction due to a health condition may qualify for home instruction or an extended school year (instruction during the summer).

A health impairment puts extra stress on a child and may result in anxiety, depression, or other social-emotional difficulties. Students with health impairments may need specialized instruction in strategies for coping with emotions that may affect learning. Students with health impairments may also have delays in social skills. Many times, students with a health impairment have fewer opportunities to interact with other children than their healthy peers do. As a result, children with health impairments may need direct instruction to learn age-appropriate social skills.

Health impairments may affect fine motor, gross motor, and language development, and some students may require physical therapies to address motor needs which occur as a result of their health condition. They may also need occupational therapies to improve fine motor skills and address daily living needs. Students whose health condition affects oral motor development or language centers in the brain may need speech-language therapy in order to effectively communicate with peers.

SAMPLE QUESTIONS

5) Cynthia is a second-grade student with diabetes. Her school team has a plan of care to address needs related to Cynthia's diabetes including glucose testing, extra snack times, insulin injections, and an emergency plan. What is this type of plan often called?

    A.   diabetes control plan

    B.   individual health plan

    C.   seizure action plan

    D.   IEP

6) Which of the following best describes the primary symptoms of ADHD?

    A.   hyperactivity and impulsivity

    B.   hyperactivity, impulsivity, and learning delays

    C.   hyperactivity, impulsivity, and inattention

    D.   impulsivity, learning delays, and inattention

AUTISM SPECTRUM DISORDER

CHARACTERISTICS OF AUTISM SPECTRUM DISORDERS

Autism is defined by IDEA as a developmental disability that significantly affects communication and social interaction. The term **autism spectrum disorder (ASD)** encompasses what used to be five separate diagnoses:

- autistic disorder
- Asperger syndrome
- Rett syndrome
- childhood disintegrative disorder
- pervasive developmental disorder not otherwise specified (PDD-NOS)

Before 2013, the *Diagnostic and Statistical Manual of Mental Disorders* (DSM-IV) listed each as a distinct condition. The DSM-5 (fifth edition) combined those five conditions, which had similar characteristics, into one diagnostic category of autism spectrum to encompass the broad range of individuals who demonstrate similar characteristics in interaction, behavior, and communication.

The DSM-5 uses five criteria for diagnosing individuals with autism spectrum disorders. First, individuals must demonstrate persistent deficits in social communication and social interactions. **Social communication** refers to the way a person uses language within social situations. Deficits may include both verbal and nonverbal communicative behaviors. In order to be considered, deficits must occur over multiple contexts. For example, the behaviors must occur at home, in the community, and at school rather than just manifest themselves in one particular setting or with one particular person.

HELPFUL HINT

The *Diagnostic and Statistical Manual of Mental Disorders, Fifth Edition* (DSM-5) is published by the American Psychiatric Association. It sets standards for the diagnosis and classification of psychiatric disorders.

Social interaction, how we interact with those around us, may be challenging for people with autism. A person with autism may have little interest in interacting with others. Other people with autism may desire such interactions but struggle to consider interests outside of their own. Failure to adhere to expectations in social interactions can make it hard for persons with autism to make friends and maintain relationships.

Difficulties with communication can make all areas of interaction harder for individuals with autism. Using socially expected **nonverbal communication** and understanding the nonverbal communication of others may be very difficult for a person with autism. Nonverbal communication includes eye contact, body language, facial expression, and gesturing. An example of a frequent nonverbal communication challenge for individuals with autism is poor eye contact. Many people with autism have difficulty making eye contact, maintaining eye contact, or using eye contact in a socially expected way.

Another nonverbal communication difficulty is maintaining socially appropriate personal space. Some individuals with autism fail to respect others' personal space by standing too closely when speaking or grabbing something on another person that catches their interest (like glasses, jewelry, or hair) rather than offering a compliment. In contrast, other individuals with autism may totally avoid nonverbal behaviors that require touching another person, such as shaking hands or giving high fives. Other nonverbal communication challenges include a lack of facial expression or difficulty using gestures.

In addition to having difficulty using nonverbal communication in socially expected ways, persons with autism may have trouble understanding the nonverbal communication of others. Many people with autism struggle to read nonverbal cues, such as facial expression and body language, which communicate important messages. For example, a person with autism might not understand nonverbal cues that suggest a person is angry or upset. In another instance, a person with autism might miss typical cues that an individual needs to end a conversation. Failure to read nonverbal cues can result in awkward and even unsafe social interactions. People on the autism spectrum are much more likely than their neurotypical peers to be hurt, victimized, or wander off.

Some people with autism spectrum disorders also have difficulty with **verbal communication** or spoken words. Many individuals with autism are **nonverbal**, using no verbal communication. Other people with autism use assistive technology or American Sign Language to communicate. People with autism who use verbal language may have difficulty initiating social interactions or responding according to social expectations. For example, a person with autism might have difficulty participating in a back-and-forth conversation by either failing to respond to another's inquiry or by talking for long periods without giving the other participant a turn.

A second criterion for a diagnosis of autism spectrum disorder is the presence of **restricted**, **repetitive patterns of behavior**, interests, or activities. Individuals must display restricted, repetitive behaviors in at least two areas in order to be diagnosed with autism spectrum disorder. One type of repetitive behavior observed in people with autism is **stereotyped motor movements**. Repetitive motor movements include stereotypic simple motor movements, often called *stimming*, which is short for *self-stimulatory behavior*. Common stereotypic behaviors include hand-flapping, rocking, or spinning. Another stereotypic behavior is **echolalia**—the repetition of words and phrases. Echolalia includes immediate repetition of words spoken by another person as well as repetition of lines from movies or other media.

Another form of a restricted behavior pattern observed in individuals with autism is insistence on routine. A person with autism may display **ritualized patterns of behavior**, insisting on following the same routine each day. Ritualized behaviors include eating the same foods daily, repeating verbal scripts or interactions, and doing activities in the exact same order or way each day. Many people with autism have difficulty with transitions or changes in routine. In some cases, changes in routine may cause extreme distress.

Restricted behavior includes behavior that arises from a very **narrow range of interests**. Much of the time, attachment to a particular interest is much more intense than what is typical. A person with autism may be extremely focused and passionate when working in their areas of interest, sometimes achieving an impressive level of expertise. In contrast, it may be difficult for them to take interest in things outside their special interests.

Finally, restricted patterns of behavior may be due to hyper- or hyporeactivity to **sensory input**. Areas of sensory input include visual (sight), auditory (hearing), olfactory (smell), gustatory (taste), tactile (touch), vestibular (sense of head movement in space), proprioceptive (sensations from muscles in body) and interoceptive (sense of what internal organs are feeling). In any area of sensory input, a person with autism may be hyperreactive and actively avoid input in that area. For example, a person who is hyperreactive to visual input may avoid bright lights, or a person hyperreactive to auditory input may wear noise-cancelling headphones. Individuals may also be hyporeactive in any of the areas of sensory input and require increased intensity of input in order to get a sensory response. For example, a person who is hyposensitive to proprioceptive input may seek deep pressure (often provided through weighted blankets or compression clothing) while a person with a hyporeactive gustatory system may seek heavily spiced foods.

> **DID YOU KNOW?**
>
> Over half of children with autism experience chronic sleep challenges while as much as 75 percent of children on the autism spectrum experience feeding problems.

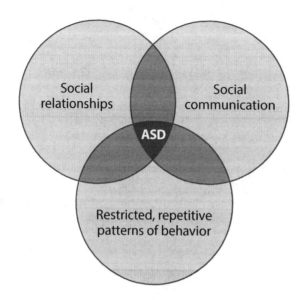

Figure 2.3. Triad of Impairment

When diagnosing ASD, medical professionals specify the severity level for each of the first two criterion (social interaction and restricted behaviors). Individuals may be rated according to the different severities for each criterion.

▶ Level 1 "requires support."

▶ Level 2 "requires substantial support."

▶ Level 3 "requires very substantial support."

The final criteria for diagnosis of an ASD are guidelines for how the symptoms above must manifest to be considered part of an ASD.

1. Symptoms must be present early in a person's development. (Most characteristics of ASD usually appear by age three.)

2. Symptoms must cause significant impairment in functioning across areas of life (social, occupational).

3. Behaviors are not better explained through a different diagnosis, such as intellectual disability or global developmental delay.

ASDs frequently co-occur with other physical and mental health conditions, intellectual disabilities, and language impairments. Individuals with autism experience epilepsy at a much higher rate than the general population. Other physical health conditions commonly occurring with autism include gastrointestinal problems, feeding issues, and disrupted sleep. Mental health conditions which can co-occur in people with autism at a higher rate than in the general population include ADHD, anxiety disorders, depression, schizophrenia, obsessive compulsive disorder, and bipolar disorder.

ELIGIBILITY AND IDENTIFYING AUTISM SPECTRUM DISORDERS

Eligibility criteria for qualifying for services under the category are not defined in IDEA, so there is some variation from state to state; however, most states have similar criteria. In some states, the student does not have to have a medical diagnosis of autism in order to qualify for special education services.

For a student to qualify for services under the category of autism, educational teams assess whether the student exhibits behaviors associated with ASD. (Many schools will have a team specifically trained to identify students with autism.) The educational team must determine that the student has difficulties with communication and forming social relationships. Teams may look for unusual responses to sensory input, repetitive behaviors, or a narrow range of interests.

> **DID YOU KNOW?**
>
> There are many reasons a student's guardian may want special education services but hesitate to seek out a medical diagnosis, including social stigma, insurance coverage, or local availability of qualified medical professionals.

During an educational evaluation, teams will assess cognitive development as well as observed behaviors that may indicate autism. Finally, the educational team must determine that the student's educational progress is adversely affected by any signs associated with the characteristics of an ASD.

EDUCATIONAL PRACTICES FOR STUDENTS WITH AUTISM SPECTRUM DISORDERS

Educational researchers have identified many evidence-based interventions which are effective in improving outcomes for students with autism. Students with autism often require a range of interventions to ensure that they are being educated in a way that best fits their strengths while minimizing potential adverse effects of ASD. Evidence-based interventions for students with autism include behavioral, language, and instructional interventions as well as environmental supports.

Almost all educational interventions utilized with students with autism use the instructional strategies of modeling, prompting, and visual support. **Modeling** is the demonstration of the target behavior by the instructor to encourage the imitation of the behavior by the learner. After frequent practice with modeling, the learner may become independent in the desired behavior.

In many cases, **prompting** helps ensure that the student with autism performs the behavior appropriately. A prompt is verbal, gestural, or physical assistance which ensures a student correctly performs the target behavior. Many learners with autism have difficulty coping with making mistakes, so it is important that learners have many repetitions of the correct behavior rather than practicing incorrectly. Prompting is used to ensure that the student practices the behavior correctly until he or she is able to perform it independently.

Finally, students with autism are often very visual learners; therefore, almost all interventions should include some type of **visual support**. Visual supports are any visual provided to the learner to promote the acquisition of new skills or the demonstration of a desired behavior. Visual supports should be used throughout the environment of a student with autism. Supports such as picture cards can aid in communication while task lists, visual schedules, maps, and labels can assist learners with autism in navigating their environment and handling changes in routines. Cue cards, pictures, and videos can help students learn new material and understand behavioral expectations.

Students qualify for special education services under the category of autism due to difficulties with building social relationships and the presence of restrictive or repetitive behaviors. Therefore, behavioral interventions are very important to enable learners to fully access their education. **Applied behavior analysis (ABA)** is a research-based system of educational and behavioral interventions that is often used with students with autism. ABA interventions apply principles from the science of behavior analysis to improve learning and behavior. Behavioral analysts view behavior as a three-term contingency: antecedent, behavior, consequence (ABC). Interventions used as part of an ABA program directly address any of the three parts of behavior.

STUDY TIP

The three-term contingency of ABA can be easily remembered by thinking of it as the ABCs of behavior: **A**ntecedent, **B**ehavior, **C**onsequence.

Individual behavioral interventions are most effective when based on a **functional behavior assessment (FBA)**. FBAs use a variety of data to ascertain the function, or purpose, behind a behavior. Sources of data to determine behavior function may include observations, behavioral inventories, ABC behavioral data, and even experimental investigation of behavior. Some common functions of behavior include attention, escape or avoidance of an activity, or access to a tangible item. Once function is determined, a behavioral strategy may be put in place to address the behavior. FBAs are discussed in detail in chapter 4.

Antecedent-based interventions address circumstances that precede a behavior. Antecedent-based interventions are used to arrange events or environmental stimuli to lead to a reduction of problem behavior or an increase in desired behavior. For example, if a student gets overwhelmed and shuts down when given a worksheet, the teacher may give the student fewer problems or allow the student to choose to do half of the problems. By reducing the amount of work, the teacher is controlling the antecedent which leads to the problem behavior. Conversely, if an instructor is working on teaching a student to greet others, the teacher may set up situations in which the student can practice in order to increase the behavior.

Positive behaviors may also be increased through **reinforcement**. Reinforcement is an event that follows a behavior and results in an increase of the behavior in the future. Common reinforcers for behaviors are social reinforcement (attention), tangible reinforcement (toys, candy), or escape from something adverse (avoiding an activity that the student does not want to do). When working with students with autism, reinforcement can increase learning and develop social behaviors.

Teachers must determine what reinforcement is most motivating for an individual student and ensure that reinforcement is being immediately provided for desired behaviors (and withheld for negative behavior). One type of reinforcement—**differential reinforcement of alternative behavior**—involves reinforcing a specific or acceptable behavior other than the problem behavior. **Extinction** is a method used to reduce problem behavior. In extinction, the teacher ceases outside reinforcement by ignoring the behavior. Eventually the student will stop engaging in the behavior. A teacher who ignores the student who is dropping pencils for attention, rather than providing that attention by picking up the pencils, is using extinction. Extinction is often used in combination with a differential reinforcement intervention.

Another effective behavioral intervention based on ABA principles is self-monitoring. **Self-monitoring** interventions put students with autism in control of monitoring their own behavior and reinforcing themselves for behaving according to a pre-set expectation. The first step in a self-monitoring program is to define the expected behavior with the student and provide examples and nonexamples of the behavior. Then, the student receives a way to track or record their behavior and a plan for how often it should be recorded. The teacher and student work together to decide on a reinforcement plan for meeting target behavior goals. Teachers may want to provide occasional check-ins with the student to discuss outcomes.

One area where self-monitoring interventions have been used effectively is for on-task behavior. In **on-task behavioral interventions**, students are given a cue (such as a beeping or vibrating watch) which signals them to record if they were on task when the cue occurred or not.

Many effective behavioral interventions for students with autism seek to improve social skills in order to improve deficits in building social relationships. **Social skills training** is direct instruction in expected social behaviors, often provided in a small group or one-on-one setting. Social skills training groups typically use direct instruction, modeling, role-playing, and feedback to help students improve their ability to interact with peers. One very effective way to structure a social skills training group is through a **structured play group** which pairs students with autism with typically developing peers. In the structured play group, an adult guides and structures the play to support appropriate social interactions among all learners.

> **DID YOU KNOW?**
>
> Research indicates that self-monitoring interventions are effective in altering behavior. Simply providing the structure to draw the student's attention to the behavior is often enough to initiate change.

Other effective interventions for improving social skills in students with autism include scripting, social narratives, and video modeling. In **scripting** interventions, a student receives a verbal or written script to follow in order to perform a certain skill. A student typically practices the script until mastering the skill and then applies the skill to a generalized setting. Scripting interventions teach social skills (such as approaching a peer and asking to play) or academic skills (like letter formation).

Social narratives use a story about a specific situation to provide students with a description of environmental cues, others' thoughts and feelings, and behavioral expectations. Social narratives (also called social stories) are usually short and individualized according to a specific learner's needs in a certain situation or setting. Most social stories include picture support to facilitate understanding of cues, feelings, and appropriate behavior.

Many students with autism are drawn to videos as a medium of information and will sometimes imitate a video—especially one of themselves—more readily than they will imitate another person. **Video modeling** interventions use a video recording to model a targeted behavior or skill. A peer or the student with autism will model the expected behavior on camera. Then, the video is used to teach and prompt expected behavior.

Communication interventions are also very important in promoting educational achievement for students with autism. Most often, special education teachers collaborate with speech-language pathologists to provide communication interventions for students with autism. One effective intervention for students, especially those with minimal verbal skills, is the use of **alternative and augmentative communication (AAC)**. AAC is the use of any additional communication method (beyond traditional speech) to improve someone's ability to communicate. AAC can range from low-tech options, like pictures or American Sign Language, to high-tech speech-generating devices.

In the **picture exchange communication system (PECS)**, students hand pictures to a partner as a way to communicate. Picture communications in the PECS system often begin with making requests but can be expanded to using sentences and commenting as part of a conversation. More high-tech AAC interventions teach students with autism to use a computer or tablet system with speech output to communicate with others.

Educational interventions for students with autism are most

Figure 2.4. Picture Exchange Communication System (PECS) Cards

effective when they provide direct instruction, visuals, and structure beyond what is used in typical educational instruction. **Discrete trial teaching** (sometimes called **discrete trial training** or **DTT**) is an educational intervention based on ABA principles and usually delivered in a one-on-one setting. It consists of an antecedent stimulus, prompt (if needed), student response, and consequence. Discrete trial teaching is fast paced and uses **errorless learning**, meaning a student is prompted to give the correct response until they can do so consistently. For example, a discrete trial teaching session to teach the letter *A* would involve the teacher showing the student a letter flashcard and asking, "what letter" (stimulus); the teacher would then give a vocal prompt, stating the letter *A*. If the student responds correctly, the teacher provides reinforcement. If the student responds incorrectly, the teacher corrects him or her and begins the trial again.

A frequent complaint about discrete trial teaching is that it is contrived and does not promote the generalization of skills (extension of skills to other people and environments). **Natural environment training (NET)** is an instructional system that uses many of the same ABA principles as DTT, but instruction occurs using items readily available in the student's environment (rather than contrived). During NET, an instructor identifies behavioral and educational targets and then uses circumstances that naturally occur in the student's environment to teach those targets. Instructors use modeling, prompting, and reinforcement to teach skills to the student and may involve peers in the training. An example of natural environment training would be to teach the student the names of foods (using a similar stimulus, prompt, and reinforcement method) while playing with a kitchen set.

Structured teaching, or the TEACCH method (*Treatment and Education of Autistic and Communication Handicapped Children* method), is a strategy for educating students with autism. Structured teaching begins with providing a physical layout that clearly labels and separates learning areas, such as teacher-time area, independent work area, group-time area, sensory area, or break area. Students move through the physical structure using a visual schedule. During work time, each student navigates a system that uses visual structures to encourage independence. An example of a structured teaching work task might be counting out Velcro items onto a ten frame or spelling words using letters on connecting cubes. Students are often responsible for independently following a task list to retrieve, complete, and turn in assigned work. All areas of structured teaching rely on visual supports to enable students to navigate the school environment and demonstrate what they know.

To support the education of students with autism spectrum disorders, special education teachers must provide a broad range of interventions. Students with autism spectrum disorders often require behavioral interventions that will teach them the skills they need to build social relationships and demonstrate behavioral expectations in the classroom. Teachers need to work with speech and language pathologists to ensure that social communication needs are being met. Finally, special education teachers need to be able to structure instructional interventions to provide information to students with autism in a way that they can learn according to their strengths.

Table 2.3. Summary of Educational Practices for Students with ASD

Intervention	Description
Alternative and augmentative communication (AAC)	any communication method (beyond traditional speech) which improves a person's ability to communicate
Antecedent-based interventions	interventions which address circumstances that precede target behavior to either increase or decrease the likelihood of the behavior
Differential reinforcement	reinforcing a specific alternative to undesired behavior
Discrete trial teaching (DTT)	instructional method featuring a consistent antecedent stimulus, prompt (if needed), student response, and consequence in fast-paced trials
Errorless learning	student is prompted with correct response until they consistently respond correctly and independently
Extinction	removal of all reinforcement from an undesired behavior
Functional behavior assessment (FBA)	assessment to determine the purpose behind a behavior
Modeling	demonstration of the target behavior to encourage imitation by the learner
Natural environment training (NET)	instruction in behavioral and educational targets using opportunities within a student's environment
Picture exchange communication system (PECS)	AAC communication system in which an individual uses pictures to communicate
Prompting	verbal, gestural, or physical assistance to ensure a target behavior is performed correctly
Reinforcement	anything that follows a behavior resulting in the increase of said behavior
Scripting interventions	a student receives verbal or written instructions to perform a certain skill
Self-monitoring	behavioral intervention in which a student is in charge of monitoring their own behavior and reinforcement
Social narratives	provide students a description of environmental cues and behavioral expectations using a story about a specific situation
Social skills training	direct instruction of expected social behaviors

Intervention	Description
Structured play group	pairs a student with autism with typically developing peers to teach appropriate social interactions
Structured teaching (TEACCH)	educational structure featuring clearly defined learning areas and visually supported learning tasks
Video modeling	using a video of a person (or the student) performing the targeted behavior to encourage imitation by the learner
Visual support	any visual provided to promote the acquisition of a new skill or demonstration of a desired behavior

SAMPLE QUESTIONS

7) Zane is a student with autism who has difficulty transitioning between classes. What would be an appropriate antecedent intervention to improve Zane's ability to transition?

  A. visual schedule

  B. keep Zane in one classroom

  C. give Zane his favorite toy once he transitions

  D. provide Zane with a one-on-one aide

8) Which criteria are necessary for students to qualify for special education services under the category of autism?

  A. deficits in social communication, building social relationships, and a cognitive disability

  B. deficits in social interaction and communication and restricted, repetitive behaviors which adversely affect educational progress

  C. deficits in social interaction and communication, cognitive disability, and restricted, repetitive behaviors which adversely affect educational progress

  D. deficits in social interaction and communication which adversely affect educational progress

DEVELOPMENTAL DELAY

CHARACTERISTICS OF DEVELOPMENTAL DELAY

Developmental delay describes failure to meet developmental milestones. Typical areas of development include language, cognition, and social-emotional, motor, and adaptive skills. (See Chapter 2 for a detailed discussion of childhood development milestones.) Children whose development does not meet age-level expectations in at least one of the areas may be described as having a developmental delay. Developmental delays in children are generally identified by the age of five.

Eligibility and Identifying Developmental Delay

Eligibility under the category of developmental delay is used to service young children, often in early intervention programs. Developmental milestones are assessed during well-child checks through a child's pediatrician. Children who do not meet developmental milestones may be referred for early intervention services by the pediatrician. Other students are identified as having developmental delays through **Child Find** activities.

Children with a developmental delay in at least one area are eligible for early intervention services (under IDEA, Part C) from birth through age three. Although it varies by state, students are generally eligible for special education services (under IDEA, Part B) under the category of developmental delay from ages three to nine (and beyond in some cases). Once a child turns nine, the school must determine if special education services are still necessary. If the student is functioning at a level similar to typically developing peers, the child may be dismissed from special education services. If the student has not caught up to typical peers, schools may identify a student as eligible for services under a different disability category.

Educational Practices for Students with Developmental Delays

Interventions for students with developmental delays often occur in preschool or early intervention settings. Teachers who work with children with developmental delays should collaborate with families to create consistent expectations between home and school. Interventions for children with developmental delays should specifically target the area, or areas, in which a child is delayed.

Many students with developmental delays respond well to interventions delivered through play as well as interventions delivered in a student's natural environment. Students who have motor delays may benefit from play activities such as jumping, dancing, and climbing. Teachers should incorporate activities into the daily routine which require targeted gross and fine motor movement. Students with motor delays that affect everyday living should be provided with additional opportunities to practice adaptive behavior skills. For example, a dress-up activity could be used to encourage practice of independent dressing skills while handwashing and hygiene skills may be practiced each time a student uses the restroom.

Students with cognitive and social-emotional developmental delays benefit from classrooms with structured procedures and routines. It is important for children with developmental delays to be taught concepts in concrete ways, such as through hands-on experiences and the use of manipulatives, prior to abstract instruction. Often, active learning opportunities are most effective for students with developmental delays. Learning supports for students with cognitive delays should include visual ones, such as timers, schedules, and picture cues. Specific skill deficits can be addressed through direct instruction. For example, teachers may provide students guided practice and/or allow role-playing to teach them expected classroom and playground behavior, friendship skills, conflict resolution, and how to express feelings in appropriate ways.

Interventions should be provided in short instructional periods with frequent breaks. Students with developmental delays benefit from a highly structured learning environment. Classroom areas and behavioral expectations should be clearly defined and practiced with students

on a regular basis. Most importantly, teachers should collaborate with a variety of team members, which may include physical therapists, occupational therapists, SLPs, and a student's family to provide comprehensive interventions addressing every area of need for a student.

SAMPLE QUESTIONS

9)   In most states, children in which age range are served under the category of developmental delay?

   A.   three to nine years

   B.   birth to three years

   C.   birth to nine years

   D.   birth to twelve years

10)   Which of the following would NOT be identified as an area of developmental delay?

   A.   reading skills

   B.   communication skills

   C.   motor skills

   D.   adaptive skills

INTELLECTUAL DISABILITIES

CHARACTERISTICS OF INTELLECTUAL DISABILITIES

An **intellectual disability** describes when an individual has general intellectual functioning significantly below average with co-occurring deficits in adaptive behavior. For individuals with intellectual disabilities, a cognitive impairment—often measured using an IQ score—results in deficits in **adaptive behavior** like communication, self-care, and social skills. Deficits are usually evident during an early developmental period and adversely affect several areas of life, including educational performance. In the past, intellectual disabilities were referred to as **mental retardation**. In some areas, intellectual disabilities are referred to as **cognitive disabilities**.

Intellectual disabilities are characterized by intellectual impairment resulting in daily functioning delays in conceptual, social, or practical areas. **Conceptual skills** encompass the ability to think about and understand concepts through creativity, analysis, memory, and attention. Individuals with intellectual disabilities may demonstrate varying levels of ability in any area of cognitive functioning but lag behind typical peers in the acquisition of skills related to cognitive ability in at least one area. Deficits in cognitive functioning can result in difficulty with skill acquisition, memory recall, and retention and generalization of learning.

The areas of social and practical functioning are often referred to as **adaptive skills**, the everyday skills individuals use to function in the environment. Adaptive skills include conceptual, social, and practical areas. **Social skills** relate to the ability of an individual to form relationships with others through emotional understanding and communication. **Practical skills** concern the ability of an individual to perform skills of daily living, such as self-care, hygiene, feeding, finance, or even utilizing transportation.

Identified causes of intellectual impairments include genetic conditions, issues during pregnancy and birth, and poverty and cultural factors. **Genetic conditions** result from abnormal genes which may be inherited from a parent or caused by environmental factors (infections, exposure to toxins or radiation, etc.). The most common genetic conditions associated with intellectual disabilities are Down syndrome and fragile X syndrome. Less common genetic causes of intellectual disabilities include Williams syndrome, Angelman syndrome, phenylketonuria (PKU), Bardet-Beidle syndrome, Laurence-Moon syndrome, and Prader-Willi syndrome.

> **QUICK REVIEW**
>
> What might adaptive skills of a typically developing six-year-old look like? What about a sixteen-year-old?

Down syndrome is the most common genetic cause of intellectual disabilities. It is caused by a genetic mutation which results in an extra third chromosome 21, called trisomy 21. Down syndrome is associated with a unique set of symptoms and physical features. Generally, a person with Down syndrome has a brain that is smaller than average and shaped slightly differently. Common physical characteristics include eyes with an upward slant, facial features that are flat in profile but full around, a shorter neck, uniquely shaped ears, Brushfield spots (white spots on the iris), and a crossways crease on the hand. Down syndrome may cause varying levels of difficulty in cognitive and adaptive functioning. Each individual is different, but those with Down syndrome frequently demonstrate strong social skills, with a strong interest in making friends and building relationships.

Fragile X syndrome is the most common genetically inherited cause of intellectual disabilities in males. Fragile X syndrome is caused by a genetic anomaly of the FMR1 gene, which is inherited in an *X*-linked dominant pattern. Males are much more likely to have fragile X syndrome because of the presence of only one X chromosome. (That is, the genetic anomaly only needs to occur once rather than be inherited from both parents.) Females are much less likely than males to show symptoms of fragile X syndrome and often have more mild levels of intellectual impact.

Individuals with fragile X syndrome share common physical features, such as a face that is elongated with larger-than-typical ears. Other common physical features include a large forehead, a pronounced jaw, and an overall large stature with poor muscle tone. Individuals with fragile X syndrome also have varying levels of cognitive deficits and may demonstrate behavioral traits like those of autism, including stereotyped movements, reluctance to make eye contact, and delayed social and communication skills.

Intellectual disabilities may also be caused by pregnancy or birth issues. Use of alcohol during a pregnancy can result in **fetal alcohol syndrome (FAS)**. Individuals with FAS share common facial features, such as small eyes and a thin upper lip with a smooth philtrum (no groove between the nose and lip). FAS results in varying levels of developmental delays, behavioral problems, and intellectual impairments.

Intellectual disabilities may also occur as a result of smoking or other drug use. A mother's exposure to environmental toxins (like lead) may also result in intellectual disability. Other pregnancy complications which may result in intellectual disability include malnutrition and infections of the mother. Premature birth, low birth weight, and oxygen deprivation or other birthing injuries may also result in complications which lead to intellectual disabilities.

Finally, intellectual disabilities can be the result of environmental or accidental factors which occur during childhood. Near-drowning is an example of an accident that may result in intellectual disabilities. Children who live in poverty face a higher risk of intellectual disability due to increased risk of malnutrition, less access to preventative healthcare, later treatment for illness, and the risk of exposure to environmental toxins.

Intellectual disabilities may be accompanied by other conditions. In addition to academic and language interventions, many people with cognitive disabilities require behavioral interventions. People with intellectual disabilities may experience fine and gross motor delays and have co-occurring mental and physical conditions, including cerebral palsy, epilepsy, anxiety disorders, depression, ADHD, and ASD.

ELIGIBILITY AND IDENTIFYING INTELLECTUAL DISABILITIES

The multidisciplinary team conducts evaluations in several areas to provide a thorough description of a student's overall functioning. An assessment of cognitive ability (IQ score) provides a description of a student's capacity to learn, make sense of information, and problem-solve. Academic achievement assessments should be done to measure student progress in areas such as math, reading, and writing. Further evaluations should be done to assess areas of functioning, including social skills, daily living skills, communication, fine motor skills, and gross motor ability.

For a student to qualify as having an intellectual disability, the evaluation team must determine that there is a deficit in cognitive functioning. Generally, a deficit in cognitive functioning is determined by an IQ standard score below 70 (or below 75 with significant adaptive impairments). Cognitive assessments have a mean of 100 with a standard deviation of 15, making the average a range of 85 – 115. A score of 70 is two standard deviations below the mean, representing a cognitive functioning level that is significantly below average. Students with IQs in the range of 70 or below likely have extreme difficulty learning and problem-solving at the same level as their peers.

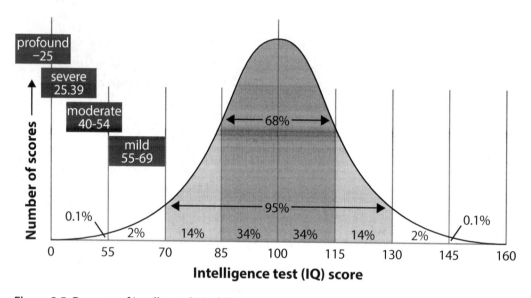

Figure 2.5. Degrees of Intellectual Disability

The evaluation team must also determine that the student has a delay in at least one area of adaptive functioning. A student may have an expressive or receptive language delay and difficulty communicating ideas or responding to the verbal communication of others. Another adaptive behavioral area is daily living skills. A delay in daily living skills might include toileting, dressing, self-care, or feeding skills that are developmentally below typical peers. Students may also have adaptive functioning delays in their ability to relate to others or follow developmentally appropriate behavior expectations. Students with intellectual disabilities may demonstrate social skills significantly below those of peers or have difficulty demonstrating independent learning behaviors. If the multidisciplinary evaluation team determines that a student is performing significantly below typical peers in cognitive functioning and at least one area of adaptive functioning, the student may qualify for special education services under the category of intellectual disabilities.

EDUCATIONAL PRACTICES FOR STUDENTS WITH INTELLECTUAL DISABILITIES

Students with an intellectual disability may require specialized and more intensive instruction (for example, more direct instruction, smaller student-to-teacher ratio) than typically developing students. Furthermore, students with intellectual disabilities often require intervention across areas of functioning, including adaptive behavior, communication, and social and daily living skills, in addition to academic interventions. Students with intellectual disabilities may also have motor delays or sensory needs that must be addressed through specially designed instruction.

While students with intellectual disabilities commonly require instruction beyond what a typical student might need, this instruction may be delivered in a variety of settings. As much as possible, students with intellectual disabilities should be exposed to the general education curriculum and given opportunities to learn with peers. Many students with intellectual disabilities make progress with supplemental supports and instructional needs provided in the general education setting. In some cases, individuals with intellectual disabilities may need instruction in an alternate location to ensure all learning needs are met. Decisions about least restrictive environments should be made by school teams based on individual student needs and should not be determined by qualification in any disability category, including intellectual disability.

In any educational setting, teachers can use many different instructional strategies to improve learning for students with intellectual disabilities. The educational environment should include many visual supports, and classroom schedules, areas, and materials should be clearly labeled. As needed, written visuals should include picture supports. Students with intellectual disabilities may require extra prompting and support to follow classroom routines and complete academic activities. Support for students can be provided by a designated peer helper, through a peer-mediated intervention, or by an instructional aide.

Teachers should avoid presenting too much information at once. Instead, they should present information or instruction one step at a time. One strategy to help students with intellectual difficulties learn is to break tasks into smaller steps using a task analysis. Then, steps may be taught one at a time until the entire skill is mastered. Another strategy is to present information at the concrete level, using manipulatives and visual supports. It is easier for students with disabilities to retain information which is presented in a concrete and hands-on way.

In some cases, students with intellectual disabilities require modifications to the general education curriculum or follow a curriculum based on alternate learning standards. Teachers should allow these students to demonstrate their knowledge in alternate ways, such as using manipulatives or by giving verbal, rather than written, responses. Students with intellectual disabilities typically require frequent reteaching of concepts to maintain mastery.

Assistive technology tools may help students with intellectual disabilities make progress in and have access to the general education curriculum. One beneficial assistive technology tool is **text-to-speech**. Text-to-speech technology scans and reads written words aloud for students who may have difficulty reading. **Speech-to-text** technology transcribes spoken words into written text. Speech-to-text may allow students who have difficulty with spelling or the fine motor aspects of writing or typing another avenue to communicate using written response. Students with intellectual disabilities who experience communication delays may benefit from alternative and augmentative communication systems to aid in expressive communication.

Students with intellectual disabilities benefit from many of the same instructional strategies that are effective for individuals with autism spectrum disorders. Systematic instruction based on ABA principles (for example, discrete trial teaching or natural environment training) is effective for teaching novel skills to individuals with intellectual disabilities. Systematic instruction may also be used to teach skills of daily living, such as handwashing or zipping a jacket.

Curricula for students with intellectual disabilities may include direct instruction in adaptive skills to improve long-term independence. For example, young students may need direct instruction on expected behavior in the classroom or on using the restroom independently. As students with intellectual disabilities progress toward middle and high school, interventions may focus on functional academics. **Functional academics** teach students skills they will need to function independently at home, work, and in the community. These skills include balancing a budget, laundry, and cooking. Interventions to improve functional work skills include résumé writing, interview training, or prerequisite skills for a job of interest to a student. Interventions to improve community access include exploration of community activities, practice purchasing from a grocery store, and orientation in a public transportation system. Functional academics are most effective when taught through hands-on, experiential learning activities.

Individuals with intellectual disabilities may benefit from instruction in skills of daily living that improve opportunities to live on their own, such as washing clothes or preparing food. Employability skills, such as interviewing, completing a résumé, and understanding workplace expectations may also be an important part of the curriculum for students with intellectual disabilities.

Students with intellectual disabilities should also receive direct instruction in social skills. Peer groups help students learn new social skills while building relationships. Strategies such as video modeling and social narratives are also effective ways to build social skills. Students with intellectual disabilities require multiple opportunities for role playing, guided practice, and immediate feedback in order to build new social skills.

Table 2.4. Educational Practices for Students with Intellectual Disabilities

Intervention	Description
Alternative and augmentative communication (AAC)	any communication method (beyond traditional speech) which improves a person's ability to exchange information
Concrete representation	instruction using hands-on strategies to demonstrate abstract concepts
Functional academics	instruction in skills of daily living in order to improve long-term independence
Increased intensity of services	examples include smaller student-to-teacher ratio, more minutes of direct instruction
Modifications	instruction and assessment that alter learning expectations
Peer-mediated intervention	intervention in which a peer is trained to support the social and educational interactions of a student with a disability
Prompting	verbal, gestural, or physical assistance which ensures a target behavior is performed correctly
Reteaching	frequent review of concepts
Social skill instruction	direct instruction of expected social behaviors
Speech-to-text	technology which transcribes speech to written text
Systematic instruction	intensive and direct instructional strategies, such as discrete trial teaching or natural environment training
Task analysis	breaking a skill into smaller, more manageable components
Text-to-speech	technology that reads written words aloud
Visual supports	any visual provided to promote the acquisition of new skills or the demonstration of a desired behavior; picture supports may be especially needed for students with intellectual disabilities

Often, students with intellectual disabilities require targeted behavioral interventions that should be based on the results of an FBA. Once an FBA has been completed, an intervention should be implemented based on the function of the behavior. Behavioral interventions for students with intellectual disabilities should focus on building new skills, such as social or communication skills, to replace inappropriate behavior. As much as possible, interventions should focus on positive reinforcement of appropriate behaviors rather than consequences for inappropriate behaviors.

11) **Which is the most common inherited cause of intellectual disability?**

    A.   FAS

    B.   Down syndrome

    C.   fragile X syndrome

    D.   muscular dystrophy

12) **Which strategy may be beneficial before beginning to teach laundry skills to a high school student with an intellectual disability?**

    A.   functional behavior assessment

    B.   task analysis

    C.   scripted reading intervention

    D.   touch cues

EMOTIONAL DISTURBANCE

CHARACTERISTICS OF EMOTIONAL AND BEHAVIORAL DISORDERS

The primary characteristic of students with **emotional and behavioral disorders (EBD)** is the presence of behaviors that are significantly different from age expectations or social norms. To be considered to have an EBD, a child's behavior must significantly impact normal life functions. Behaviors can be externalizing or internalizing.

Externalizing behaviors are those which are readily observable to another person. Common externalizing behaviors that characterize EBD include physical aggression, verbal aggression, hyperactivity, and noncompliance.

▶ **Physical aggression** includes behaviors which may cause physical harm to the student or another person. Examples include hitting, kicking, throwing items, and biting.

▶ **Verbal aggression** includes verbally threatening behaviors or those that may cause emotional harm to another person. Examples include yelling, tantrums, profanity, threats, or intentional humiliation of another.

▶ **Hyperactivity** includes behaviors associated with impulsiveness. A student may have difficulty completing a task, be constantly in motion, have difficulty keeping hands to self, or frequently talk out of turn.

▶ **Noncompliance** includes behaviors in which students refuse to follow instructions. Examples include refusing to move or speak in response to a request.

Internalizing behaviors are behavioral characteristics that primarily occur within a person and are not easily observable. Common internalizing behaviors include anxiety, depression, and social withdrawal. **Anxiety** is primarily characterized by excessive worrying while **depression** is characterized by a persistent feeling of sadness interfering with normal activities. **Social withdrawal** is characterized by a student spending most of their time alone, reluctant to interact with others. Students with EBD who internalize may exhibit other symptoms, such as irritability, changes in appetite, disturbance in sleep patterns, difficulty concentrating, fatigue, crying, or physical complaints (e.g., headache or stomach ache) that do not respond to treatment (known as somatization).

In some cases, students with EBD have a related mental health diagnosis. One possible diagnosis is an anxiety disorder. Anxiety disorders include generalized anxiety disorder (GAD), obsessive-compulsive disorder (OCD), panic disorder, post-traumatic stress disorder (PTSD), and phobia disorders.

Generalized anxiety disorder (GAD) is characterized by exaggerated and chronic worry, often with little provocation. To be diagnosed with a generalized anxiety disorder, an individual must report significant daily worry over a long-term period (at least six months). A person with GAD often worries over routine life situations in addition to circumstances that would be stressful for anyone.

People with **obsessive-compulsive disorder** may experience obsessions, compulsions, or both. **Obsessions** are relentless thoughts or urges that cause fear or anxiety. **Compulsions** are repetitive behaviors, often in response to an obsessive thought. For example, a person who has an obsession with germs may exhibit the compulsion of excessive cleaning. For a person with OCD, obsessions and compulsions far exceed typical habits or routines. People with OCD often spend over an hour each day on their obsessions and compulsions, experiencing little relief to their anxiety. Both the thoughts and behaviors pose significant problems to daily living.

The main characteristic of **panic disorders** are repeat, unexpected panic attacks. **Panic attacks** are sudden moments of intense fear which leave a person unable to perform typical life activities until the attack subsides. When having a panic attack, a person may experience a pounding or accelerated heart, trembling, shortness of breath, excessive sweating, intense fear or hopelessness, or feelings of being out of control. In some cases, panic attacks occur based on a known trigger, like a specific fear or circumstance. In other cases, panic attacks occur unexpectedly. For a person with a panic disorder, the fear of having a panic attack compounded with the attacks themselves may cause significant disruption to typical daily functioning.

Post-traumatic stress disorder is an anxiety disorder which develops as a result of a traumatic event. PTSD is characterized by symptoms of re-experiencing, avoidance, reactivity, and mood. A person with PTSD may re-experience events through flashbacks, nightmares, or re-occurring frightening thoughts. People with PTSD may actively avoid any situation that reminds them of their traumatic experience. A person with PTSD might have difficulty with cognition, such as trouble remembering important information, especially about the traumatic event. PTSD may also cause mood symptoms, such as negative thoughts about oneself, intense guilt, or loss of interest in activities. Young children with PTSD may have toilet training or language regression, act out the traumatic event in play, or become clingy toward trusted adults. Older children may develop disruptive or destructive behaviors.

Phobia disorders are characterized by an intense fear of a specific object or situation. While many people have fears, a person with a phobia disorder experiences excessive anxiety that interferes with daily life. **Social anxiety disorder** is a phobia condition characterized by an intense fear of social or performance situations. Individuals with social anxiety disorder actively avoid social situations, which often results in social withdrawal. **Separation anxiety disorder** is a phobia disorder primarily exhibited by children. Youngsters with separation anxiety have an extreme fear of being parted from people who are important to them (often a parent). Extreme fears related to separation anxiety disorder may result in tantrums, nightmares, or even physical symptoms of being unwell when separated.

Other students with EBD may be diagnosed with mood disorders such as major (clinical) depression or bipolar disorder. **Major depression** is characterized by persistent, long-term sadness (nearly every day for at least two weeks). Symptoms of major depression include loss of pleasure in activities, extreme fatigue, low self-esteem, or thoughts of harming oneself.

Bipolar disorder is a serious mental illness characterized by extreme mood changes. Sometimes referred to as *manic depression*, people with bipolar disorder experience feelings of **mania** followed by depression. During manic times, a person is generally extremely happy and often has excessive energy, sometimes with exaggerated self-confidence and impulsiveness. Following a period of mania, a person with bipolar disorder may experience an episode of depression or a normal period in mood.

Students with psychotic disorders may also be characterized as having EBD. **Schizophrenia** is a psychotic disorder characterized by hallucinations and delusions.

When a person experiences **hallucinations**, they hear or see things that are not actually real. **Delusions** are steadfast beliefs in things that are not true (paranoia, for example). Schizophrenia symptoms generally appear in a person's late teens to twenties. The onset of schizophrenia under the age of twelve is extremely rare. Early symptoms of schizophrenia may include children talking about strange ideas or fears, increased sensory sensitivity, withdrawal from others, or extreme difficulty with routine tasks.

Disruptive behavior disorders are another mental health diagnosis common to children with EBD. One type of disruptive behavior disorder is **oppositional defiant disorder (ODD)**. ODD is characterized by repeated defiant and disobedient behaviors toward authority lasting over a long period of time (at least six months). Children with ODD often become angry or resentful toward others. When given an instruction, they may refuse or intentionally disobey. While all children occasionally exhibit disobedient behaviors, a child with ODD exhibits behaviors consistently over an extended period of time to the point where defiance severely impacts functioning.

A second type of disruptive behavior disorder is **conduct disorder**. Conduct disorder is often considered a more serious disruptive behavior disorder because it includes willful cruelty toward others. Conduct disorder is characterized by behavior that violates social rules and sometimes harms others. Students with conduct disorder might exhibit aggressive behavior toward others and destructive behavior toward property. They may also ignore or deliberately violate established rules or act deceitfully toward others.

Table 2.5. Summary of Mental Health Diagnoses That Can Qualify as EBD

Anxiety disorders	generalized anxiety disorder (GAD)	chronic, exaggerated worry with no provocation
	obsessive-compulsive disorder (OCD)	relentless thoughts or repetitive behaviors
	panic disorder	sudden periods of intense fear, usually accompanied by physical symptoms such as rapid heart rate and breathing
	post-traumatic stress disorder (PTSD)	anxiety that develops in response to a traumatic event; often includes re-experiencing the event through flashbacks or nightmares
	phobia disorders	an intense fear of a specific object or situation
Mood disorders	major depression	persistent, long-term sadness
	bipolar disorder	extreme changes in mood between depression and mania
Psychotic disorders	schizophrenia	hallucinations and delusions that result in behavior and mood changes
Disruptive behavior disorders	oppositional defiant disorder (ODD)	repeated defiant and disobedient behaviors toward authority
	conduct disorder	defiant behavior that violates social rules and harms others

Students with emotional and behavioral disabilities may experience co-occurring difficulties. Behavioral disruptions can lead to delays in learning or coexist with learning disabilities. Students with EBD may also have delays in other developmental areas, such as communication, motor, or social skills.

Eligibility and Identifying EBD

IDEA defines emotional disturbance as a condition in which behavioral challenges occur over a long period of time to such intensity that it adversely affects a child's education. Behavioral challenges covered under the IDEA definition include the inability to maintain interpersonal relationships, behavior or feelings that are inappropriate in typical circumstances, depression, or the development of physical symptoms or anxiety related to perceived problems. The category of EBD is intended to serve students with significant emotional and behavioral disturbances. It is not meant to include students who are socially maladjusted and who may need social or behavioral interventions.

The multidisciplinary team evaluation should include information about the student's academic performance, cognitive functioning, social-emotional skills, and behavior. Depending on the student, other areas, such as language or fine motor skills, may be addressed. For a student to qualify as EBD, socio-emotional and behavioral rating scales must indicate long-term challenges differing significantly from typically developing skills. The team also needs to determine that behavioral difficulties have adversely affected the student's educational performance. Even if there is a behavior that significantly impacts educational performance, the multi-disciplinary team must rule out other disabilities, such as intellectual disabilities or autism. Further, the team must determine that behaviors occur as a result of an emotional disturbance and not as a result of social maladjustment, socio-economic circumstances, chemical dependency, or cultural differences.

Educational Practices for Students with EBD

Environmental supports play a large role in promoting classroom success for students with EBD. Teachers are instrumental in creating a classroom environment which is welcoming and supportive of students with all needs, especially those with EBD. A positive classroom environment begins with the way teachers interact with students. The teacher should consistently model cooperation and respect for others and help guide students to treat each other respectfully. Teachers should provide positive feedback and reinforcement at least four times as often as they provide correction. Students with EBD often react to tone and body language much more than to verbal communication, so it is important that teachers always keep a calm and nonjudgmental tone, even in challenging situations. Teachers must build relationships with students, taking time to learn about their interests, strengths, and needs. When such a relationship of trust exists, teachers are better able to support students during times of emotional crisis.

The classroom arrangement can also make a meaningful difference for students with EBD. The classroom should be well organized without too much visual stimuli. Materials should be labeled and have an established location. An array of seating and grouping options is often helpful for students, who should have the opportunity to sit in a group and work with peers as well as a space where they can work by themselves if they need some time away. For younger students, it is helpful to have a "quiet corner" or "sensory station" within the classroom where they can go if their feelings escalate. A **sensory station** is usually a quiet space, such as a bean bag in a corner or a tent, that provides a variety of sensory options based on the needs of the students in the classroom.

For most students with EBD, predictability can help prevent behavioral crises. Teachers can provide predictability to students by having consistent routines for them to follow; these should be established and taught on the first day of school. Examples of daily routines include how to transition in the hallway, where to turn in work, or how to transition between classroom activities.

Another important factor in daily predictability is a consistent daily schedule visible to students at all times. When there is a schedule change, teachers should provide early warning about what is changing and why. Schedules should be posted daily and used to aid transitioning between activities. During lessons and activities, teachers should provide clear expectations and objectives to students about the purpose of the activity. Even when an activity is meant to be open-ended to allow for student creativity, students with EBD may benefit from additional scaffolds and supports so that expectations are clear to them.

Students with EBD may have difficulty responding to high-pressure situations within the classroom. When possible, teachers should provide supports to take the pressure off of situations. For example, talking in front of the class is very stressful for many students. Teachers should avoid calling on a student who has not volunteered an answer. Instead, they should provide other ways to check for understanding, such as group-response options, think-pair-share, quick checks on paper, or other peer-supported options.

It is also important to avoid correcting the behavior of a student in front of others as much as possible. A much better option is for teachers to provide specific and immediate correction of a behavior directly to the student. Some students with EBD have difficulty communicating when they do not understand or need help. These students should be given signal or response cards to indicate when they do not understand without drawing the attention of their peers. Guided notes may help students follow instruction while avoiding the pressure of keeping up.

There are many school-wide, classroom-wide, and student-specific interventions for addressing student behavior. Interventions that are effective for students with ESB include token economies, behavioral contracts, and check-in/check-out systems. (Chapter 4 contains a detailed discussion of behavioral intervention strategies.)

In addition to behavioral management interventions, students with EBD often require direct instruction in social skills and self-regulation strategies. Teachers should provide students with strategies to interact with others in socially expected ways through modeling, guided instruction, and role playing. Social skill instruction includes identifying choices and consequences. Students may work with teachers to identify pathways to making good choices in situations that are often difficult. Other social skill strategies that may be effective include video modeling and peer social groups. Students with EBD should also be taught to self-regulate to handle overwhelming emotions safely. It is important for students to be able to self-identify upsetting situations or physiological signs they are becoming upset or about to "lose control." Students may be taught strategies such as mindfulness, deep breathing exercises, or sensory strategies (for example, swinging, rocking, deep pressure) to calm themselves when overly upset.

Table 2.6. Summary of Educational Practices for Students with EBD

Intervention	Description
Behavioral contracts	contracts which clearly define opportunities for reinforcement of expected behavior and consequences of unexpected behavior
Check-in/check-out system	behavioral system in which a student checks in with a teacher at the beginning and end of the day to discuss behavioral expectations and performance
Choices	opportunities for students to make choices throughout their day
Established routines	classroom schedules and routines that are predictable in nature and explicitly taught
Positive behavioral supports	reinforcement for demonstration of expected behavior
Relationship-building	establishing oneself as a person of trust with students by learning about their interests, strengths, and needs
Role playing	acting out social situations to practice appropriate responses
Self-regulation strategies	direct instruction of strategies to calm oneself when experiencing overwhelming emotion
Sensory station	quiet space with a variety of sensory options where students self-regulate
Social skill instruction	direct instruction of expected social behaviors
Token economies	students acquire tokens for appropriate behavior which may later be exchanged for other reinforcers

In many cases, supporting students with EBD means working with a team of professionals to meet a variety of needs. Special education teachers must collaborate with general education teachers and possibly paraprofessionals to ensure that behavior management plans are consistent throughout the day. School staff may need to collaborate with outside counselors, mental health professionals, and families to work on consistent strategies across environments. For students to make educational progress, they may also need direct instruction in academic areas, communication, or motor skills in addition to behavioral intervention.

SAMPLE QUESTIONS

13) **Physical aggression and tantrums are examples of which of the following?**

    A.   externalizing behaviors

    B.   internalizing behaviors

    C.   autism spectrum disorders (ASD)

    D.   hyperactivity

14) **Mr. Jones has a student in his class who has frequent outbursts, and he would like to intervene. What should his first step be?**

    A.   set up a group contingency

    B.   set up a token economy

    C.   talk to the student each time the behavior occurs

    D.   determine the function of the behavior

MULTIPLE DISABILITIES

CHARACTERISTICS OF MULTIPLE DISABILITIES

Students characterized as having **multiple disabilities** have concomitant cognitive, physical, or communication impairments which require intensive supports in order to access education. Examples of multiple disabilities include combinations of other categories, like intellectual disability–blindness, intellectual disability–orthopedic impairment, autism-deafness, or a medical condition with orthopedic impairment or intellectual disability. However, the term *multiple disabilities* does not include students who have deaf-blindness.

Students with multiple disabilities may have wide variations of needs based on the combination of disabilities. For example, a student with autism–orthopedic impairment may require much different support from a student with intellectual disability–deafness. However, the categorization of multiple disabilities generally indicates intensive needs in multiple life domains.

Many students with multiple disabilities have limited speech or communication. Communication difficulties can stem from physical impairments, intellectual disabilities, ASD, or deafness. Students with multiple disabilities may need intensive language intervention in order to develop functional communication skills. Many students with multiple disabilities use alternate and augmentative communication strategies, such as picture communication cards, sign language, or voice output communication aids (VOCAs).

Students with multiple disabilities also often have orthopedic impairments and may require physical or occupational therapy in order to access school and community environments. Many students with multiple disabilities have special equipment to support mobility, such as standers and wheelchairs. Students may need assistance with activities of daily living, such as using the restroom, dressing, and eating. Students with multiple disabilities may also have medical needs beyond orthopedic impairments and might require special medical supports, such as seizure plans, a specialized diet, or catheterization.

ELIGIBILITY AND IDENTIFYING MULTIPLE DISABILITIES

The IDEA definition of *multiple disabilities* includes simultaneous impairments that combine to result in intensive educational needs that may not be adequately addressed under the category for one of the impairments. Evaluation for a student who may qualify as a student with multiple disabilities involves assessments across life areas. An evaluation for a student with multiple disabilities should include a medical and developmental history since most students with multiple disabilities have medical diagnoses and a history of developmental delays. Developmental histories may include previous interventions a child has received to promote growth in any area of development.

Evaluations for students with multiple disabilities should include assessments of cognitive ability (IQ assessments) and academic achievement. Assessments in cognitive ability help a student's support team determine which strategies could work toward a student's strengths and what accommodations and modifications might be necessary for a student to make educational progress. Academic achievement assessments can help teams determine areas where specialized instruction is needed.

Adaptive behavior assessments are important when evaluating a student who has multiple disabilities. Assessments in adaptive behavior help school teams determine if any specialized supports are required to accommodate a student's needs in any area of adaptive behavior. Fine and perceptual motor assessments may be done to determine if occupational or physical therapy is needed. Most children with multiple disabilities require speech and language assessments to determine necessary communication supports.

For a student to qualify as having multiple disabilities, the team must determine that the student meets the requirements for two or more disability categories. The team must also determine that the combination of disabilities requires more supports than what might be necessary for the student under any one of the other disability categories for which that student may qualify. The team then determines the appropriate supports needed for the student to access and make progress in their educational setting.

EDUCATIONAL PRACTICES FOR STUDENTS WITH MULTIPLE DISABILITIES

Providing supports for students with multiple disabilities involves collaboration between a team of professionals (special education teachers, general education teachers, physical therapists, SLPs, occupational therapists, medical personnel, and vision or hearing consultants) and a student's family. Because the category of multiple disabilities covers a range of disability combinations that affect students in many ways, the needs of students with multiple disabilities are both intensive and diverse. Often, the special education teacher plays a primary role in managing the various supports that benefit a student with multiple disabilities. Special education teachers must work with other professionals to ensure that a student's physical and medical needs are met while providing opportunities for social-emotional and academic growth within the school setting.

Students with multiple disabilities may need a spectrum of adaptive equipment and instruction to support areas of daily living. When working with a student with multiple disabilities, teachers should look for opportunities to use adaptive equipment or teach a new skill which can build independence. Some students may need adaptive equipment (like modified seating or cutlery) or have dietary needs, such as thickeners or cut-up food, to enable them to eat independently. Others may require more intensive supports, such as tube feeding or adult assistance. Similarly, some students may be able to use the restroom with adaptive equipment while others might require changing or catheterization.

Students with multiple disabilities may utilize a range of mobility equipment, such as wheelchairs, crutches, walkers, or ankle-foot orthoses (AFOs) to access the school environment. For students with limited mobility, physical therapists can provide recommendations to ensure that students' positioning needs are met in the school setting. Special education teachers should collaborate with all professionals who work with a student to build student independence across daily living areas.

Communication is often an area that requires specific intervention for students with multiple disabilities. Effective language interventions for students with multiple disabilities are determined by considering the students' strengths while mitigating the effects of their disabilities. Many students with multiple disabilities benefit from AAC devices. Some students with multiple disabilities use American Sign Language or PECS as a communication system; other students use **voice output communication aids (VOCAs)**, electronic devices with voice output that replace or supplement speech for students with severe speech impairments. Depending on a student's physical strengths and needs, they may access a VOCA device using touch (for example, a touch-screen tablet) or through an **adaptive switch**. Adaptive switches are devices that allow students with physical impairments to use areas of strength to access technology. Examples of adaptive switches include push buttons, joysticks, foot switches, sip-and-puff switches, or voice/sound activated switches.

It is important for students to have the opportunity to practice communication skills in a natural environment. Teachers of students with multiple disabilities should facilitate opportunities for students with multiple disabilities to practice communication and social skills, especially with peers.

Academic instruction for students with multiple disabilities may include adaptive aids and equipment. Often, hands-on and experiential learning opportunities are most beneficial since students gain more through concrete instruction of concepts and the use of visuals or manipulatives than they do through symbolic instruction. In some cases, students need adaptations made to visuals (contrasting background, raised images, magnification) or manipulatives (contrasting colors, mixed textures to diversify sensory input). Students may use adaptive switches to access instruction or to demonstrate knowledge of material. Often, direct instruction with frequent review is necessary for students to master and maintain understanding of academic concepts.

> **QUICK REVIEW**
>
> Which assistive technology supports might help a student with multiple disabilities interact with peers?

When designing a classroom environment, the teacher should consider a student's medical, dietary, and sensory needs as well as mobility. Classrooms should have appropriate spacing to allow a student with mobility equipment to easily navigate the room. For students who use a wheelchair, it may be necessary to provide opportunities for them to learn outside of their wheelchair (for example, wedge supports on a carpet). A teacher may also need to provide accommodations for special dietary needs (refrigeration, for example) or classroom restrictions in cases of allergies or sensitivities. In all situations, a teacher should work closely with families and other professionals to ensure students' needs are met.

SAMPLE QUESTIONS

15) **Which of the following students would be LEAST likely to qualify as a learner with multiple disabilities?**

    A. Jeff, a student with an intellectual disability who is living with cerebral palsy

    B. Lyla, a student who is deaf and who has autism

    C. Shawn, a student who is deaf and blind

    D. Nicole, a student with an orthopedic impairment who is blind

16) **Mo is a student living with cerebral palsy and an intellectual disability. He uses a sip-and-puff switch with auditory scanning to speak with peers. What type of device is this?**

    A. voice output communication aid

    B. auditory voice output device

    C. speech-to-text

    D. text-to-speech

DEAFNESS AND HEARING LOSS

CHARACTERISTICS OF DEAFNESS AND HEARING IMPAIRMENT

Two separate educational categories under IDEA—hearing impairment and deafness—serve students who have some level of hearing loss. Under IDEA, a **hearing impairment** is a partial or total inability to hear sounds, which interferes with daily functioning. When hearing loss is severe enough that a person is not able to process language through sound, that person is considered to be **deaf**. The degree of hearing loss is described based on the loudness of sound (measured in decibels) required for a person to hear.

- ▶ **Mild hearing loss** requires sounds to be 25 to 40 decibels (dB) higher than normal.

- ▶ **Moderate hearing loss** requires sounds to be 40 to 55 dB higher than normal.

- ▶ **Moderate-to-severe hearing loss** requires sounds to be 55 to 70 dB higher than normal.

- ▶ **Severe hearing loss** requires sounds to be 70 to 90 decibels higher than normal.

- ▶ A person who requires sounds to be at least 90 dB higher than normal has a **profound loss**; individuals who are deaf have a profound hearing loss.

According to the World Federation of the Deaf, referring to hearing loss or deafness as an "impairment" is no longer acceptable. Because IDEA does still use the term "hearing impairment" as a category, it is sometimes used in this text for clarity and accuracy in reference to legal categories.

> **HELPFUL HINT**
>
> In the Deaf community and among those who are hard of hearing, the term *hearing impairment* may be considered offensive. "Hard of hearing" is preferred to describe people who have low or moderate hearing loss, and "deaf" for those with profound hearing loss.

Hearing disorders are often categorized based on the location of the disorder within the auditory system. **Conductive hearing loss** is caused by damage to the external or middle ear. Conductive hearing loss causes may include earwax build-up, ear malformations, fluid in the middle ear, or ear infections. The damage prevents conduction of sound through those ear chambers. There are medical treatments—such as ear tubes or flushing—for many conditions that cause conductive hearing loss. However, depending on the length of the conductive loss, a child may have delays in language development or learning.

Damage to the cochlea (inner ear) or auditory nerve results in **sensorineural hearing loss**. Sensorineural hearing loss is often more severe and permanent, with a lasting impact on language development and learning. Common causes of sensorineural hearing loss include exposure to loud noise, head trauma, aging, auto-immune inner ear diseases, malformation of the inner ear, and Ménière's disease. Sensorineural hearing loss may be managed with hearing aids.

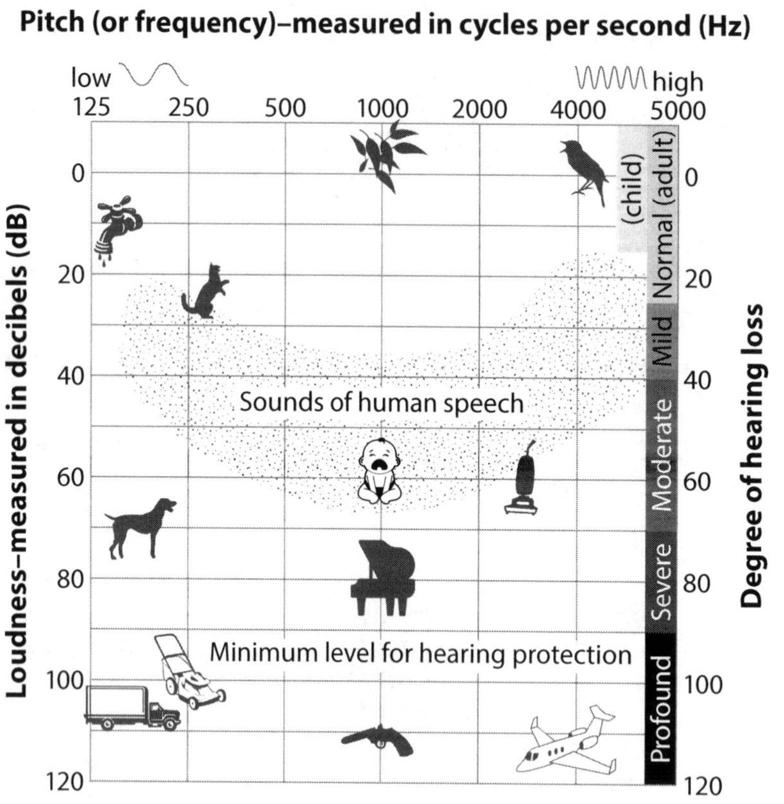

Figure 2.6. Degree of Hearing Loss

Congenital hearing loss, which is present at birth, is often caused by genetic traits passed from parents to children. Prenatal infections, illnesses, or exposure to toxins (including drugs and alcohol) are other congenital causes. Some sensorineural hearing loss may be treated surgically, with cochlear implants, as well as with corticosteroids or drug therapies. A **cochlear implant** is a medical device that does the job of the cochlea by using electronic signaling to send impulses to the brain to be interpreted as sound.

Mixed hearing loss is caused by damage to the outer or middle ear (conductive damage) as well as the inner ear or auditory nerve (sensorineural damage). Birth defects, disease, infections, and head injuries may all be causes of mixed hearing loss. Most often, treatments for mixed hearing loss begin with addressing the conductive damage, then the sensorineural damage.

Central hearing disorders cause hearing loss through dysfunction within the central auditory system between the brain stem and auditory cortex. Central hearing loss, which is much rarer than other types of hearing loss, is sometimes referred to as *cortical deafness*. Individuals with central hearing loss may respond to environmental sounds (such as startling to a loud noise) but be unable to process daily sounds in a functional way.

Hearing impairment impacts development in many ways. Individuals are affected differently depending on the type and degree of loss as well as the onset of the impairment. Hearing impairments impact speech and language, especially for students who are deaf from birth. Students who are born deaf are unable to process auditory information, causing delays in the development of speech and language. Students with less severe hearing loss may have difficulty with communicating at socially expected volume levels, matching patterns of intonation, or hearing and articulating specific sounds which are quieter or higher frequency (e.g. *f, th, s, sh*).

Hearing impairments that result in communication delays may impact the social-emotional development of learners. If students lack an effective and socially appropriate way to communicate, they may use maladaptive behaviors (such as tantrums or aggression) to communicate their wants and needs. Furthermore, delays in communication may make it difficult for a student who is hard of hearing or deaf to form social relationships with others. As a result, typical play and cooperative behaviors may be delayed.

Difficulty processing auditory information often impacts the educational achievement of students with hearing loss. Less sensory input results in less opportunities for students with hearing loss to learn the same information as their peers. Additionally, difficulty hearing, processing, and blending sounds may result in delays in learning to read and access written information. Students who are deaf or hard of hearing often require specific educational supports to make adequate progress.

> **QUICK REVIEW**
>
> How might hearing loss in different levels or frequencies affect a student's ability to produce speech sounds? How might it affect reading decoding?

Up to 40 percent of students living with hearing loss have coexisting disabilities and are diagnosed with learning disabilities and ASDs at a higher rate than the general population. Genetic and prenatal disorders that can cause deafness may also result in additional disabilities, such as cerebral palsy, visual impairment, EBD, and/or those which are intellectual.

ELIGIBILITY AND IDENTIFYING DEAFNESS AND HEARING IMPAIRMENTS

Eligibility for special education services under the category of deafness or hearing impairments is determined by a multidisciplinary evaluation team. In addition to typically required team members, educational teams for students with any type of hearing loss should include input from an audiologist and a teacher of the Deaf and hard of hearing, and may potentially include an educational interpreter, especially for students who are deaf.

First, the team must consider the level of hearing loss based on evaluations done by an audiologist. Students with profound hearing loss which impairs their ability to process linguistic information—with or without amplification—may be serviced under the category of deafness. Students with mild-to-severe hearing loss who are able to process linguistic information (with or without amplification) may be serviced under the category of hearing impairment.

Second, the team must determine that the student's hearing loss has an adverse educational effect. Adverse educational effects may be demonstrated through academic performances which are below those of typically developing peers as measured by assessments of academic achievement. Adverse educational effects may also include impairments in speech and language or other adaptive behaviors which may affect a child's educational performance and ability to access the general education environment. Cognitive evaluations should also be done to identify areas of strength and need in determining appropriate types and levels of support.

Students whose hearing loss adversely affects educational achievement to the extent that they need specially designed instruction in order to make educational progress are serviced under IDEA through an IEP. Students with hearing loss who require accommodations (for example, an amplification system) in order to make educational progress but who do not require specially designed instruction usually receive such accommodations through a Section 504 plan under the Rehabilitation Act.

Many states require schools to provide hearing screenings (often yearly) for all students to determine if hearing might be affecting access to educational services. For students with any type of disability, hearing must be evaluated a minimum of every three years.

> **STUDY TIP**
>
> The need for specially designed instruction is key for determining whether a student with a disability qualifies for special education services under IDEA or accommodations under Section 504 of the Rehabilitation Act for any disability.

EDUCATIONAL PRACTICES FOR STUDENTS WITH DEAFNESS AND HEARING IMPAIRMENTS

IDEA requires IEP teams to make several considerations when designing supports for students who are deaf or hard of hearing. The IEP team must take into account the student's communication needs and the preferred mode of communication for the student's family. Communication considerations should include linguistic needs and opportunities for direct communication with peers, family, and professionals in the child's preferred method of communication. Teams should consider the severity of the hearing loss, the potential for using residual hearing, and what supports (if any) may maximize opportunity to use hearing to access the educational environment. Finally, the IEP team must determine the academic, social, and emotional needs of the student when designing services.

Communication options are often a primary concern for students who are deaf or hard of hearing. A preferred communication method should be chosen based on the level and nature of a student's hearing loss. Social factors, including family preference, also play a large role in determining communication options. For example, a child who has at least one parent who is deaf may have more opportunity to communicate using American Sign Language. Communication options for students who are deaf or hard of hearing include the oral method, cued speech method, manual communication methods, and total communication methods.

▶ When using the **oral method** of communication, a student is taught to pair speechreading (lipreading) with residual hearing for receptive understanding and production of speech.

▶ The **cued speech method** supports speechreading with hand gestures to improve receptive understanding of speech, especially for sounds which are visually similar on a speaker's lips.

▶ **Manual communication methods** such as **American Sign Language (ASL)**, **Manually Coded English (MCE)**, and **finger spelling** use hand movements, gestures, and body language to convey meaning. ASL differs from MCE in that it has its own unique grammatical structure, while MCE uses many of the same signs but mimics English grammar. Fingerspelling, or using hand shapes which symbolize letters to spell words, often supplements other forms of manual communication.

▶ **Total communication** combines any of the oral and manual communication methods to enhance a student's communication.

Some students, especially those who are deaf and whose primary form of communication is ASL, receive educational services in schools that specialize in teaching students who are deaf. Receiving educational services in a school for the Deaf has several potential benefits for students in the Deaf community. One of the most important benefits is the opportunity for students to be immersed in a method of communication like ASL. Instead of communicating through an interpreter as they might in another setting, students at a school for the Deaf receive all instruction and communicate directly with teachers and peers using ASL. In a school for the Deaf, students learn more specifically about the Deaf community and culture, an important consideration for many individuals. Further, students can work with professionals who are highly qualified in providing effective education for students who are deaf.

Other students who are deaf or hard of hearing receive educational services within a general school setting. In any educational setting, an important educational consideration for students who are deaf or hard of hearing is the use

> **DID YOU KNOW?**
>
> Many individuals who are deaf identify with a Deaf culture that differs from the that of the hearing population. Deaf culture includes its own set of social beliefs, behaviors, art, and values along with sign language (ASL in the United States) as a means of communication.

of specialized equipment or assistive technology. Students may use amplification devices such as assistive listening devices, FM amplification systems, audio loops, and cochlear implants. Teachers often play a role in ensuring that amplification devices are functioning properly for a student. It is important that teachers minimize background noise to avoid discomfort for students using an amplification device and to maximize auditory input of important material. Other technology devices such as a teletypewriter (TTY), closed captioning, real-time captioning, speech-to-text, and visual or vibrating alert systems may assist students who are deaf or hard of hearing in accessing education.

Students who are deaf or living with hearing loss may require other supports to facilitate communication. For example, students who communicate using ASL may need an educational interpreter in the classroom. Teachers should ensure that students have specialized seating, with the teacher always facing the student when talking if the student relies on speechreading to receive communication. Regardless of their level of hearing loss, students should be provided with visual supports for learning. Whenever possible, teachers should provide visual supports such as pictures, graphics, text labels, or captioning to any information that is being given through auditory means.

Teachers are responsible for ensuring students who are deaf or hard of hearing have access to all educational materials and the chance to interact with peers. A classroom teacher may help peers learn about an amplification device and understand what it is used for. If a student with hearing loss communicates using ASL, it is appropriate for the whole class to learn some basic signs in order to facilitate peer-to-peer communication in the classroom. Teaching a student who is deaf or hard of hearing often requires collaboration among families and professionals (for example, audiologists, SLPs, interpreters) to ensure that all a student's educational needs are being met.

Students who are deaf or hard of hearing often require direct instruction in language and communication provided by a SLP. If hearing loss has affected academic performance, a student may require direct instruction in academic areas such as reading, writing, or math. Some students with hearing loss may also need instruction in social skills or other areas of adaptive behavior because of developmental delays resulting from hearing loss. In any case, specialized instruction for students who are deaf and hard of hearing should include instruction using their preferred method of communication with ample visual supports for learning.

Table 2.7. Summary of Educational Practices for Students with Deafness and Hearing Impairment

Intervention	Description
Alerting devices	visual or vibrating systems (such as flashing lights) designed to alert individuals who are deaf or hard of hearing
Amplification devices	devices that improve ability to process auditory input, such as assistive listening devices, hearing aids, FM amplification systems, audio loops, and cochlear implants
Closed captioning	subtitling of audiovisual material
Cued speech method	supports speechreading with hand gestures to improve receptive understanding of speech
Direct instruction	explicit instruction techniques to teach a targeted skill
Educational interpreter	individual who translates speech into sign language in a school setting
Manual communication methods	using hand movements, gestures, and body language to communicate; includes ASL, MCE, and finger spelling
Oral method of communication	paired speechreading with residual hearing for receptive understanding and production of speech
Social skills training	direct instruction of expected social behaviors
Speech-to-text	transcription of auditory input to text format
Teletypewriter (TTY)	an electronic device for text communication over a telephone line
Total communication	combination of any oral and manual communication methods
Visual supports	any visual provided to promote the acquisition of a new skill or demonstration of a desired behavior

SAMPLE QUESTIONS

17) **Which professional is most qualified to evaluate hearing loss?**

   A. special education teacher

   B. speech-language pathologist (SLP)

   C. teacher of the Deaf

   D. audiologist

18) **Which support is educationally necessary for all students who are hard of hearing?**

   A.   educational interpreter

   B.   visual supports

   C.   FM amplification system

   D.   sign language instruction

ORTHOPEDIC IMPAIRMENT

CHARACTERISTICS OF ORTHOPEDIC IMPAIRMENT

Children with **orthopedic impairments** have a range of musculoskeletal disabilities that adversely affect educational performance. Orthopedic impairments may be the result of congenital anomalies, disease, or other causes. The category of orthopedic impairments covers a wide variety of disorders that have varying impacts on functioning. Disorders resulting in orthopedic impairments may be categorized as neuromuscular impairments or musculoskeletal disorders.

Neuromuscular impairments are diseases that impair muscle function as a result of abnormalities of or damage to the nervous system (brain, spinal cord, peripheral nerves). One common neuromuscular impairment is **spina bifida**. Spina bifida is a neural tube birth defect in which the neural tube fails to close, resulting in a gap in the spine. Further complications associated with spina bifida include meningitis, Chiari malformation type II (elongated brainstem), sleep disorders, and latex allergies. There are three types of spina bifida: occulta, meningocele, and myelomeningocele.

1. **Spina bifida occulta** is the mildest and most common type of spinal bifida. It occurs when there is a small gap in the back, but no fluid escapes through the opening. Children with spina bifida occulta have limited to no symptoms.

2. **Meningocele** spina bifida occurs when nerve fluid escapes through an opening in the back, causing a fluid sac in the back. Children with meningocele spina bifida often experience few symptoms and no neural damage.

3. **Myelomeningocele** causes the most developmental impact. In myelomeningocele spina bifida, a gap in the spine results in both nerve fluid and a portion of the spinal cord protruding through the gap, causing spinal cord damage. Myelomeningocele spina bifida may result in partial or complete motor paralysis, sensory deficits, and bladder or bowel dysfunction. Most children with myelomeningocele spina bifida also have too much fluid on their brain because the fluid around the brain and spinal cord cannot drain as it should, which may result in cognitive or learning impairments.

Another common neuromuscular impairment is cerebral palsy. **Cerebral palsy (CP)** is actually a group of disorders affecting balance, movement, and muscle tone beginning in infancy or early childhood. It occurs when the area of the brain which controls muscle movement does not develop as it should or is damaged (often during birth). Cerebral palsy may be congenital or acquired. Acquired CP results from damage occurring sometime after birth. Problems which may cause CP include genetic conditions, infant or fetal seizures, bleeding in the brain, or a lack of blood flow to important organs. CP is classified according to the extent, type, and location of motor impairments. CP may be spastic, athetoid, ataxic, or mixed.

> **DID YOU KNOW?**
>
> Spina bifida occulta is sometimes called *hidden spina bifida* because some people have no symptoms at all. In fact, many people have spina bifida occulta without ever realizing it.

- ▶ **Spastic CP** is characterized by very tight muscles causing stiff and awkward movements.
- ▶ **Athetoid CP** is characterized by involuntary writhing movements.
- ▶ **Ataxic CP** includes poor balance with uncoordinated movement.
- ▶ **Mixed CP** describes CP that combines any two movement impairments.

The type of CP is further identified by which limbs are affected and to what extent.

- ▶ Muscle or motor weakness in an area is considered **paresis**.
- ▶ Paralysis of the area is labeled as **plegia**.
- ▶ **Hemiplegia/hemiparesis** refers to one side of the body (left or right) being affected.
- ▶ **Diplegia/diparesis** describes CP that predominantly affects the legs with less severe effects in the arms and face.
- ▶ **Paraplegia/paraparesis** affects only the legs.
- ▶ **Quadriplegia/quadriparesis** affects all four limbs.

Charcot-Marie-Tooth disease (CMT) is an inherited neuromuscular impairment that damages the peripheral nerves responsible for relaying information between the central nervous system and the rest of the body. CMT impairments typically begin with loss of sensation or weakness in the feet and legs and later progresses to hands and arms. Damage to the peripheral nerves by CMT may result in muscle weakness and atrophy, stiff joints, curvature of the spine, or loss of sensation in the limbs.

Degenerative diseases refer to medical conditions which worsen over time. One degenerative neuromuscular impairment which affects school-age children is **muscular dystrophy**, a group of nine inherited diseases during which muscles progressively weaken. The most common types of muscular dystrophy which affect school-age children include congenital, Duchenne and Becker, and limb-girdle.

▶ **Congenital muscular dystrophy** progresses slowly, potentially resulting in spinal curvature, seizures, respiratory difficulties, and learning disabilities.

▶ **Duchenne muscular dystrophy** is caused by the absence of dystrophin, a protein that supports muscle cells. It mostly affects boys. Duchenne muscular dystrophy begins with muscle weakness in the limbs around age three and eventually progresses to weakness in the heart and respiratory muscles, resulting in a shortened life expectancy.

▶ **Becker muscular dystrophy** is like Duchenne but milder; onset is usually late teens.

▶ **Limb-girdle muscular dystrophy** is characterized by weakness and atrophy of limb-girdle muscles of the shoulder and pelvic areas. Limb-girdle muscular dystrophy may result in difficulty with mobility and activities of daily living, such as self-feeding, walking, or standing up from a chair because of weakness in the hips and shoulders.

Spinal muscular atrophy (SMA) is a genetic, neuromuscular disease which attacks motor neurons in the spinal cord. There are three types of SMA which are determined by the severity of symptoms and age of onset. The earlier the onset of SMA, the more severe the type.

▶ Children with type I SMA have floppy limbs and trunk, feeble limb movements, swallowing difficulties, and impaired breathing which begin within the first few months of life. Babies with type I SMA usually have a life expectancy of about two years.

▶ Type II SMA usually begins at six to eighteen months of age with limb weakness, especially in the legs. Children with type II SMA may need assistance sitting, standing, and walking and have a reduced life expectancy (adolescence to young adulthood) due to the respiratory effects of SMA.

▶ Type III SMA begins in children aged between two and seventeen years. Children with type III SMA generally have a normal life span but may have difficulty running, climbing, or rising from a chair.

Musculoskeletal disorders are conditions that affect muscles, bones, and joints. Musculoskeletal disorders may be inherited or occur as a result of injury or lifestyle (for example, during play, athletics, or traumatic events such as motor vehicle accidents or severe burns).

▶ **Clubfoot** is a birth defect in which the foot is twisted and turned inward while calf muscles are underdeveloped. Children with clubfoot may need supports for mobility.

▶ **Limb deficiencies** describe when a child is missing all or part of a limb due to birth defects, disease, or trauma. Limb deficiencies may result in fine or gross motor impairments and difficulties in areas of daily living.

▶ **Juvenile idiopathic arthritis** is another musculoskeletal disorder in children. Juvenile idiopathic arthritis is caused by the body's immune system attacking its own cells and characterized by persistent joint pain, swelling, and stiffness. It may result in problems with growth and bone development, motor impairments, and eye problems due to eye inflammation.

Children with orthopedic impairments do not necessarily have any cognitive, learning, or language difficulties; however, orthopedic impairments can co-occur with other disabilities. Some causes of orthopedic impairment—such as cerebral palsy and spina bifida—also result in cognitive, learning, visual, hearing, or language impairments.

ELIGIBILITY AND IDENTIFYING ORTHOPEDIC IMPAIRMENT

Educational teams within a school district conduct a multifactored evaluation across academic, motor, and cognitive areas to determine if students meet criteria for eligibility. Eligibility criteria require that a student has an orthopedic condition which may require adaptations and specialized instructions. Evaluation of physical eligibility should include a diagnosis from a medical doctor. Impairments may include those resulting from congenital anomalies, disease, trauma, or other causes. Teams must also assess how the orthopedic condition affects motor function in the educational environment. Often, physical therapists and occupational therapists conduct observations and assessments to determine how an orthopedic impairment may affect student learning.

Students qualify for services when needs stemming from an orthopedic impairment cannot be met through environmental accommodations and must be addressed through specialized instruction. Students who qualify under the area of orthopedic impairments are generally able to have their needs met through physical, occupational, and speech therapies paired with environmental supports. Students who have significant orthopedic impairments co-occurring with intensive cognitive, learning, or emotional disabilities are more likely to be serviced under the Multiple Disabilities category.

EDUCATIONAL PRACTICES FOR STUDENTS WITH ORTHOPEDIC IMPAIRMENTS

For students with orthopedic impairments, interventions often center on ensuring the learner can access and interact in the educational environment. Teachers working with students who have orthopedic impairments must address special seating and positioning requirements to promote student learning in the classroom. The classroom environment should be arranged to ensure that students navigate the classroom as independently as possible. Teachers should consider width of doorways and walkways, the height at and ways in which materials are stored, bathroom accessibility, and flooring.

When planning instruction, teachers should consider how an orthopedic disability may affect a student's ability to participate. Students with orthopedic disabilities may tire easily and need extended time to complete an activity, or breaks during challenging activities. Activities requiring refined fine or gross motor skills may need to be modified to ensure a student with an orthopedic impairment is able to participate. When transitioning between school environments, a student with an orthopedic impairment will likely need more time than other students. Teachers should plan all instruction in a way that allows students with an orthopedic impairment to participate as fully and independently as possible.

Students with orthopedic impairments benefit from adaptive tools and technology to support education. These tools and technology may address the following:

▶ mobility (canes, walkers, crutches, wheelchairs, exercise equipment, and specialized cushions, chairs, desks, and tables for posture)

▶ sensory needs (weighted or deep pressure vests or reduced lighting)

▶ writing (slant boards, special paper, grips and pencil holders, and specialized writing utensils)

▶ communication (speech recognition software, screen readers, AAC devices, VOCAs, and adaptive switches)

▶ medical needs (catheterization)

Specialized interventions for students with orthopedic impairments often involve specialists beyond special education teachers, including physical therapists, occupational therapists, and SLPs. Adapted physical education teachers may work with other therapists to ensure the physical education program meets the needs of a student with a disability. Because therapists may only work directly with students a small percentage of a school week, special education teachers play an important role in ensuring the student receives consistent intervention and exercise. A special education teacher must work with all professionals on a student's team to identify ongoing needs and ensure those needs are met throughout the school day.

SAMPLE QUESTIONS

19) **Which best describes the necessary requirements for a student to qualify for special education services under the category of orthopedic impairment?**

    A.   motor impairment that requires environmental modifications for a student to have productive participation in school

    B.   motor impairment that requires specially designed instruction for a student to have productive participation in school

    C.   motor impairment with cognitive or learning disabilities

    D.   motor impairment with emotional behavioral disability

20) **Ali is a middle-school student who works on grade-level academics and has spastic cerebral palsy with paraplegia. She qualifies for special education supports under the category of orthopedic impairment. Which of the following supports is most likely necessary to help Ali in her middle school classroom?**

   A.   specialized mobility and positioning equipment

   B.   specialized reading instruction

   C.   behavior intervention plan (BIP)

   D.   orientation and mobility training (O&M)

BLINDNESS AND VISUAL IMPAIRMENT

CHARACTERISTICS OF BLINDNESS AND VISUAL IMPAIRMENT

A **visual impairment** is a loss of sight which impacts a person's ability to complete daily life activities, including education. Visual impairment is often defined by the level of impairment.

▶ Visual impairments that can be corrected with lenses, such as refractive errors, would not qualify a student as having a visual impairment.

▶ **Partially sighted** refers to any visual impairment which adversely affects educational performance, even when corrected as much as possible.

▶ **Low vision** describes visual acuity between 20/70 – 20/160 which cannot be corrected. Students who are partially sighted or have mild visual impairments still use vision as a primary sensory channel for learning.

▶ Students at the higher end of the low-vision range may be considered **functionally blind**, using residual vision for functional tasks but relying on other senses for learning.

▶ A person who is **legally blind** has visual acuity lower than 20/200, or a field of vision that is 20 degrees or less at its widest point.

▶ A person who lacks any light perception is considered **totally blind**.

Loss of visual acuity is a primary characteristic of vision loss; however, other visual concerns may impact the ability of a student to access the educational environment. Students may have **tunnel vision**, or a narrowed range of vision due to loss of peripheral vision. Other learners may have blind spots within their visual fields. Other vision issues may include light sensitivity, night blindness, poor color separation, or blurred vision.

Visual impairments occur when the eye or visual processing centers in the brain are diseased or damaged. Some eye conditions result from dysfunction of muscles in the eye. **Amblyopia**, or lazy eye, is caused by weak eye muscles. Students with amblyopia may have reduced visual acuity as a result. **Strabismus** occurs when eyes are unable to focus on the same object at the same time due to a muscle imbalance.

Cortical visual impairments (CVIs) are caused by a problem within the visual cortex area of the brain. Students with cortical visual impairments have inconsistent vision depending on their health, mood, and environmental characteristics. People with cortical visual impairments often have other developmental delays as a result of the damage to the brain which resulted in the CVI.

Another cause of visual impairment is damage to any part of the eye because of disease, infection, or trauma. **Retinopathy** refers to retinal damage, which often results in loss of vision. Two types of retinopathy which may affect children include retinopathy of prematurity and diabetic retinopathy. **Retinopathy of prematurity** is an eye condition of babies born prematurely who require a high concentration of oxygen at birth. As a result, the retina may scar or detach. **Diabetic retinopathy**—a complication of diabetes—is caused by excess sugar in the blood which blocks the tiny blood vessels in the retina. Effects of diabetic retinopathy range from mild vision loss to blindness.

There are several other congenital and adventitious eye conditions which may result in permanent vision loss. **Retinitis pigmentosa** is a degenerative condition that results in a gradual loss of peripheral vision. It often begins with difficulty seeing in low-light situations and later progresses to severe tunnel vision. A **cataract** is a cloudy area in the lens of the eye. Children may be born with cataracts or may develop them later, often as a result of trauma to the eye. Many cataracts are treated through surgical removal but may result in amblyopia, strabismus, or permanent loss of vision. **Glaucoma** is a condition resulting from excess fluid in the eye that causes pressure which damages the optic nerve. Glaucoma may cause amblyopia, strabismus, tunnel vision, or significant and permanent vision loss.

Children rely on visual stimuli as a basis for learning, and vision is one of two senses (with hearing) that a child can use at a distance. Sight is the primary sense children use to attach meaning to sensory stimuli. For example, babies use sight to understand that a bottle means they will soon be fed. Visual cues, such as the sight of a desired or interesting object, like a bottle, provide the primary motivation for students to explore their environments. A student who has limited visual input misses out on those motivating visual cues, resulting in fewer learning opportunities than a typical peer would enjoy. Consequently, visual impairments often have sweeping impacts across areas of development, including motor, language, social, and cognitive development. Impact of a visual impairment on development varies based on the severity, onset, and type of vision loss.

> **DID YOU KNOW?**
>
> Visual cues account for 80 percent of learning in children.

Visual impairments and blindness may result in significant motor delays in children. Infants with visual impairments, especially those who are blind, have difficulty building hand coordination. Instead of eye-hand coordination, a child with severe visual impairments must learn to use hearing in coordination with hand movements. The consequent delay in hand utilization affects other areas of motor functioning which require hand coordination to master. Furthermore, children with severe visual impairments lack visual stimuli to motivate their mobility in their environment. Thus, students who are blind may demonstrate more repetitive, self-stimulating movements (like hand-flapping or rocking) while taking longer to master skills such as crawling and walking. Once mobile, children with severe visual impairments may need assistance or training to ensure that they are able to navigate the environment in a safe way.

Visual stimuli play a primary role in the development of cognitive constructs. A child with typical vision uses visual information to connect other forms of sensory input, coordinating and organizing information to form higher-level cognitive concepts. Without vision to tie other sensory stimuli to a common construct, children with severe visual impairments often have delays in cognitive development. Important cognitive concepts such as object permanence, causation, classification, and conservation may be delayed by a year or more.

Visual stimuli also play an important role in social development. A large percentage of social behaviors are learned through imitating behaviors seen in others. For example, an infant smiles regularly in response to the smile of another. Beyond smiling, a child with a severe visual impairment may fail to exhibit learned facial expressions and body language which convey important social meanings. As a result, others may have difficulty understanding the abnormal body language demonstrated by the child, making it difficult to form relationships.

Imitation and visual stimuli also play an important role in language development. Language development relies on the ability to understand and describe increasingly complex concepts. A child who is blind or severely visually impaired often imitates sounds and learns early words for requesting (often nouns or verbs) at a typical rate. However, a child with a visual impairment might have difficulty learning language associated with visual stimuli, such as adjectives, prepositions, or abstract words with no concrete tie.

Imitation is also important to the development of self-help skills. Self-feeding, dressing, brushing teeth, and using the bathroom are skills which are typically learned by watching adult models. Without the ability to see the model, daily self-care activities such as brushing teeth and using the bathroom may become activities which are uncomfortable—and maybe even frightening—sensory experiences.

Students with visual impairments often have one or more coexisting conditions, resulting in cognitive or learning disabilities which further impact learning. Others may have speech-language impairments, orthopedic impairments, autism, hearing impairments, or social-emotional disabilities.

ELIGIBILITY AND IDENTIFYING BLINDNESS AND VISUAL IMPAIRMENT

In addition to typical team members, teams evaluating students with visual impairments should include a **teacher of the visually impaired (TVI)** who specializes in educating students with visual impairments. The team may also include an orientation and mobility specialist, especially for students who are blind or who have degenerative eye diseases. The team will likely also include physical and occupational therapists who can work closely with orientation and mobility specialists to assess and recommend strategies to improve motor performance for students with visual impairments.

In order to qualify as a student with a visual impairment, the student must have medical documentation of a visual impairment. Students may qualify as having a visual impairment due to reduced visual acuity even with best correction (usually 20/60 or less with correction), a reduced visual field of 20 degrees or less, blind spots that severely impede vision, or a congenital or degenerative eye condition. The evaluation should also include a functional evaluation of visual abilities which may include near and distance acuity, peripheral visual field, print functioning, light sensitivity, color perception, convergence, eye movements, depth perception, and visual efficiency.

In addition to functional vision assessments, a student's cognitive, academic, and adaptive behavior should be evaluated. For many students with visual impairments, assessments of language, fine motor, and gross motor skills should be completed. A student qualifies for special education services when the school team determines that visual impairment is present and that the impairment impacts educational performance. A student with a visual impairment that affects educational performance qualifies for service under the category of visual impairment. However, if the visual impairment coexists with other disabilities, such as orthopedic impairments, hearing impairments, or intellectual disabilities the student qualifies under the category of multiple disabilities or deaf-blindness.

EDUCATIONAL PRACTICES FOR STUDENTS WITH BLINDNESS OR VISUAL IMPAIRMENT

Educational interventions for students with blindness or low vision must address each of the developmental areas delayed as a result of the impairment. A TVI plays an important role in designing interventions and ensuring adequate supports are in place for students who are visually impaired. Interventions and supports should address mobility, language, social skills, daily living, and academic learning needs.

Students who are blind or visually impaired require specialized instruction to improve their motor skills and ability to independently navigate environments. **Orientation and mobility training (O&M)** is specialized instruction to improve the ability of an individual with a visual impairment to move within an environment.

O&M should be delivered or overseen by a person certified in O&M. **Orientation** is the understanding of where one is in space and where one would like to go. **Mobility** is the ability to carry out a plan to move from one location to another. O&M teaches students sensory awareness, special concepts, and searching skills to improve orientation. Mobility skills include strategies for independent movement (crawling and walking) and techniques for protecting oneself when moving in unfamiliar environments. O&M teaches a variety of modes for mobility, including sighted guide techniques, dog guides, electronic travel aids, and cane travel.

Students with visual impairments often require direct instruction in the area of social skills since many of these skills are typically learned through observing the behavior of others. Students who are blind or who have low vision may therefore need to be directly taught expected behaviors that are typically learned through observation. For example, these students must be directly taught body language expectations, such as facial expressions and gestures, which they are unable to learn through imitation. An important part of social education for students with visual impairments is self-advocacy. Students with visual impairments must know strategies for seeking help when needed, how to advocate for adaptations and materials to access an environment, and how to explain their needs to others.

Direct instruction in activities of daily living may also be necessary for individuals with low vision. Skills such as dressing, self-feeding, using the bathroom, and personal hygiene may need to be addressed. It is important that teachers encourage and instruct students with visual impairments to be as independent as possible in daily activities to avoid learned helplessness.

Academic instruction for students who are visually impaired should include direct instruction in a manner which utilizes a student's strengths while minimizing effects of the visual impairment. Auditory descriptions should be included with all information presented. Students with CVI or mild visual impairments may benefit from information with contrasting backgrounds, enlarged print, or raised print. Students who are blind or severely visually impaired need to be given instruction in reading and writing in braille.

Assistive technology tools are very important for students with visual impairments. For students with low vision, devices such as magnifiers and closed circuit televisions (which enlarge images) may provide access to visual information. Screen readers convert text on a screen to speech. Higher-tech screen readers even provide information about graphics and serve as a mouse or pointing device. Braille translation software may be used to convert print into braille and braille into print. Braille printers and braille embossers can convert text on a computer to braille. Braille notetakers are lightweight devices that can move with a student across school environments and later be connected to a printer or braille embosser to print notes. Devices that provide auditory access to everyday resources, such as talking calculators, personalized digital assistants, and electronic book players, are important for students with visual impairments.

Teachers should organize the learning environment to maximize independence and accessibility for students with visual impairments. An accommodating learning environment begins with knowledge of a student's specific learning requirements. A student with low vision should be given preferential seating with magnification when needed. Teachers should control lighting according to individual needs—reduced lighting for sensitivities and bright lighting for students with night blindness. Consistent classroom organization of furniture is important to allow a student with low vision to independently navigate within the environment. Materials should also remain in a consistent, easily accessible place with labels which include braille or tactile information.

Teachers must ensure that students have timely access to all instructional information through auditory means or adapted text options. For example, teachers may provide audiobooks or braille text for a student with a visual impairment. Teachers may also need to provide expanded options for students to demonstrate what they know, such as oral responses or the use of assistive technology.

Table 2.8. Summary of Educational Practices for Students with Blindness or Visual Impairment

Intervention	Description
Auditory supports	auditory description of any information otherwise delivered through visuals
Braille	tactile reading and writing system
Braille notetakers	lightweight devices that students can use to take notes in braille
Braille printers	convert computer text to printed braille
Braille translation	technology that converts print into braille and braille into print
Contrasting backgrounds	changing the background and/or print color
Enlarged print	using a larger font size or magnification system
Functional academics	instruction in skills of daily living in order to improve long-term independence
Orientation and mobility training (O&M)	specialized instruction to teach individuals with visual impairments to move within an environment
Raised print	printing raised above the surface of the paper (as in embossing)
Screen readers	convert text on a screen to speech
Self-advocacy training	teaching students when and how to seek help when needed
Social skill instruction	direct instruction of expected social behaviors

SAMPLE QUESTIONS

21) **Mrs. Long wants to ensure that she is correctly adapting materials for her student who has a visual impairment. Which specialist is most qualified to provide recommendations for modifying academic materials for students with visual impairments?**

    A.   orientation and mobility specialist

    B.   school psychologist

    C.   board-certified behavior analyst (BCBA)

    D.   teacher of the visually impaired (TVI)

22) **What is a primary reason that social skills are difficult to master for some students with visual impairments?**

    A.   inability to observe and imitate social behavior

    B.   difficulty discriminating tone of voice

    C.   sensory overstimulation

    D.   avoidance of social contact

DEAF–BLINDNESS

CHARACTERISTICS OF DEAF–BLINDNESS

Deaf-blindness is defined by the co-occurrence of hearing and visual impairments resulting in a range of needs that cannot be met through supports designed for students with only one of the two impairments. Individuals with deaf-blindness may have varying levels of residual hearing and sight: they may be totally deaf and totally blind; totally deaf with limited vision; totally blind with limited hearing; or able to use some residual hearing or vision. The level of hearing and sight impairments plays a role in how an individual is able to learn and develop. Further, deaf-blindness may occur at varying times in a person's life.

A student may have **congenital** deafness or blindness, meaning one is deaf or blind from birth. Deafness or blindness may also be **adventitious**, meaning that deafness or blindness occurs sometimes after a child is born. Generally, a congenital impairment in one or both areas has a greater impact on development than if a person has exposure to the sense(s) during some period of his or her life.

Students with deaf-blindness often experience developmental delays resulting from access to much less stimuli than a typical child might experience. Developmental delays may occur in the area of motor skills, cognitive skills, social-emotional skills, and communication. Degree and onset of the impairment play large roles in how a student develops in relation to his or her peers. Students—especially those with congenital deaf-blindness—may be delayed in motor skills such as crawling or walking. Children with visual impairments often have delayed motor skills as a result of lack of distance input which motivates movement (for example, reaching for an interesting object or moving to obtain a desired item). Children with deaf-blindness lack both the visual and auditory stimuli that would typically motivate them to move, often resulting in significant delays in motor skills.

> **DID YOU KNOW?**
>
> Internationally, there is a debate whether it is more appropriate to hyphenate the term "deaf-blind" or to merge the words as "deafblind" since the combination of the two sensory impairments is a unique experience. While the terms are often merged in other countries, the hyphenation of the words is currently more prevalent in the United States.

A child who is deaf-blind experiences much fewer stimuli than a typical peer would in the same situation. As a result, the child with deaf-blindness has fewer opportunities to process and learn new information. Children with deaf-blindness may require extra time to process information and have difficulty learning object permanence or causality without direct input into what happens to an object when they are no longer touching it. **Object permanence** is the understanding that objects still exist when they cannot be seen (or touched). **Causality** is the understanding that actions have consequences. Both object permanence and causality are early learning experiences which greatly impact ability to master more complex concepts.

Students who are deaf-blind may have more difficulty establishing and maintaining relationships. They may have limited ability to interact with others, except through touch, which often makes it difficult for them to connect with others. Furthermore, a child with deaf-blindness may not even know that a person is available to communicate with unless that person makes his or her presence known to the child. Social skills may be further impacted by limitations in communication. Individuals with deaf-blindness often have significant communication delays, including difficulty developing communication strategies both in making wants and needs known and in receiving information from others.

People with deaf-blindness often react to sensory information in an atypical way. For students with some residual use of sight or hearing, they may have inconsistent responses to sound or visual images and difficulty using remaining senses in a functional way. A student with deaf-blindness may be hyperreactive to tactile input and demonstrate tactile defensiveness, or the avoidance of touch. Individuals with deaf-blindness might startle easily, especially if they have no residual auditory or visual input to warn of an approach before they are touched.

If individuals with deaf-blindness are not given access to sensory experiences, they may experience **sensory deprivation**, or a scarcity of sensory input. Individuals with deaf-blindness might experience higher levels of fear or anxiety when they do not receive the sensory input which lets them know they are safe and secure. Those with deaf-blindness may also have repetitive or stereotyped behaviors as a result of anxiety or in order to provide themselves with sensory input. Lack of cues to indicate the passage of time, such as light, could cause a distorted sense of time. As a result, individuals with deaf-blindness might have disrupted sleep patterns or difficulty following a regular schedule.

In some cases, deaf-blindness is a result of a genetic disorder. The most common genetic disorders associated with deaf-blindness include Down syndrome, CHARGE syndrome, trisomy 13, and Usher syndrome.

▶ **CHARGE syndrome** is caused by mutations in the CHD7 gene. CHARGE stands for the identifying features of the disorder: **C**oloboma (gap or hole in eye structure), **H**eart defects, **A**tresia choanae, growth **R**etardation, **G**enital abnormalities, and **E**ar abnormalities.

▶ **Trisomy 13,** also called Patau syndrome, results when a child has three copies of chromosome 13 instead of the usual two. Trisomy 13 results in severe intellectual disabilities and physical abnormalities, including heart defects, brain abnormalities, weak muscle tone, cleft lip or palate, and poorly developed eyes. Only 5 – 10 percent of children with Trisomy 13 live past the age of one.

▶ **Usher syndrome** is characterized by hearing and vision which deteriorates over time. There are three types of Usher syndrome. For individuals with Usher syndrome, hearing loss is caused by abnormalities of the inner ear while vision loss is caused by **retinitis pigmentosa (RP)**, an eye disease which affects the retina. Type I is characterized by severe to profound hearing loss at birth with progressive vision loss beginning in childhood. Individuals with Usher syndrome type II experience hearing loss from birth with the beginning of vision loss in adolescence or adulthood. Usher syndrome type III is characterized by hearing and vision loss which begins during late childhood or adolescence and becomes more severe over time.

Deaf-blindness can also be caused by issues during pregnancy or birth, such as FAS or maternal drug abuse. Other causes of deaf-blindness include congenital exposure to diseases such as AIDS, herpes, rubella, syphilis, and toxoplasmosis; hydrocephalus—the build-up of fluid in the ventricles of the brain; and microcephalus (in infants).

Post-natal injuries, illnesses, or accidents can also result in deaf-blindness. These include asphyxia (due to near-drowning or other accidents); inflammation of the brain (caused by encephalitis or meningitis); and strokes or head injuries.

Deaf-blindness often co-occurs with other physical or mental impairments, and many of the causes of deaf-blindness often result in intellectual disabilities. Other coexisting disabilities of deaf-blindness include orthopedic impairments, specific learning disabilities, and traumatic brain injury.

Eligibility and Identifying Deaf–blindness

In order to qualify under the IDEA category of deaf-blindness, a student is assessed by a school multidisciplinary team. In addition to required team members, such as a school psychologist, an administrator, a general education teacher, and a special education teacher, the multidisciplinary team often includes an audiologist, a teacher of the Deaf, and/or a TVI with expertise in hearing and vision loss.

Evaluations should also include assessments of cognitive ability, academic performance, communication, and any other areas of need. A student qualifies as having deaf-blindness when the educational team determines concomitant visual and hearing impairments combine to result in significant deficits in the ability to access education. A student does not have to be fully deaf and/or blind to qualify for deaf-blindness; however, deficits in both hearing and vision must have a compounding effect to the point that educational needs may not be met by educational programs designed to support either area individually (for example, students who are deaf or students who are blind).

Educational Practices for Students with Deaf–blindness

Students who are deaf-blind may be serviced in a variety of locations. Because of the need for highly specific and intensive support, some students with deaf-blindness attend schools that specialize in servicing students who have visual impairments and hearing loss. However, due to the low incidence of deaf-blindness, only a few schools specialize in deaf-blindness, often only one per state.

Students with deaf-blindness may also receive services within a regular school setting. A school may hire a teacher or a consultant who specializes in working with students who are deaf-blind, a teacher of the visually impaired, and/or a teacher of the deaf. No matter the location, teachers working with students who are deaf-blind must use the learner's strengths to help him or her make educational progress.

One of the most critical skills teachers of students who are deaf-blind must develop is a strategy for meaningful communication. Often, teachers must use touch-based strategies to develop and teach a communication system. Students who are deaf-blind should be allowed to freely explore objects through touch in order to develop understanding of objects and the ability to communicate about them.

One form of communication used with students with deaf-blindness is the use of object or picture symbols from a choice board. Depending on the level of hearing and vision loss, several other communication methods can be effective for students who are deaf-blind. Auditory or visual training may help students use the vision and hearing they do have in functional ways. Students with functional vision may be taught to communicate using ASL or other forms of sign language. Students with little-to-no vision may use tactile sign language or print-on-palm. When using **tactile sign language**, the person who is deaf-blind puts their hands on the hands of the person signing to feel the shape of the sign or fingerspelling.

When communicating with a person who does not sign, a person with deaf-blindness may use **print-on-palm** communication, which involves printing block letters onto the other person's palm. Students who have not mastered sign language may use signaling, gesturing, or coactive movement to communicate with others. Some students who are deaf-blind may be taught **Tadoma**, a method that uses touch (fingers on chin and cheek of the speaker) to speech read using vibrations and lip movements. In many cases, alternate communication methods such as sign language or picture communication may be paired with verbalizations and vocalizations.

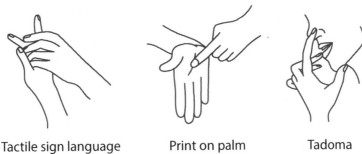

Tactile sign language   Print on palm   Tadoma

Figure 2.7. Strategies for Communicating with Students with Deaf-Blindness

Students who are deaf-blind should also be taught written forms of communication. In some cases, large print with contrasting background or raised text may be effective accommodations. Other students should learn written communication through braille. Braille technologies, such as braille notetakers, TTYs with braille display, screen braille communicators, and electronic braille writers allow individuals with deaf-blindness to communicate with others.

A key strategy in developing cognitive skills for students with deaf-blindness is providing consistent stimuli that allow students to anticipate what is occurring and use known information to build new skills. A teacher might use consistent **touch cues** to communicate specific information to a student. For example, a teacher working with a student with deaf-blindness may touch the student on the same place on the arm each time to indicate his or her presence. A different type of touch or object cue may alert a student with deaf-blindness to transitions to activities throughout the day. Using touch and object cues consistently with students with deaf-blindness helps them anticipate routines, demonstrate appropriate behavior, and build upon known skills.

QUICK REVIEW

What steps might a teacher take to build a communicative relationship with a student who is deaf-blind?

Environmental supports are extremely important for students who are deaf-blind. The classroom environment must be designed to maximize engagement so that students do not feel isolated. It is helpful for students who are deaf-blind to be seated in a group where they are near and facing other students rather than in an isolated desk where they may have no opportunity to interact with classmates. Teachers should help build social skills in students with deaf-blindness by providing access to and facilitating positive social interactions. Teachers should model ways in which peers can communicate with a student who is deaf-blind and set up opportunities for interaction.

Classroom set-up should remain dependable, with materials stored in consistent locations and predictable routines. Adequate lighting and landmarks within the classroom may be used to foster independent mobility for students who are deaf-blind. Classroom materials may need to be modified or provided in alternative formats (for example, object choices, braille, raised-line print and graphics) to support inclusion of students with deaf-blindness. Finally, depending on hearing and visual ability, many of the strategies used for students with low vision or hearing loss may also be effective for students who are deaf-blind.

SAMPLE QUESTIONS

23) **Which of the following is the genetic disorder which most often causes deaf-blindness?**

   A. Usher syndrome

   B. fragile X syndrome

   C. FAS

   D. retinitis pigmentosa (RP)

24) **Mrs. Jackson is setting up her classroom, which will include a student who is deaf-blind. Which of the following supports might best benefit the needs of her student?**

   A. a safe desk where the student can sit without being bumped by peers

   B. light covers to minimize visual stimuli

   C. tactile landmarks for important areas in the classroom

   D. a classroom set-up that can be easily moved to encourage flexible arrangements

TRAUMATIC BRAIN INJURY

CHARACTERISTICS OF TRAUMATIC BRAIN INJURY (TBI)

Traumatic brain injury (TBI) occurs when an external force damages the brain, resulting in partial or total functional disability or psychosocial maladjustment. Impairments related to TBI vary greatly in severity and may be temporary or permanent in nature. TBI may be caused by external blows to the head (for example, falling from a height) or the internal impact of the brain hitting the skull (for example, shaken baby syndrome or car accident, even when no external blow occurs). A TBI is generally divided into three levels of severity based on duration of loss of consciousness and **post-traumatic amnesia**, which is the time period immediately following unconsciousness when a person is alert and awake but behaving in an abnormal manner with no continuous memory of events.

▶ **Mild TBI** is trauma to the head which results in a confused state or loss of consciousness for less than thirty minutes with posttraumatic amnesia which may last up to twenty-four hours.

▶ **Moderate TBI** is trauma to the head which may result in loss of consciousness for up to twenty-four hours with posttraumatic amnesia for up to a week.

▶ **Severe TBI** may result in loss of consciousness for over twenty-four hours and posttraumatic amnesia for over a week.

Traumatic brain injury, especially when severe, may result in cognitive, physical, or behavioral impairments. Following a severe TBI, a person may have impaired attention, concentration, and memory. Other cognitive deficits resulting from a TBI include slowed processing speed and impaired ability for abstract thinking and concept formation. Individuals with a TBI may have challenges with organization and planning and difficulty with problem-solving and decision-making skills.

Traumatic brain injury may also lead to abnormal social behavior. Individuals with a TBI may experience disinhibition, resulting in poor social judgment and socially inappropriate behavior. Often, individuals with a severe TBI have increased impulsivity with difficulty connecting behaviors to consequences. A TBI may cause other social-emotional difficulties, such as aggression, anxiety, depression, or intense mood swings. As a result, individuals with a TBI may have difficulty demonstrating the social-emotional behaviors required for learning or building relationships with others.

A severe TBI may have significant impacts on a range of physical abilities. A TBI may result in quadriplegia/quadriparesis or hemiplegia/hemiparesis. Even with normal muscle functioning, a person with a TBI may experience **apraxia**—difficulty carrying out motor planning in order to perform tasks. Apraxia can affect both speech and mobility. A person with a TBI may also experience **ataxia**, or difficulty coordinating muscle movements. Ataxia may result in loss of balance, slurred

QUICK REVIEW

How might a TBI affect a student's relationship with friends and family?

speech, poor coordination, and/or difficulty with fine motor tasks or swallowing. A severe TBI may also cause sensory impairments, including vision and hearing loss and double vision.

A TBI can result in emotional, physical, and educational needs that differ greatly from what the student required prior to the injury. Many times, a TBI results in the loss of skills which a student had previously mastered, including those which came very easily. Recovery of lost skills and the addition of new skills may be inconsistent, with a student frequently "losing" skills he or she seemed to have (re)mastered. Often, a student with a TBI can remember the ease with which they used to perform tasks that are now a struggle, adding another layer of emotional difficulty. Consequently, a TBI results in a unique array of learning needs which may differ from those of students with other types of disabilities.

Eligibility and Identifying Traumatic Brain Injury

The IDEA definition for a TBI includes any acquired brain injury caused by an external physical force, resulting in psychosocial impairment or functional disability (total or partial), or both. In order to qualify for special education services, the brain injury must adversely affect a student's educational performance. The term *traumatic brain injury* applies to both open- and closed-head injuries. Students may qualify based on impairments that either immediately follow brain injury or are delayed. However, the term does not apply to brain injuries that are caused by congenital conditions, birth trauma, or degenerative brain disorders.

A multidisciplinary evaluation team should conduct a full assessment to determine if a student has a TBI and, if so, what effects the TBI has on a student's functioning. When appropriate, the evaluation should include a summary of information relating to the student's functioning prior to the injury. The evaluation should also include information about the nature of the TBI. Verification of and information about a TBI often requires an evaluative report from a medical professional. An evaluation should also include information about how the TBI affects areas of functioning. Areas to be specifically addressed in an evaluation of a student with a TBI include cognitive functioning, social/behavioral functioning, and physical/motor functioning.

Following the completion of the evaluation, the school team must determine if a student's TBI affects the child's educational progress. If the team determines that special education services are necessary, the evaluation should inform which areas of specialized instruction the student with a TBI may require in order to make academic progress.

Educational Practices for Students with Traumatic Brain Injury

Educational strategies for students with a TBI should address the cognitive, social, and physical impacts of the injury. Traumatic brain injury often impacts cognitive processes such as attention, memory, and organization. To support attention, a teacher may take steps, such as preferential seating, to reduce extraneous stimuli to avoid learning distractions. A teacher may also divide work into smaller sections to help the student focus on one task at a time. In addition, the teacher may provide attention cues or implement a self-monitoring plan with students to increase the amount of time they concentrate on a task.

Because memory is often affected in students with a TBI, teachers should perform frequent checks of understanding. To do this, teachers should have students with a TBI repeat back information in their own words. It is beneficial for students with a TBI to have repeated opportunities to practice to ensure that mastery is maintained. Whenever possible, new information should be linked to prior knowledge to help a student build mental concepts. Students with a TBI may also benefit from direct instruction of techniques to improve memory, such as mnemonic devices and mental rehearsal. Hands-on, experiential learning with concrete levels of instruction may be easier for a student with a TBI to retain than more abstract concepts. Students with a TBI might need opportunities for direct, small group instruction with repeated practice in order to make academic progress.

Many students with a TBI struggle with organization. Teachers can help by providing a visual schedule with consistent daily routines. Students with a TBI should be taught organizational strategies, such as creating checklists, writing down information, using an assignment book, or color-coding materials. Teachers may also help students with a TBI by slowing the pace of instruction, highlighting important information, giving directions one step at a time, providing written instructions, and giving them time to organize materials.

Students with a TBI may require significant social-emotional supports as a result of the injury. Supports that promote positive behaviors in students with autism, emotional disabilities, or ADHD may also benefit students with a TBI. Teachers can conduct an FBA to target specific behaviors in an effective way and use the FBA to create a behavior intervention plan (BIP) to address behavioral challenges associated with TBI, such as aggression, impulsiveness, and emotional outbursts. BIPs, discussed in chapter 4, should focus on antecedent strategies, behavioral skill instruction, and positive consequences for appropriate behaviors. Teachers should plan for antecedents that promote success (for example, limited distractions, breaking tasks into small steps) while avoiding antecedents that trigger inappropriate behavior. Behavioral skill instruction may include guidance with social skills and self-regulation strategies.

Research indicates that punishment is an ineffective method of behavior change for students with a TBI because they blame the person delivering the punishment rather than connecting it to the inappropriate behavior. As much as possible, teachers should provide positive reinforcement (such as praise or behavioral incentives) of appropriate behavior and redirection and prompting (rather than punishment) when inappropriate behavior occurs.

Students with a TBI may require related service therapies to address physical needs related to their injury. Speech-language therapy may be necessary to address speech and language difficulties, including apraxia of speech. Students may also require physical therapy to improve muscle coordination and strength in order to regain as much mobility as possible. Occupational therapy is often necessary for a student to build fine motor skills and (re)master daily living skills which may have been lost following the TBI.

Table 2.9. Summary of Educational Practices for Students with a Traumatic Brain Injury (TBI)

Intervention	Description
Antecedent-based interventions	interventions aimed at circumstances that precede target behavior to increase or decrease the likelihood of the behavior
Concrete representation	instruction using hands-on strategies to demonstrate abstract concepts
Frequent checks of understanding	teacher frequently checks in with student to ensure understanding of material taught so far
Mental rehearsal	visualization of a task
Mnemonic devices	technique a person can use to improve memory
One-step directions	using brief, direct instructions rather than instructions containing multiple steps
Organizational strategies	strategies such as visual schedules, checklists, and color-coding to help a student organize information
Positive behavioral supports	reinforcement for demonstration of expected behavior
Reteaching	repeated opportunities to practice a concept after it is initially taught
Self-monitoring	behavioral intervention in which a student is in charge of monitoring their own behavior and reinforcement
Self-regulation strategies	direct instruction of strategies to calm oneself when experiencing overwhelming emotion
Social skill instruction	direct instruction of expected social behaviors

SAMPLE QUESTIONS

25) What is the term for the period immediately following loss of consciousness due to trauma to the brain, when a person may act bizarrely and have little-to-no ongoing memory?

   A. post-traumatic amnesia

   B. post-traumatic stress disorder

   C. coma

   D. traumatic brain injury

26) Stephen is a student with a traumatic brain injury as a result of a car accident. Since the accident, Stephen frequently has emotional outbursts in class when he is frustrated with difficult work. His teacher would like to implement a BIP to help decrease Stephen's emotional outbursts. Which of the following would be LEAST likely to help modify Stephen's behavior?

A. direct instruction for Stephen on calming strategies, such as deep-breathing methods

B. requiring Stephen to leave the classroom if he has an emotional outburst

C. allowing Stephen time with a preferred reinforcer (e.g., a computer game) for class periods when no outburst occurs

D. breaking activities into smaller chunks

Answer Key

1) A.   Incorrect. Dyslexia may impact written expression based on difficulties with word and letter decoding, not motor movements.

    B.   Correct. Dysgraphia is a learning disability characterized by difficulty performing motor movements required for written expression.

    C.   Incorrect. Dyscalculia is a learning disability characterized by difficulties with mathematical concepts.

    D.   Incorrect. Dysrhythmia is not a type of learning disability.

2) **A.   Correct.** Concrete/semi-concrete/abstract instruction is characterized by using three-dimensional objects to represent problems before depicting concepts using pictures or numerical symbols.

    B.   Incorrect. Scaffolding is an instructional technique in which a teacher provides temporary support to help students progress toward greater understanding.

    C.   Incorrect. Problem-solving strategies assist students with thinking processes required to solve word problems.

    D.   Incorrect. Mnemonic techniques are methods a student may use to improve memory.

3) A.   Incorrect. Voice disorders are characterized by abnormal pitch, tone, or volume of voice.

    B.   Incorrect. Speech fluency impairments are characterized by interruptions to the regular flow of speech.

    C.   Correct. Apraxia is a speech sound production impairment caused by central nervous system difficulties in motor planning.

    D.   Incorrect. Language impairments are difficulties in the form, function, or use of language while apraxia is an impairment in speech sound production.

4) A.   Incorrect. Reading from cue cards is not likely to be enough to ease the anxiety which may cause disfluency difficulties.

    B.   Correct. Allowing Billy to pre-record his presentation maintains the expectation of oral reporting but allows Billy to participate in a way that minimizes the impact of his disability.

    C.   Incorrect. Excusing Billy from the assignment is not appropriate because it would be a modification that changes learning expectations in the class.

    D.   Incorrect. Deep breathing exercises may help Billy be calmer and more successful giving the presentation, but this is not the best option because of the potential emotional distress the situation causes for Billy, which may be alleviated through video accommodations.

5) A. Incorrect. A diabetes control plan is not a type of health care plan provided for students in schools.

  B. **Correct.** Many schools create individual health plans to support the needs of students with specific healthcare needs.

  C. Incorrect. A seizure action plan addresses needs specifically related to seizure disorders.

  D. Incorrect. IEPs address specialized learning needs. Healthcare needs are most often addressed in a separate health plan which may be attached to an IEP.

6) A. Incorrect. The symptom of inattention is missing.

  B. Incorrect. ADHD may result in learning delays, but these are not a primary symptom of ADHD; the primary symptom of inattention is missing.

  C. **Correct.** The three primary symptoms of ADHD are hyperactivity, impulsivity, and inattention.

  D. Incorrect. ADHD may result in learning delays, but these are not a primary symptom of ADHD; the primary symptom of hyperactivity is missing.

7) **A.** **Correct.** Providing Zane with a visual schedule prior to his expected transition (antecedent) may help him know what is coming and transition more effectively.

  B. Incorrect. Keeping Zane in one classroom may prevent behavior but does not improve his ability to transition.

  C. Incorrect. Giving Zane a toy would be a reinforcer (consequence) rather than an antecedent.

  D. Incorrect. Providing a one-on-one aide does not directly address the transition behavior.

8) A. Incorrect. An adverse effect on educational progress in a necessary component.

  B. **Correct.** All necessary criteria are listed.

  C. Incorrect. A cognitive disability is not a necessary criterion.

  D. Incorrect. Restricted, repetitive behaviors are a necessary component of qualifying for special education services under the category of autism.

9) A. Incorrect. Children may also receive services from birth to age three under IDEA, Part C.

  B. Incorrect. Children may also receive services under IDEA's category of developmental delay from ages three to nine.

  C. **Correct.** Under IDEA, Part C, children may receive services from birth to age three; under IDEA, Part B, students may receive services from ages three to nine.

D.   Incorrect. Students are generally no longer eligible for services under the category of developmental delay after age nine.

10) **A.**   **Correct.** Developmental delays are typically identified before age five— younger than most children learn to read.

B.   Incorrect. Children may be identified as having a developmental delay based on their level of communication skills.

C.   Incorrect. Children may be identified as having a developmental delay based on their level of motor skills.

D.   Incorrect. Children may be identified as having a developmental delay based on their level of adaptive skills.

11) A.   Incorrect. FAS is not an inherited cause of intellectual disability.

B.   Incorrect. Down syndrome is the leading genetic cause of intellectual disability but is not inherited.

C.   **Correct.** Fragile X syndrome is the leading inherited cause of intellectual disabilities in males.

D.   Incorrect. Muscular dystrophy is an *X*-linked inherited disease but often does not impact intellectual ability.

12) A.   Incorrect. A functional behavior assessment (FBA) is a strategy that determines the function of a behavior to plan effective behavioral interventions.

B.   **Correct.** Doing a task analysis to break down the skill of doing laundry into small steps may be a beneficial way to teach the student one skill at a time.

C.   Incorrect. A scripted reading intervention would not be an effective strategy to directly impact laundry skills.

D.   Incorrect. Touch cues are generally used to signal information to students who have a combination of hearing loss and visual impairments.

13) **A.**   **Correct.** Physical aggression and tantrums are readily observable behaviors.

B.   Incorrect. Internalizing behaviors are difficult to observe or unobservable.

C.   Incorrect. Students with autism spectrum disorders (ASD) may exhibit externalizing behaviors such as physical aggression and tantrums, but these are not a defining characteristic of ASD.

D.   Incorrect. Hyperactivity is also an example of an externalizing behavior but does not necessarily include physical aggression or tantrums.

14) A.   Incorrect. A group contingency would be most effective if the function of the behavior is known.

B.   Incorrect. A token economy may be ineffective if it does not address the function of the behavior.

C.   Incorrect. Talking to the student may reinforce the inappropriate behavior if it is caused by attention-seeking.

D.   Correct. An intervention will be most effective if the function of the behavior is known.

15) A.   Incorrect. Jeff's combination of disabilities would likely qualify him as a student with multiple disabilities.

B.   Incorrect. Lyla's combination of disabilities would likely qualify her as a student with multiple disabilities.

C.   Correct. Shawn would not qualify as a student with multiple disabilities because deaf-blindness is a separate category.

D.   Incorrect. Nicole's combination of disabilities would likely qualify her as a student with multiple disabilities.

16) **A.   Correct.** Voice output communication aids (VOCAs) are assistive communication devices that use technology, including adaptive switches, to create speech.

B.   Incorrect. "Auditory voice output device" does not describe any alternative and augmentative communication (AAC) device.

C.   Incorrect. Mo is not using speech to create text.

D.   Incorrect. Mo is not typing text to create speech.

17) A.   Incorrect. Special education teachers do not receive specific training in evaluating hearing loss.

B.   Incorrect. Speech-language pathologists (SLPs) often provide hearing screening, but an audiologist is better qualified to fully evaluate hearing loss.

C.   Incorrect. Teachers of the Deaf receive specialized training in educational supports for students who are deaf or hard of hearing but not in evaluating hearing loss.

D.   Correct. Audiologists specialize in evaluating and providing rehabilitation services for individuals with hearing loss.

18) A.   Incorrect. Educational interpreters are necessary for a small percentage of students who are hard of hearing.

B.   Correct. Visual supports should be an educational accommodation for any student who is living with hearing loss.

C.   Incorrect. FM amplification systems benefit many students with hearing loss, but some students use other forms of amplification.

D.   Incorrect. Sign language is a communication system for some students who are hard of hearing, but depending on level of hearing loss and family communication preferences, it is not necessary for all students with hearing loss.

19) A.   Incorrect. A motor impairment that requires only environmental modifications is more likely to be addressed through a Section 504 plan.

   B.   Correct. Students with motor impairments that require specially designed instruction qualify for special education services under the category of orthopedic impairment.

   C.   Incorrect. Students with motor impairments paired with cognitive or learning disabilities are more likely to be served under the category of multiple disabilities.

   D.   Incorrect. Students with motor impairments paired with emotional disabilities are more likely to be served under the category of multiple disabilities.

20) **A.   Correct.** Ali likely needs specialized equipment to support her mobility and positioning needs in the educational setting.

   B.   Incorrect. Ali is working on grade-level academics; there is no indication that she needs specialized reading instruction.

   C.   Incorrect. Ali qualifies under orthopedic impairment with no indication of emotional or behavioral needs that may require a BIP.

   D.   Incorrect. Ali qualifies under orthopedic impairment with no indication of vision loss that might require orientation and mobility (O&M) training.

21) A.   Incorrect. Orientation and mobility (O&M) specialists focus on issues related to mobility and would be less likely to provide recommendations for modifying academic materials.

   B.   Incorrect. While school psychologists may provide some recommendations, they do not have the specialized training in teaching students with visual impairments that TVIs have.

   C.   Incorrect. A board-certified behavior analyst (BCBA) is unlikely to be specifically qualified to make recommendations in this instance.

   D.   Correct. TVIs are trained to support the educational development of students with visual impairments.

22) **A.   Correct.** Many social skills are learned through observation and imitation of social behavior.

   B.   Incorrect. Students with only visual impairments should have no difficulty discriminating tone of voice.

   C.   Incorrect. While sensory overstimulation may impact opportunities for interactions, it is not the best choice for a primary cause.

   D.   Incorrect. While mobility difficulties might impact social opportunities, students with visual impairments don't necessarily avoid social contact.

23) **A.   Correct.** Usher syndrome is a genetic disorder which causes deaf-blindness.

   B.   Incorrect. Fragile X syndrome is not a common cause of deaf-blindness.

C.   Incorrect. FAS is not a genetic disorder.

D.   Incorrect. Retinitis pigmentosa (RP) is an eye disease that causes blindness.

24) A.   Incorrect. It is important for students with deaf-blindness to sit near others to encourage engagement within the classroom.

B.   Incorrect. Students with deaf-blindness often benefit from bright lighting to maximize visual input.

C.   Correct. Tactile landmarks may help the student navigate the classroom environment independently.

D.   Incorrect. Frequent rearranging of the classroom set-up would interfere with the student's ability to navigate within the classroom.

25) **A.   Correct.** Post-traumatic amnesia is the period immediately following loss of conscious in which a person has difficulty with memory and may act abnormally.

B.   Incorrect. Post-traumatic stress disorder is an ongoing mental health condition that follows a traumatic event.

C.   Incorrect. A coma is a period of prolonged unconsciousness.

D.   Incorrect. Post-traumatic amnesia may occur as the result of a TBI, but the description does not describe the full effects of a TBI.

26) A.   Incorrect. Stephen would likely benefit from direct instruction in alternate behaviors for emotional outbursts.

B.   Correct. Punishment is usually ineffective for students with TBI. If leaving the room is a punishment, Stephen is more likely to blame the teacher than his behavior. In fact, asking Stephen to leave the room may actually act as a reinforcer if Stephen gets out of doing difficult work.

C.   Incorrect. Reinforcement of appropriate behaviors may help decrease inappropriate emotional outbursts.

D.   Incorrect. Breaking activities into smaller chunks is likely an effective antecedent strategy for when a student with a TBI becomes frustrated.

3

Planning and the Learning Environment

LESSON PLANNING

ROLE OF SPECIAL EDUCATION TEACHERS IN LESSON PLANNING

The role of the special education teacher varies depending on the students he or she serves. Special educators can teach in **substantially separate classrooms**, where students do not integrate with the general education classes for core content, or an **inclusion setting**, where the students are a mix of both special and general education students. Regardless of the setting, special education teachers provide targeted and scaffolded instruction to their students. While it is not necessary for a substantially separate classroom teacher to plan alongside a general education teacher, the partnership is an important one. General education teachers may need strategies the special educator uses, while special educators could benefit from analyzing grade-level instruction that general educators provide.

The structure of special education instruction is also commonly described as either push-in or pull-out. **Push-in services** are provided in the general education classroom, while **pull-out services** are provided outside the general education classroom.

Whether or not special educators use the pull-out or push-in approach, communication with the general education teacher is very important. Services provided within the classroom will align with content being taught by the general education instructor; therefore, special educators must be involved in the lesson planning to make instruction targeted and meaningful. The same rule applies for pull-out services, as small group lessons must be relevant to the content being taught in the classroom.

Table 3.1. Comparing Push-In and Pull-Out Services

	Push-In	Pull-Out
Description	Teachers and specialists work together to provide instruction and support in the general education classroom.	Specialists work one-on-one or in small groups with students outside the general education classroom.
Benefits	▶ Keeping the student in one classroom is less disruptive for the student. ▶ Students do not miss general education instruction. ▶ The special educator and general education teacher can work more closely together.	▶ Students receive instruction tailored to their needs. ▶ Special educators can remove distractions from the classroom. ▶ Individual attention allows special educators to build trust with students.
Challenges	▶ General education classrooms may include more distractions. ▶ Students may not receive the tailored instruction they need. ▶ Effective collaboration or co-teaching can be challenging for some teachers.	▶ Students may feel uncomfortable being singled out for special services. ▶ The special educator and general education teacher will have less time for collaboration. ▶ Students may miss general education instruction.

SAMPLE QUESTION

1) **Which of the following is an example of a pull-out service?**

   A.   a special education teacher pulling a group of students from the inclusion setting to a smaller classroom to teach a specific skill

   B.   a general education teacher asking a special education teacher to take a group of absentees to make up a test

   C.   a special education teacher pulling a small group to the back of the classroom for clarification on directions

   D.   a special education teacher temporarily pulling a student who is exhibiting dangerous behaviors from the inclusion setting

BUILDING A LESSON PLAN

Lesson planning is a crucial piece to creating a safe and fruitful learning environment. Without well-planned lessons, instruction is ineffective. To begin planning for a week of learning, teachers should start with the unit framework.

Framework	State Standards
Standard	Grade Three Reading Standards for Information Text Key Idea and Details: Determine the main idea of a text; recount the key details and explain how they support the main idea.
Objective	Students will be able to determine the main idea of a passage and give three details to support their meaning.
Task Analysis	1. Students will review key terms (main idea and key details). 2. Students will read passage independently at desk. 3. Students will read passage again with a buddy at desk. 4. Each buddy pair will receive four sticky notes. 5. Students will place one sticky note labeled *main idea* next to the main idea in the text. 6. Students will place three sticky notes labeled *supporting details* in the text. 7. Students will write the main idea at the top of a graphic organizer. 8. Students will write each key detail in a box underneath the main idea in the graphic organizer. 9. Students will raise their hands for teacher approval.

Figure 3.1. Building a Lesson Plan

The **framework** is a set of standards defined by the district, local department of education, or state. A framework, or curriculum, is rigid and comprised of content standards that all students are expected to reach. A **content standard** can be simply defined as a target point for planning, teaching, and learning. Standards are the end goal of curriculum and answer the question "what do we want students to take away from instruction?"

The **scope** is the bigger picture: it consists of standards that must be taught within the framework. The **sequence** is the order in which content is taught for effective practices. The sequence of content can be determined by school, district, or state using curriculum mapping. The sequence of content should be built upon **prior knowledge**, or knowledge gained by students in formal and informal settings. For example, fourth-grade curriculum should build upon skills taught in third grade; third grade should build upon second grade, and so on.

Once content has been determined and organized, it can be broken down into learning objectives. A learning **objective** is the overarching goal of instruction. Learning objectives, or outcomes, can be designed as mastery or lesson objectives. **Mastery objectives** are typically larger scale, carrying over across a unit of study. **Lesson objectives** are smaller goals created for individual activities or lessons that eventually lead to mastery. **Language objectives** are also an integral part of planning, especially when working with students who are language learners or are diagnosed with a communication disability. Many states use standards defined by WIDA, an organization that focuses on identifying language needs and planning intervention through the use of language learning standards for English language learners and early language development.

Teacher's Name: **Grade**: 3 **Room**: 215	**Dates**: 1/11/2011 – 1/11/2011
Lesson Time: 30 minutes	**Subject**: Reading
Standards Addressed	LAFS.3.RL.3.7 Explain how specific aspects of a text's illustrations contribute to what is conveyed by the words in a story (e.g., create mood, emphasize aspects of a character or setting). LAFS.3.RL.1.1 Ask and answer questions to demonstrate understanding of a text, referring explicitly to the text as the basis for the answers.
Learning Objectives	Mastery Objectives: Students will be able to... compare and contrast their lives with Romie from *Me and Uncle Romie.* Lesson Objectives: Students will be able to... scan a text and predict the subject based on illustrations, headings, and text features. use metacognitive strategies to show questioning and understanding of a text.
Scaffolds	Clear directions Model all activities Small groups Peer tutors Pre-written sticky notes for matching
Assessment of Student Learning	Formative Assessment: Complete a diagram Summative: Engage in classroom debate on preference of city versus countryside living. Give 3 clear reasons, stating evidence from the text, why the city/country is better.
Materials	Story: *Me and Uncle Romie* Ten sticky notes per child Pencil Blank Venn diagram

Figure 3.2. Sample Lesson Plan

Objectives can be broken down using **task analysis**. Task analysis is the process of breaking tasks into smaller steps. During task analysis, the educator identifies the task and breaks it down into component steps. The educator can then provide instruction for each component step, helping the student to complete tasks that are too complex to learn all at once. Task analysis can be used in planning activities to be sure all accommodations for varying steps are in place. Task analysis is also an area in which students can be involved, as planning out activities and projects step-by-step increases independence.

The tasks can be academic or routine oriented. Below is an example of a task analysis of a classroom's morning routine:

1. enter classroom quietly
2. walk to your desk
3. unpack backpack
4. deliver materials to teacher
5. zip backpack
6. hang backpack on hook
7. walk to breakfast table
8. take one cereal, one juice, and one milk
9. bring breakfast to desk
10. sit down
11. eat quietly

When planning for a lesson using objectives, it is important to make the information accessible to all students with the use of scaffolds. **Scaffolds** are accommodations and instructional strategies that allow all students to master standards. Scaffolds make content available to students of all abilities and increase independence and confidence in the classroom. Many students with exceptionalities have learning gaps, or spaces in their learning where their performance is not in line with typical grade- or age-level performance. Scaffolds are meant to close those gaps while pushing students toward their end goal.

Accommodations are one way of scaffolding lessons to meet student needs. Accommodations are put in place to support students with exceptionalities and ensure success and comfort in the classroom. When planning materials and activities for a lesson, it is imperative to consider students who require extra support. Content should always be taught to meet individual student needs as determined by IEP goals and objectives. The IEPs contain a list of accommodations specific to each student, which must be followed when delivering instruction to that particular individual.

In general, accommodations are the most effective way to bring the curriculum to students of varying abilities and levels. Accommodations should be listed for every lesson and learning objective. If it is age-appropriate, students can be involved in accessing their accommodations. For example, a student who is allowed to use fidgets in the classroom will know where to go to get a fidget and the expectations of accessing that accommodation (for example, silently, no sharing, and so forth).

Once content has been taught, student learning should be measured. In order to determine whether or not a student demonstrates understanding of a standard, **assessments** must be used regularly and purposefully. Assessments can be informal or formal. An informal assessment can vary from a simple oral questioning between teacher and student, to an exit ticket at the end of the lesson to demonstrate student understanding. Informal assessments are driven by student performance. Formal assessments are data driven and can be teacher created (checkpoints, unit exams, weekly quizzes) or state assigned (benchmarks, standardized testing).

SAMPLE QUESTIONS

2) **Which of the following best describes scope?**
   A.   the final assessment after a unit
   B.   the set of accommodations within a framework
   C.   the prior knowledge needed by students before a lesson begins
   D.   the set of standards that must be taught within the framework

3) **Which of the following is an example of an informal assessment?**
   A.   a weekly test given to assess student learning
   B.   questioning a student to check for understanding
   C.   a state benchmark
   D.   a quick checkpoint that assesses student understanding

SCHEDULING

Student IEPs should be referenced regularly when lesson planning, which is an essential component to the overall function and flow of a classroom. When planning for the week, it is important to keep service providers' schedules in mind and note times during which students will be pulled or where providers will push-in. Simple notes alongside a lesson plan allow for the teacher to stay on track and know when to expect to lose students to pull-out services. These disruptions can be minimized when planned for, leaving more time for learning. When lesson planning is detailed and structured, classroom instruction is nearly seamless.

In Figure 3.3, it is clear that the teacher has planned for students' activities based upon their pull-out schedules. For example, the instructor notes when students receive push-in and pull-out services but also plans for what the rest of the class is doing during those times.

Reading Schedule			
Time	Group A (SPED)	Group B (SPED)	Group C (Gen. Ed.)
9:20 – 9:40	Speech pull-out	Peer activity	Teacher-led small group
9:40 – 10:00 *SPED push-in*	Teacher phonics lesson	SPED teacher-led small group	Peer activity
10:00 – 10:20 *SPED push-in*	SPED teacher-led small group	Teacher phonics lesson	Independent reading

Figure 3.3. Sample Schedule

SAMPLE QUESTION

4) A teacher is given a class with six students who receive services for occupational therapy thirty minutes per week. The occupational therapist only has time during the classroom's math block. How should the teacher plan for this situation?

   A. The teacher should continue with the originally planned lessons and allow the other students to catch up later.

   B. The teacher should stop the lesson and have the students who remain in the class do something independently until the rest of the class comes back.

   C. The rest of the class should continue learning, but the whole group lesson should be postponed until the entire class is present.

   D. The teacher should refuse to send students to pull-out services.

ORGANIZING THE LEARNING ENVIRONMENT

While classroom sizes and shapes vary, there are basic rules that special education teachers must consider when designing the layout of the classroom. All special education classrooms must be designed so that there is ample room for small-group instruction. For instance, furniture like a horseshoe table could face the teacher and be placed away from distractions, or there could be a larger instruction area with a partition to assist in focus. Students with attention difficulties will become easily distracted, so it is imperative that instruction be as uninterrupted as possible. Computer screens should face away from any instruction areas to avoid extra stimuli. Desk groupings, or pods, may pose problems when working with students with attention challenges.

HELPFUL HINT

Organization is key for both teacher and students. When materials are prepared, readily available, and accessible, more time can be spent on instruction and learning.

In order to move through lessons and transition from one activity to another seamlessly, the teacher must be organized and have regularly used materials accessible. Depending on the population a teacher is serving, the readily available materials will vary. For example, if the classroom is composed of students with social and/or emotional diagnoses, it would be logical to keep sharp and blunt objects out of student reach in case of a crisis. The grade level also defines which objects would be appropriate, such as crayons and washable markers in elementary school art classrooms and pastels and paints in middle and high school art classrooms.

> **HELPFUL HINT**
>
> Clutter in the classroom creates anxiety for both teachers and students.

If students are expected to gather materials independently, it can help to color-code areas. This system of labeling is accessible to a variety of students, regardless of communication capabilities or physical disabilities. Visuals and labels can allow students with exceptionalities and students who are language learners to access classroom materials and routines while also reinforcing sight words, high-frequency words (HFW), and classroom vocabulary.

STUDENTS WITH PHYSICAL DISABILITIES

For classrooms designed for students with physical disabilities who require mobility aids or more room, all paths to and from student desks must be accessible. The location of classroom materials should also be accessible to all students, even if some students are unable to transport themselves. Small gestures, like grabbing a book off of the shelf or putting trash in the waste bin, help increase student confidence and independence.

STUDENTS WITH SOCIAL, EMOTIONAL, AND/OR BEHAVIORAL CHALLENGES

When designing a classroom suited for students with social, emotional, and/or behavioral challenges, safety is the top priority. The first component to consider is all entrances and exits in the classroom. If there are multiple access points, it is important to decide which one will be the main door. Students with social, emotional, and/or behavioral challenges or trauma histories have "fight or flight" responses that may result in an attempt to flee the classroom, so measures must be in place to ensure safety.

If a sensory room or similar therapeutic break room is not available in a building, these spaces must be placed in the classroom. An area free of doors, windows, breakable objects, cabinets, and so forth is perfect for students in need of a sensory break or de-escalation. These spaces should have padded areas in case of student aggression or an event during which physical management is necessary. Students and staff should also have clear access to and from the door to avoid any interaction with the rest of the class during a crisis. Any expectations or classroom rules should be posted in a visible area of the classroom for easy referencing. Rules must be written in student-friendly language.

AUTISM SPECTRUM DISORDERS

In classrooms designed for students diagnosed with autism spectrum disorders (ASD) or sensory needs, it is especially important to scan for any possible triggers in the classroom. Something as simple as fluorescent lighting can be overstimulating for students with autism spectrum disorders; such triggers should be considered prior to the start of school.

Wall coverings or classroom decor should be less distracting than typical classrooms since these can divert students' attention during learning time. Classroom materials should fit the needs of the students in the classroom, and if any students are working on occupational therapy goals, adaptive equipment must be accessible. Anchor and reference charts should be placed at eye level with easy-to-read fonts and colors. These charts should display clearly defined rules and expectations that are practiced and reinforced daily. Visuals on labels, diagrams, rules, and reference charts increase student independence in the classroom. As in a social-emotional classroom, an ASD classroom must have a sensory area for de-escalation or therapeutic breaks. Due to the unpredictability of student behavior in times of crisis, all entrances and exits should be evaluated and planned for in case of an emergency.

STUDENTS WHO ARE VISUALLY IMPAIRED AND/OR HARD OF HEARING

For students who have hearing loss or visual impairments, small classroom setup changes will allow for accessible instruction. Students with visual impairments may require accommodations such as specific lighting, braille, and a variety of adaptive equipment. Students with low vision or who are blind benefit from a variety of textures in the classroom. From tables to rugs, any minor textural differences can help a student understand his or her space in the classroom. For students who have low vision, small gestures such as placing the rules and expectations at eye level or in a large, readable font can make a big difference in student accessibility in the classroom.

Students living with moderate hearing loss may also require accommodations, such as an interpreter and adaptive equipment. Rules and directions should be detailed and clear when presented to students to ensure their understanding. Students who are hard of hearing or deaf may also benefit from increased lighting in the classroom to assist in American Sign Language (ASL) communication. There should not be any background noise or music in these classrooms.

ENGLISH LANGUAGE LEARNERS

English language learners (ELL) benefit from many classroom accommodations to support learning. Visuals and labels make the classroom accessible. Labels on common items like doors, cabinets, desks, chairs, sinks, pencils, and so forth help to increase sight word and high-frequency word recognition and reading. Visuals assist ELLs in associating text with meaning and reinforce early reading skills.

EMERGENCY SITUATIONS

In the event of a lockdown or school emergency, district protocols should be followed. However, it is important to practice these routines so students are informed of what to do in case of an event. This should include practicing with students who use mobility aids, since their response time to an emergency will be delayed, and students with sensory sensitivities who may require extra assistance evacuating. English language learners, students who are deaf or hard of hearing, and visually impaired or blind students should have appropriate directions available to them in such scenarios.

SAMPLE QUESTIONS

5) **Which of the following should have the highest priority when laying out a classroom for students with social and/or emotional disabilities?**

   A.   organization

   B.   safety

   C.   accessibility

   D.   functionality

6) **Why is it important for language learners to have labels on common classroom items?**

   A.   Labels assist ELLs in learning decoding strategies.

   B.   Labels assist ELLs with text-meaning association.

   C.   Labels assist ELLs reinforce location and directionality skills.

   D.   Labels force ELLs to use English rather than their native language.

MANAGING STUDENT BEHAVIOR

DEFINING AND RESPONDING TO BEHAVIORS

Student behavior is defined as observable activity in the classroom. When behavior is referenced, it is typically in a negative light since negative behaviors are more easily recognized than positive ones. For example, a student who pushes a desk over and throws a chair is more likely to be noticed as compared to a student sitting appropriately in the classroom. Negative behavior seeks attention, and how adults and peers respond determines the likelihood of the behavior occurring again.

Negative student behavior is simply the noncompliance to classroom, school, and/or district expectations. Behaviors can range from refusal to work to physical aggression and must be responded to appropriately depending upon the type of behavior witnessed. Each school should have a tiered behavior system, usually ranging from tier 1—simple disruptions and failure to follow directions—which require redirection, to tier 3—aggression, threats, pulling of emergency alarms—which require intensive interventions.

If these tiers do not exist or a building does not follow a positive behavioral interventions and supports (PBIS) or response to intervention (RTI) framework, the special educator may need to create a tiered system. District handbooks should be followed when responding to behaviors outlined in the rules and regulations as protocols differ from school to school. Consequences for specific behaviors are outlined in handbooks. Understanding the behavior and the tier in which it falls determines how teachers should respond.

In order to appropriately respond to a behavior, student disabilities should always be considered. If behaviors are reoccurring, a **manifestation meeting** may be held in order to review the student's diagnosis and determine whether the behavior is a manifestation of the disability. By law, students with disabilities cannot lose learning time due to behaviors associated with their disability. If the meeting determines that the behaviors are a manifestation of the student's disability, the student cannot be withheld from the school environment. Similarly, students cannot be withheld if their behavior is the result of improper implementation of the IEP.

Manifestation meetings are conducted after a student is removed from his or her learning environment for ten or more consecutive days or fifteen days annually for one or more reasons, such as drug possession, violation of school code, weapons possession, bodily injury upon another person, and so forth. Manifestation meetings are required by the Individuals with Disabilities Education Act (IDEA) and must be carried out within ten days of the decision to withdraw a student from the learning environment.

Schools are moving toward alternatives to typical in- or out-of-school suspensions. Alternatives to suspension that have gained popularity are Saturday school, "mindfulness" detentions, and youth court. **Saturday school** requires students to attend class for a number of hours on a Saturday in order to make up missed work or complete assignments related to their behavior. **Mindfulness detentions** involve having students stay after school for activities regarding mindfulness techniques, such as de-escalation, self-awareness, and deep-breathing strategies. This is both reactive and proactive since it is a response to behavior but also prevents possible future behaviors.

Youth court is an option for students who have repeatedly displayed high-risk behaviors. Youth court involves students in a judicial process led by a jury of their peers. This jury decides a just punishment for the action, which is typically some form of community service. The student will then serve on a jury for other cases in the court.

7) **Which of the following best describes the purpose of a manifestation meeting?**

    A.   to determine whether a disability is the cause of a school conduct violation

    B.   to decide if a student has a behavioral disability

    C.   to create a behavior intervention plan (BIP)

    D.   to evaluate if the punishment for a school conduct violation is warranted

ASSESSING BEHAVIOR AND INTERVENTION

A **functional behavioral assessment (FBA)** is a series of observations and reports that determines the driving forces behind undesired behaviors. FBAs are conducted by the school with permission from a parent or guardian when a behavior is dysregulated and cannot be managed with typical interventions. FBAs are often requested within ten days after a punishable offense (such as aggression). The outcome of an FBA is a plan for intervention.

The **behavior intervention plan (BIP)** is a guide for all team members to reference when working with a student. The BIP form will differ by state or district, but each form will have similar components.

An example of a situation that may warrant an FBA is as follows:

> The assessment dives into the "why" of a behavior and observes what the child's desired outcome is. For example, if a student is refusing to write an open response in English language arts (ELA) and puts his or her head down on the desk, the student may be sent out of the room to see a guidance counselor or administrator. If his or her desired outcome was to get out of doing the assignment, the behavior earned the student what he or she wanted.

After a behavior occurs, the functional assessment team will work together to gather data. There are five steps when conducting an FBA:

1. **Identify**: The first step in the FBA process is to identify the undesired behavior. These behaviors must be observable and measurable, meaning there are specifics as to when, where, and how often a behavior takes place.

2. **Gather**: Once the target behavior is identified, data collection must begin. Data collection can be done indirectly or directly. Indirect data collection methods can be student interviews, student records, educator

interviews, or anything that gives information on events and the setting surrounding the occurrence. Direct data collection methods are usually observations that record all factors present when a behavior occurs. Direct methods also collect data such as frequency and duration of behaviors. One specific direct method is **ABC sequencing**. This organizer lists the Antecedent or stimulus, Behavior or action, and Consequence.

3.   **Analyze**: After data is collected, the team must work together to analyze it. This includes searching for patterns or triggers, discovering the behavior's purpose, looking at environmental variables, medication changes, and emotional variables.

4.   **Hypothesize**: The team will use the data that was analyzed to form a hypothesis. This hypothesis is the team's best guess at the reasoning behind a behavior.

> **STUDY TIPS**
>
> The FBA interviewer should try to answer four questions:
>
> ▶ Who is present when the behavior takes place?
> ▶ What is occurring in the classroom before and after behaviors?
> ▶ When is the behavior displayed?
> ▶ Where does the behavior occur?

5.   **Plan**: After a hypothesis has been formed, the BIP is written. The BIP will outline the behavior and positive behavioral supports to help diminish negative behaviors and encourage appropriate ones. Behavior plans may include accommodations to teaching strategies, lists of appropriate consequences, and ways to teach students replacement (positive) behaviors that get them the same "reward" as negative behaviors.

Student Information: Joan Arc			
Setting Description: Classroom during math block			
Behavior Description: Joan is seemingly upset by a worksheet she received.			
Time	**Antecedents**	**Behaviors**	**Consequences**
9:00 a.m.	Student was handed worksheet.	Student became upset and pushed the worksheet off the desk.	Student was told to pick the worksheet up and get to work.
9:12 a.m.	Student was told (for the second time) to pick up the worksheet and get to work.	Student ripped the worksheet in half and threw it in the trash.	Student was sent to the office.

Figure 3.4. ABC Tracker

After a BIP is in place, the work does not end. Student progress should be continuously tracked and shared with team members. Review dates for the plan ensure that the team will meet regularly to discuss student progress and look at data collection. If a BIP becomes ineffective or the child is displaying a new behavior, the FBA can be conducted again.

BIPs should be followed by anyone serving the student in need. Frequency of meetings and persons involved will be decided at the initial team meeting, during which all service providers are involved to discuss the child's needs prior to implementation of the BIP.

Student Name	John Smith		
Target Behavior	John becomes disruptive and disrespectful when demands are put on him in the classroom. An FBA determined that John is most dysregulated during writing.		
Goals	The team will work together to help John reach his goals: John will be able to write a 5-sentence paragraph, with accommodations, with fewer than 3 prompts from the teacher in 8 out of 10 opportunities. John will be able to ask for a break when feeling upset in 7 out of 10 opportunities.		
Intervention Methods	**Check-ins:** The teacher will check in with the student at 10-minute increments in the classroom during writing block. **Access to supports:** John will be able to seek assistance from school adjustment counselors and social workers. These services will also be provided to him for the duration determined in his "Services Provided" section. **Peer tutor:** Student assigned will assist John in completing his classwork with the use of graphic organizers.		
Accommodations	Frequent breaks Extra time to complete assignments Sentence starters Peer tutor Graphic organizers		
Services Provided	**Service**	**Provider**	**Weekly Sessions**
	SEL skills	School social worker	2 days × 30 minutes
	Peer lunch group	School adjustment counselor	5 days × 15 minutes

Figure 3.5. Example of a Behavior Intervention Plan (BIP)

The **target behaviors** are behaviors witnessed in the FBA that require intervention through the BIP. This section should be detailed and have specific data to support each target behavior. The goals will be the end result, or the ideal outcome, after implementation of the BIP. Intervention methods will cover the services and/or supports in place in order to help the child reach his or her BIP goal.

Accommodations, as mentioned earlier in the chapter, will be any adjustments to help the child succeed in his or her learning environment. This could be anything from extra time on a test to graphic organizers while note-taking. The section concerning services provided will outline the schedule of services the student will receive in accordance with his or her BIP, including the name of the provider, duration of intervention, and frequency of services.

SAMPLE QUESTIONS

8) **Which of the following should be the end result of an FBA?**

   A. a BIP

   B. an ABC chart

   C. an IEP

   D. a mastery objective

9) **Which of the following is a target behavior?**

   A. Michael asks to use the bathroom more than three times a day.

   B. Joseph will put his head down and refuse to work on math assignments.

   C. Kayla is able to ask for breaks when she is feeling upset.

   D. James is a student diagnosed with oppositional defiant disorder.

POSITIVE BEHAVIOR SUPPORTS

When positive behavior occurs, it must be recognized. Rewiring the brain to think that good behavior translates to praise and bad behavior translates to no attention after years of getting attention from negative behavior is difficult, but it is possible. Rewarding positive behavior is the most effective way to do this. Rewards can range from a five-minute break after completing a writing activity (using an "if/then" chart), to a pizza party for the classroom after goals are reached.

Many schools use **positive behavioral interventions and supports (PBIS)** to promote positive behavior for all students. Briefly discussed in chapter 2, PBIS offers universal early intervention for all students in self-regulation and social skills. It also features a multitiered model to provide an appropriate level of services according to each student's need, with some students receiving more intensive, targeted intervention as necessary. PBIS systems use direct instruction and positive reinforcement of appropriate behavior to improve school culture and behavior school-wide.

A **token economy system** is a system in which "tokens" (points, beans, stars, and so forth) are used as a means of positive reinforcement. These tokens act as a form of currency and "pay" for a variety of desired rewards. Tokens are given when students are following expectations as defined by classroom rules or goals outlined in their IEP or BIP. There are a variety of token economy systems. These may include:

▶ Points: Students earn points throughout the day as monitored by a behavior tracker, which is designed around their IEP or BIP goals. Students can use points to "cash out" in a classroom "store" for a variety of items, which could range from intangible rewards like lunch with the teacher, to tangible rewards like bouncy balls or pencils.

▶ Beans: Students can earn beans as a class when the entire group is on task and meeting expectations. There may be a jar where the beans are stored after they are earned, and once a certain number of beans are acquired, the students can earn extra recess, a movie day, pizza party, and so forth.

▶ Tickets: Students can earn tickets when exceeding expectations in the classroom and use these tickets to cash out (similar to the points system).

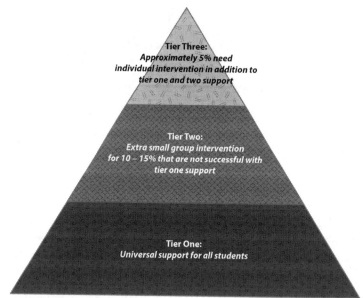

Figure 3.6. Tiered Behavior Management System

To involve students more in the token economy system, when appropriate, students can track their own points/tickets/beans in a banking-style method. They can "withdraw" or "deposit" tokens as they spend/earn them in the classroom. This holds the students accountable and makes the system even more engaging. Tokens could also be distributed weekly in a "paycheck" model.

The reward should always be something that is highly desired by the student(s). Some schools may allow consumables (candy, chocolates, juices) in their classroom "store," but it is best to check with district policy before purchasing these items.

While taking tokens away for bad behavior may seem appropriate, few studies show that this is meaningful in the token reward system. For that reason, tokens should not be taken away once earned by a student. Token economy systems should be used only as a positive reinforcement and never as a consequence.

Check-in/check-out (CI/CO) interventions are another effective PBIS intervention (usually used at tier 2). When implementing a CI/CO intervention, the teacher selects two or three behaviors to be targeted and creates a daily behavior report card. Incentives for meeting a behavioral target may be included as part of the report card. At the beginning of a day or class session, the student checks in with a teacher (the classroom teacher, special education teacher, or another trusted teacher in the building). At check-in, the teacher reviews behavioral expectations and reinforcements for meeting behavioral targets. During class, the teacher monitors the student's behavior and fills out the student behavioral report card. At the end of class or the school day, the teacher meets with the student again to review behavior and provide reinforcement or encouragement to do better the next day.

Teachers can also use PBIS to promote cooperation among students by using **group contingencies** to reward multiple students at a time. **Dependent group contingencies** reward the entire group or class based on a specific student meeting a pre-set goal. An example of a dependent group contingency would be to have a "mystery student" whose behavior in a specific situation (such as walking in the hallway) determines whether the entire class earns a reward. **Interdependent group contingencies** reward the group only if every member of the group meets the criterion. For example, if every member of the group must learn the parts of a cell in order to receive the reward, the group members may work together to ensure everyone learns the material. **Independent group contingencies** provide rewards to members of the group who meet a criterion. For example, every student who is quiet in the hallway earns extra time at recess.

When working with a token economy or any range of reward system, both the goals students must meet and the behaviors tracked should revolve around what is outlined on their IEP or BIP. If a student does not have a BIP created but has shown consistent behaviors—the consequences of which have been unproductive—an FBA should be conducted.

> **HELPFUL HINT**
>
> An important aspect of reinforcing positive behavior within any reward system is to offer *specific* praise. When praising a student, it is important to specifically state what they have done well, rather than offering general praise. An example of specific praise might be, "Tom is doing an excellent job raising his hand quietly." The praise, "Tom is such a good student," is broad and not effective in promoting expected behavior.

10) **Which of the following is a behavior that would be rewarded with tokens in a token economy system?**

    A.   bringing in homework

    B.   correct answers on a test

    C.   meeting expectations as outlined by IEP or BIP goals

    D.   helping peers master learning objectives

PREVENTING BEHAVIORS

Preventing behaviors is the most effective management strategy. When an educator is familiar with their students and has clear expectations in a classroom, the number of behaviors is reduced.

Having a predictable routine can take the unpredictability out of the classroom and in turn make students more comfortable. One way to ensure students are comfortable and know what to expect in the classroom is to have a number of visual schedules. While it is important to have a general classroom schedule on the board with times and activities posted, many students would benefit from individual schedules.

A **visual schedule** can be a Velcro schedule at a student's desk that is divided by hour, activity, class period, or morning/afternoon. Students can be responsible for placing the correct events (visuals or written language) in corresponding order on the chart. This can be done with heavy supports in the

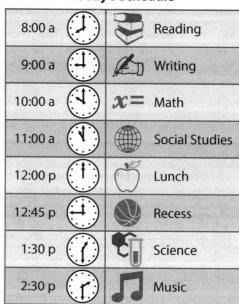

Today's Schedule

8:00 a	🕗	Reading
9:00 a	🕘	Writing
10:00 a	🕙	Math
11:00 a	🕚	Social Studies
12:00 p	🕛	Lunch
12:45 p	🕐	Recess
1:30 p	🕜	Science
2:30 p	🕝	Music

Figure 3.7. Visual Schedule

beginning of the year, but with fading supports, students can become completely independent in taking out and completing the schedule in the morning. The time periods in which the visual schedule is segmented depend on the needs of the student. For intensive intervention, ten-minute intervals may be required, but for light supports, a daily schedule broken down into morning and afternoon may suffice.

An **if-then chart**, which maps out an if-then system of tasks and rewards, can also be used to prevent or de-escalate behaviors. An if-then chart is usually a strip of Velcro that has one or two tasks that must be completed (if) before a student earns a reward activity (then). These could also track time spent on task, where a student earns a star for a certain interval of time (if), and once they receive a particular number of stars they earn the preferred activity (then).

Figure 3.8. Reward Chart

Another behavior prevention strategy is using **peer tutors**, an approach that pairs students to work together on lesson objective mastery. It could be as informal as a seat next to a model student, or as formal as a dedicated buddy with whom to work during all class activities. These tutors should display appropriate, model behavior and be willing to assist students in need rather than enable them. Tutors should be trained on when to ask an adult for assistance during work.

Another effective prevention strategy is a **behavioral contract**. When implementing a behavioral contract, the teacher should work with the student to establish expected behaviors and to identify behaviors to be reduced. On the contract, consequences for unexpected behaviors and reinforcements for expected behaviors should be specifically stated. Once the contract is agreed upon between the student and teacher, both parties sign the contract. The behavior contract may be referred back to as needed.

11) **Tom is an eight-year-old student who is having trouble staying on task. He frequently becomes upset when working and is impulsive when upset. Which of the following would benefit Tom the most?**

   A. a visual schedule so Tom knows when learning time is over

   B. a token economy system so Tom will earn rewards for good behavior

   C. an if-then chart to keep Tom focused and on track for desired activities

   D. a classroom peer tutor to motivate Tom

12) **Which of the following best describes a peer tutor?**

   A. a peer who is struggling with the same material as the student receiving the service

   B. a peer who stays after school with a struggling student to help him or her study for a specific assessment

   C. a peer who can assist in de-escalating a struggling student during a crisis

   D. a peer who works with a student in the classroom to master learning objectives

CLASSROOM MANAGEMENT

ESTABLISHING RULES

Classrooms should always contain a list of **rules and expectations** posted somewhere in the learning environment. To make this accessible to all, it helps to use simple, direct language. Classroom rules are most effective when generated together as a whole group. Having students included in the process of rule creation helps ensure greater acceptance and meaning.

Rules will vary depending on the type of classroom they are designed for. As an example, a classroom for students with social and/or emotional disabilities may have more rules regarding physical safety in the classroom, while an inclusion classroom's rules would pertain more to acceptance, patience, and kindness. In general, these classroom measures will assist in creating an accessible learning environment for students with exceptionalities.

Rules and expectations that are taught, demonstrated, and followed within and throughout the first six weeks of the school year will "make or break" a teacher's ability to manage a classroom. These first six weeks set the tone for the entire school year and show students what expected behavior and classroom functions look like. If the classroom is planning on using signs to request things like water, a bathroom break, or a new pencil, those must be introduced immediately. In addition, over the first weeks of school, everything from using glue sticks to asking to use the restroom should be **modeled**. Modeling is the act of showing the correct usage of a classroom item or displaying positive classroom behavior.

There are numerous ways to introduce items in the classroom. One way to reveal a pair of scissors, for instance, may be to put it into a "guess box." A guess box is a larger box used to encourage student questioning. Students can ask *yes* or *no* questions when guessing what item is in the box. These responses can be tracked on a whiteboard or projector while "playing" the

guessing game. The end goal is for students to identify the item; then the teacher reveals it. To introduce a bulletin board or center board, the teacher may cover up the board with a tablecloth and reveal it once he or she plans to discuss its meaning and use in the classroom.

When modeling how to use classroom objects, students should be engaged, focused, and questioned for understanding. Modeling how to sharpen a pencil might look like this:

> Teacher: "Now students, when our pencil breaks, what should we do?"
>
> Students: "Sharpen it!"
>
> Teacher: "That's right. This (points to sharpener) is a pencil sharpener. When we use the pencil sharpener, we have a few rules to follow. First, to ask to use the pencil sharpener, hold your pencil in the air silently and wait to be called on. When I give you the go-ahead, slowly walk across the back of the classroom to the sharpener. Once there, wait for a break in the speaker's talking and quickly use the sharpener. You must make sure to push the pencil in while sharpening, but not so hard that it will break. Just like this." (Teacher models.) "This is too hard." (Teacher models.) "This is too gentle." (Teacher models.)

After the teacher has modeled the expectation, he or she should call on two to three students to model the behavior. If students make an error, peers should identify and correct what went wrong. It may be necessary to model expectations repeatedly throughout the year, especially after holidays and school vacations. The expectations modeled at varying grade levels will differ, but the importance of repetition, clarity, and reinforcement remains.

In addition to modeling the use of classroom materials, behavioral expectations should also be discussed and modeled in an interactive and engaging manner. Everything from playing a game at recess to bullying must be discussed and responded to appropriately in role-playing scenarios. Teachers could pose a situation like this:

> "Let's say I'm out at recess and a boy named Billy from another class comes over and takes the chalk I was using. I get really upset. What should I do?"

In these situations, it may take the students a few times to come up with the appropriate response, but any incorrect answers are used as teaching points. Once a student generates the correct response, the action should be modeled by the teacher and numerous students. Role-playing in social-emotional scenarios leads to greater understanding of proper reactions. Again, these situations may need to be modeled repeatedly throughout the year to remind students of expectations.

SAMPLE QUESTIONS

13) **Which of the following best describes how rules should be created and introduced in the classroom?**

A. The teacher should develop the rules and introduce them during the first week of school.

B. The administrators should develop a set of school-wide rules and introduce them at an assembly.

C. The teacher should ask the students to develop a set of rules after she has gained their trust.

D. The teacher should work with students during the first week of school to develop rules.

14) **Which of the following would NOT be considered part of the modeling process?**

A. A teacher demonstrates how to light a Bunsen burner in the laboratory.

B. A teacher asks a student to write the rules of laboratory safety on the board.

C. A teacher has a student come to the front of the room to demonstrate how to light a Bunsen burner.

D. A teacher asks the students how they should behave when fires are used in the laboratory.

RITUALS AND ROUTINES

Having **rituals and routines** in place within the classroom encourages students to feel safe and welcomed at school. Students may come from homes without parental figures or be in temporary housing, so knowing what to expect takes the uncertainty out of school and provides them with a stable environment.

If rituals and routines are in place during the first six weeks of the school year, classroom management comes much easier. When students are comfortable with the classroom routine, there is less downtime, or room for error. Students are more in tune than some educators may believe: they pick up on ill-planned activities, uncertainties, and negative emotions in the classroom. Teacher preparedness and self-care are essential in creating a productive learning environment.

Rituals and routines vary from classroom to classroom, but many pieces of a ritual or routine are similar. One ritual in the classroom could be the arrival and dismissal protocols. For example, when students come in to the classroom in the morning, they are expected to hang up their backpacks, turn in homework, and take a breakfast serving. Similarly, in the afternoon, students are expected to get their backpacks, pack their homework, and put their chairs up. Another ritual may be lining up and using the bathrooms. Line orders should be established, and students will line up when called, follow hallway expectations, and use the restrooms two at a time. These rituals and routines hold students accountable and help to minimize talking between activities.

> **DID YOU KNOW?**
>
> Addressing students by name, making eye contact when speaking, and answering respectfully are essential in building relationships. When students feel valued and heard, they are invested in their education. This leads to more security in the classroom: students are willing to take risks, become involved in classroom discussions, and ask questions.

Daily schedules in the classroom should rarely shift since predictability is a component students with exceptionalities require in their schooling. Keeping many routines in place allows for easier transitions. **Transitions** are the act of moving from one activity to another, whether it is reading to writing, classroom to recess, or gym class to dismissal. Students should have a routine in place for their transition as mentioned above, but this does not diminish the anxiety some students may have in relation to changing activities. Prior to switching activities, students with exceptionalities benefit from **countdowns**. This could be a visual timer displayed on a projector, or an announcement when there are ten, five, two, and one minute(s) left of an activity.

SAMPLE QUESTION

15) Simon is a ninth grader struggling with transitions between the classroom's computer time and lunch. He frequently becomes physically aggressive and unsafe when he is asked to leave his computer and go for lunch. Which of the following would be an effective intervention for Simon?

   A. Refrain from giving him any computer time.

   B. Remove him from the computer ten minutes before the other students leave.

   C. Provide Simon with a visual timer that counts down to lunch.

   D. Allow Simon to move from computer time to lunch at his own pace.

COOL DOWN AREAS

A variety of special education classrooms benefit from social-emotional learning time. This could be something as simple as quiet time after a gym class, to a daily meditation or mindfulness activity. Devoting a piece of the school day to focus on interpersonal issues, self-regulation, and awareness strategies leads to less disruption during core instruction.

Allowing students to have a place to decompress and regain focus in the classroom results in less disruptions in the classroom and higher student success rates. While it can be difficult to give up precious moments of teaching time, breaks are a proactive approach to classroom management. Students who are able to self-regulate and ask for breaks show emotional maturity, a behavior which should be encouraged.

In a "cool down," or sensory area of the classroom, students should be encouraged to self-reflect. In these areas, reflection sheets can be placed for students to decipher what their trigger was, what their response was, and what they can do in the future to prevent the behavior or emotion that brought them to the "cool down" area. In order to keep students from abusing the sensory area, there should be a time limit and designated number of breaks each day. There will be days when teachers may need to change the duration or number of breaks in times of need, but routine procedures should be followed all other times.

SAMPLE QUESTION

16) **Which of the following statements about a "cool down" area in a classroom is NOT true?**

   A.   Students having a place to go to when they are feeling overwhelmed increases their ability to self-regulate.

   B.   "Cool down" areas are a proactive approach to behaviors.

   C.   These areas allow students to reflect on their behaviors and emotions.

   D.   Asking for a break in a "cool down" area is an acceptable form of task avoidance.

WORKING AS A TEAM

Teaching students with exceptionalities is a team effort. Teachers should remain in contact with parents throughout the school year regarding both successes and struggles in the classroom. If the student has an in-home therapist or outside services, these service providers should also be included in the student's educational meetings, if the parent consents. Meetings should begin with student performance, educational data, behavioral data, and specific progress reports that reference BIP and IEP goals. Overall, remaining organized, maintaining a routine, and being well-planned leads to higher student achievement and a more fruitful learning environment.

When a special educator pushes-in to a general education or inclusion classroom, there must be communication with both teachers. Special educators and general educators must share plans or plan together to ensure that lessons align and student needs are addressed. It is also important for the student with exceptionalities to establish a clear schedule with the general educator so a special educator's presence is not disruptive or unexpected. In addition, discussions should take place concerning which teacher will take the lead on behaviors in the classroom, since multiple directions given to a student can be overwhelming and elevate emotions.

SAMPLE QUESTION

17) **Which of the following is NOT the responsibility of a special education teacher?**

A. planning with the general education teacher to make sure lessons and objectives align

B. establishing a clear schedule with the general education teacher to minimize disruptions

C. discussing roles with the general educators to determine which teacher will lead and facilitate pieces of the lesson

D. providing pull-out services only

ANSWER KEY

1) **A.** **Correct.** A special educator pulling students from an inclusion setting to focus on a specific skill is an example of a pull-out service.

   B. Incorrect. Special educators pulling absentees to make up a test is not a pull-out service. Special educators should not be supporting students who do not have the service on their IEP.

   C. Incorrect. By pulling a small group to the back of the classroom, the special educator is not removing them from the inclusion environment, so this is not an example of a pull-out service.

   D. Incorrect. A special educator pulling a student in crisis is not an example of a pull-out service.

2) **D.** **Correct.** Scope is the set of standards that must be taught within a framework.

3) **B.** **Correct.** Questioning is an informal assessment; the other choices are all formal assessments.

4) A. Incorrect. Students must all be afforded the same education as their peers, regardless of scheduling conflicts.

   B. Incorrect. Unplanned instruction time in the classroom leads to management problems.

   C. **Correct.** When a lesson plan takes interventions and services into account, it ensures all students will have access to the same content and instruction.

   D. Incorrect. It is illegal to deprive students of services determined in an educational plan.

5) A. Incorrect. Organization is helpful, but it is not the top priority for students with social and/or emotional disabilities.

   B. **Correct.** Due to the increased risk for students with social and/or emotional disabilities, safety must be the top priority.

   C. Incorrect. Accessibility is the top priority in classrooms for students with physical disabilities.

   D. Incorrect. Functionality is a priority in all classrooms but not the top priority in a classroom for students with social and/or emotional disabilities.

6) A. Incorrect. Labels do not assist in learning decoding strategies.

   B. **Correct.** Labels encourage a text-meaning association and increase HFW recognition skills.

   C. Incorrect. Labels do not mention directionality/location; therefore, they do not reinforce those skills.

D.   Incorrect. ELLs should not be forced to use English, and labels do not support this.

7) A.   **Correct.** A manifestation meeting determines whether a student is subject to suspension or expulsion due to a behavior that is a manifestation of a disability.

B.   Incorrect. Disabilities are not determined at a manifestation meeting.

C.   Incorrect. BIPs are created after an FBA at a team meeting.

D.   Incorrect. Manifestation meetings are only related to punishments that exclude a student from his or her learning environment.

8) A.   **Correct.** The goal of an FBA is to develop a BIP.

B.   Incorrect. An ABC chart is used during the "gather" stage of an FBA.

C.   Incorrect. IEPs are separate from FBAs.

D.   Incorrect. Mastery objectives and lesson objectives are not included in FBAs.

9) A.   Incorrect. Michael asking to use the bathroom frequently is not, in and of itself, a behavior.

B.   **Correct.** Joseph putting his head down in a refusal to work is a behavior that should be targeted using a BIP.

C.   Incorrect. Kayla is displaying model behavior, not a target behavior.

D.   Incorrect. This statement does not describe the behavior James is exhibiting; therefore, it is not a target behavior.

10) A.   Incorrect. Bringing in homework is an expected behavior that does not yield a reward.

B.   Incorrect. Token economy systems do not reward correct answers.

C.   **Correct.** Students should earn tokens when they are meeting expectations as outlined by their IEP or BIP goals.

D.   Incorrect. While helping peers is an admirable behavior, only goals outlined in an IEP or BIP should be addressed in a token economy system to keep the behaviors targeted and measurable.

11) A.   Incorrect. While a visual schedule may help Tom stay on track with what's up next, it will not help him stay on task.

B.   Incorrect. Tom may benefit from a token economy system, but tokens would not assist him in staying focused on the task.

C.   **Correct.** Tom would stay most focused with a constant reinforcer, like an if-then chart, that allows him to keep the desired activity in mind and therefore motivates him to complete the task at hand.

D.   Incorrect. A classroom peer tutor may not be appropriate for an impulsive and upset student.

12) A.   Incorrect. Peer tutors should not be struggling with the material they are assisting the targeted student with.

B.   Incorrect. The peer tutor is not required to work with the student outside of school hours.

C.   Incorrect. A peer tutor should never be involved in assisting with a student in crisis.

D.   Correct. A peer tutor helps a struggling student meet learning objectives.

13) A.   Incorrect. While rules should be introduced during the first week of school, it is not effective for teachers to create these on their own.

B.   Incorrect. Classroom rules should be determined within the classroom, and while school-wide rules should be implemented as well, classroom rules should be personalized to meet the needs of the classroom.

C.   Incorrect. Students should not develop the rules on their own; the rules should be established during the first week of school.

D.   Correct. Classroom rules are most effective when teachers work with students during the first week of school to develop rules that are fair and clear to the students.

14) A.   Incorrect. Demonstration is a key part of modeling.

B.   Correct. Having students write a list of rules would not be part of modeling.

C.   Incorrect. Having students model the behavior is another key part of modeling.

D.   Incorrect. Asking the students to explain appropriate behaviors is part of modeling.

15) **C.   Correct.** The visual timer will help Simon transition from one activity to another. This intervention allows Simon to stay with the class and teaches him the importance of staying on schedule.

16) A.   Incorrect. It is true that self-regulation techniques are increased when students have a place to go when they are feeling overwhelmed.

B.   Incorrect. "Cool down" areas are a proactive approach to behaviors.

C.   Incorrect. "Cool down" areas allow students to reflect on behaviors and emotions.

D.   Correct. There is no acceptable form of task avoidance; using a "cool down" area as an avoidance strategy is a misuse of the area.

17) A.   Incorrect. A special educator must be involved in planning with the general educator to be sure lessons and objectives align.

B.   Incorrect. A special educator must be involved in establishing a clear schedule with the general education teacher.

C.   Incorrect. A special educator must work with the general education teacher to determine who is leading the lesson.

D.   Correct. Special education teachers may provide both pull-out and push-in services.

4

Instruction

INSTRUCTIONAL MODELS AND STRATEGIES

DIRECT TEACHING

Direct teaching goes by many names: direct instruction, explicit instruction, systematic instruction, and teacher-led instruction. All these terms refer to methods of instruction that share certain characteristics. Direct instruction is highly systematic and sequenced, and teachers typically control the pace and format of the interaction. In many ways the teachers are the directors, and students are those being directed. Direct instruction has proven highly effective for students with exceptionalities, especially when students are working one-on-one or in small groups with the teacher. The biggest advantage of direct instruction is that it is explicit and, as its name suggests, direct. Many students with exceptionalities respond to this type of delivery with the greatest ease.

Direct instruction is often highly effective for students in need of interventions when it is conducted in a small-group setting. Teachers can offer feedback and correction during decoding exercises for emergent readers or offer a quick vocabulary explanation for older students working on comprehension exercises. Because of its efficacy, direct instruction in a small-group setting is often the first method used for tier 2 interventions. One-on-one direct instruction is often used for tier 3 interventions or when students need significant reteaching.

> **DID YOU KNOW?**
>
> There is a formal teaching model called *Direct Instruction* (as opposed to the strategy of direct instruction as direct teaching). **Direct Instruction** emphasizes highly scripted explicit teacher-directed lessons using a standardized curriculum. Popular Direct Instruction products include Reading Mastery, DISTAR Arithmetic, and Language for Learning.

Lecture has traditionally been synonymous with direct instruction. In a lecture format, the teacher typically stands in the front of the room and gives information as the class listens and takes notes. While lecture is considered out-of-date in many circles, in many instances it can be quite effective when balanced with other methods. For example, in science or social studies, new concepts or vocabulary must often first be discussed in lecture format before students can explore and apply these concepts. In English and language arts, certain grammatical concepts have to be first explicitly explained before they can be applied.

Lectures do not have to be boring or involve only "teacher talk." Many classrooms are now equipped with a variety of multimedia aids to allow teachers to present audio, video, and digital information to students in conjunction with or in lieu of the traditional blackboard or white board. Further, lecture does not have to be continuous. Many successful lectures involve frequent breaks for any number of activities: question and answer, completing a task independently or with a partner or group, practice with a skill just learned, and so on.

Another direct instruction technique often used in tandem with lecture is **demonstration**, or modeling. In a demonstration, the teacher models the particular skill or activity the students will need to master. This might include a physical education teacher demonstrating an exercise before asking students to try it or a science teacher performing an experiment in front of the class before having students perform the experiment on their own. For younger students, demonstration might be a teacher modeling how to work with manipulatives or use materials at learning centers to meet learning objectives. Demonstration can be particularly important in mathematics learning since watching teachers work problems is a very effective instructional technique when introducing new material. For example, a math teacher might demonstrate new skills and concepts to students by working problems on a board or screen. This allows students to see problems being performed successfully before attempting similar problems on their own.

> **STUDY TIPS**
>
> Create a list of every specific method of direct instruction delivery you can think of. Which topics or concepts would be appropriate for the different types of delivery?

One advantage of direct instruction is that it can prevent mis-learning. **Mis-learning** can happen when students are involved in exploratory learning without first receiving proper guidance. They risk reaching faulty conclusions and believing something that is not true. For example, a fourth-grade student might be given the task of classifying animals into certain categories as an exploratory learning activity. Perhaps the teacher gives the student four categories of vertebrates: fish, amphibians, reptiles, and birds. She then gives students a list of animals and asks them to place these animals into categories. Some students might erroneously place eels in the reptile category and not the fish category. If the teacher never notices this and does not correct the students' mis-learning, then they might continue to believe that eels are reptiles and not fish. Had the teacher first given direct instruction to the students through a lecture or film or some other direct method, students would have had the background to distinguish a reptile from a fish. Then, perhaps fewer students would have placed the eel in the reptile category because they would know that, for example, eels must be fish because they have gills.

Another advantage of direct instruction is that student misconceptions or procedural errors can be corrected immediately. Perhaps a second-grade teacher has just demonstrated vertical two-digit addition with regrouping for the first time by working several sample problems for the class. She then asks students to work the first problem in their workbooks by first writing the correct unit in the ones place. As she walks around to check each student's answer, she can quickly redirect students who wrote the incorrect answer. If students were first asked to try the problems on their own without direction, they may believe their chosen solving method was correct and effective and would have continued using the incorrect method on other problems. In fact, research suggests that for novice learners, direct instruction is best. Consequently, in many instructional programs the teacher first gives explicit instruction to introduce the new concept and then plans more exploratory, application-based activities after students have mastered the initial learning objective.

Recently, educational technology has become quite prevalent as an instructional tool in most classrooms. While the methodology of different programs varies, many employ a direct instructional approach. These programs often involve an explanation (either through audio, text, video, or a combination of these) and then guided practice. Many educational intervention programs are now computer based because they allow more individualization and customization than even a small-group setting may allow. Frequently, these programs are most effective when they employ explicit instruction and offer immediate feedback, explanations for incorrect responses, and reteaching of foundational skills.

Of course, direct instruction is not without its critics, and it is not appropriate in all settings and situations. Most preschool classrooms use this method only minimally as very young children often learn best through play and peer interaction. Developmental appropriateness should always be considered when planning instructional techniques, and all students will need a balance of activities to keep attention and engagement.

SAMPLE QUESTIONS

1) Which of the following is NOT a method of direct instruction?
    A.   showing a video
    B.   demonstrating cracking an egg
    C.   choral reading
    D.   student experimentation

2)   Miss Shepherd is a seventh-grade English and language arts teacher. She wants to balance direct instruction for new concepts with other techniques after students have mastered a skill. Which activity would help her meet this goal?

A.   stopping her lecture every few minutes to give students the opportunity to stand up and stretch their legs

B.   having students turn to their neighbor to recap what they remember after each segment of her lecture

C.   giving students a writing prompt and then having them brainstorm ideas first before writing their essay

D.   practicing with prepositions and then having students write a descriptive paragraph using at least five prepositions

INDIRECT TEACHING

At the opposite end of the spectrum from direct instruction is **indirect instruction** (sometimes referred to as student-centered instruction). In this method, students learn without explicit direction from the teacher. If the teacher is the director in direct instruction, he can be thought of as the facilitator in indirect instruction. The teacher provides guidance as students learn new concepts through experimentation and activities.

Many methods fall under the umbrella of indirect instruction. Frequently, indirect instruction relies on a problem-solution model where students are presented with a problem and then must propose a solution. Students may also be asked to organize information in a certain form or apply information presented in one form to another situation or scenario.

There are several methods for indirect instruction, but many rely on **problem-solving**. In this method, students are given a problem to which they must find a solution. The problem might be real life ("How can we organize the desks in the classroom so that there is at least three feet of space in each aisle?"); it may involve a particular scenario ("What would you do if...?"); or it might even involve a group of students ("With your group members, decide what would happen if...").

Another popular method of indirect teaching is the use of **concept mapping**, sometimes called mind maps, webs, or graphic organizers. Concept mapping is a good way to help students organize information and establish relationships among different ideas. This is often done after students have read a chapter in a textbook or been introduced to certain information. These maps may include words, pictures, or both, but they show relationships among ideas, which aids in synthesizing information.

Using **examples** is another way to teach indirectly. This is often done by first giving students a list of examples and then asking them to determine how they are similar and different and how they illustrate certain concepts. For example, a literature teacher might give students five poems and ask them to answer certain questions about each: "Does it rhyme?" "What type of meter does it use?" "Is it telling a story?" and so on. This will help students learn about different types of poetry such as free verse, narrative poetry, lyric poetry, and so forth.

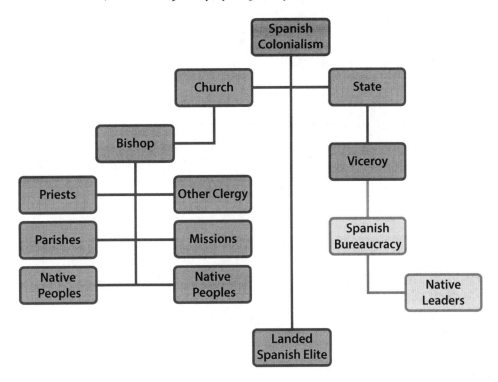

Figure 4.1. Concept Map

Another indirect teaching technique is known as **inquiry-based learning**, which involves students asking questions, conducting research or experimentation to answer these questions, and then reporting on findings. This might include questions like "What will happen if I leave a banana peel in the sun for a week?" in science or "Did Columbus really discover America?" in social studies.

Next are common examples of indirect teaching techniques frequently used for a variety of subjects.

READING

► cloze procedure, where words are deleted from a passage and students must supply the missing words

► self-assessment or self-evaluation, where students ask themselves questions as they read and determine their own level of comprehension

► concept mapping, where students organize information from what they have read into a graphic organizer

► reading for meaning, a three-phase strategy where students preview and predict before reading, search for important information while reading, and reflect on their learning after reading

► group discussion over a text

MATH

▶ Students determine the best way or all the ways to solve a given problem.

▶ Students draw a model or graphic to represent and solve the problem.

▶ Students use think-alouds in which they talk themselves through the steps of solving the problem.

SCIENCE

▶ conducting an experiment to demonstrate or glean a scientific concept such as water evaporating or properties of magnets

▶ categorization and classification

▶ listing examples and nonexamples

SOCIAL STUDIES

▶ student-led research projects

▶ oral presentations given by students

▶ case studies that illustrate certain broad concepts more specifically

Frequently, direct instruction and indirect instruction work in tandem. When learning an entirely *new* concept, students will often need direct instruction first. Students might, for example, watch a teacher demonstrate solving multiplication problems in a variety of ways using multiplication tiles. Then, students might be given multiplication tiles or other manipulatives to work with on their own after the teacher has demonstrated. In this way, indirect instruction serves as an extension and application of new knowledge that has been presented explicitly.

> **QUICK REVIEW**
>
> What are the major differences between direct instruction and indirect instruction?

There is some debate over direct and indirect instruction, particularly as it pertains to math and reading. Advocates of phonics instruction, which is generally presented through direct instruction, point to its efficacy in teaching most children to read. Others argue that pushing children to read is harmful and that they should be allowed to come to reading on their own through multiple exposures in a literacy-rich environment. New math instructional methods, especially

> **DID YOU KNOW?**
>
> Some reading programs try to bridge the gap between direct and indirect instruction. The Four Blocks Program, for example, uses what is known as balanced literacy—both whole language and phonics instruction. The program is based on the idea that not all children will learn to read in the same way. In this multimethod approach, students participate in teacher-directed guided reading, student self-selected independent reading, writing, and working with words.

inquiry-based math, focus far more on the problem-solving process than on procedural fluency and emphasize indirect instructional methods.

Most successful teachers employ both direct and indirect instruction regularly and frequently reteach concepts through direct instruction when students do not master them. It is also worthwhile to note that even when using indirect methods, teachers will still serve as facilitators and guides and offer scaffolding as needed.

SAMPLE QUESTIONS

3) A sixth-grade science teacher plans an activity in which she will break students into groups and give them supplies with the goal of building a catapult that will launch a lima bean at least 10 feet. What type of instructional method is the teacher using?

    A.   direct instruction

    B.   peer tutoring

    C.   demonstration

    D.   indirect instruction

4) A fifth-grade math teacher wants his students to work on generalizing their math knowledge. He wants to use an indirect instructional strategy. Which strategy would best meet his objectives?

    A.   Students are asked to turn to their neighbor and tell him or her at least three things they learned in class that day.

    B.   Students are given a sheet with several scenarios and asked to list which mathematical operation would be best to use.

    C.   Students are given several toilet paper and paper towel tubes of varying length and split into groups to measure and graph the lengths of the tubes.

    D.   Students are given two numbers and asked to make a list of how the numbers are both similar and different from each other.

INDEPENDENT LEARNING

Not all learning is teacher directed. Students must also learn some things independently, without the direct aid of the teacher. In **independent learning**, the activity itself serves as the teacher. Independent learning is a crucial skill for students to master as now many parts of higher education (particularly those that are in an online format) require students to learn on their own.

In a **project-based learning** assignment or classroom, students work on a project (often containing elements from all core subjects) over an extended period of time. Students have a choice both of what types of projects they

QUICK REVIEW

Is project-based learning also indirect instruction? Experiential learning? Interactive learning? Why or why not?

will take on and how they will create the finished product. The projects are often designed in response to a societal problem. The project is typically shared beyond the classroom for maximum impact. For example, high school students might be challenged to design a house that uses only alternative energy and costs less than $1,000 annually to operate. Students might then conduct extensive research on alternative energy sources for homes and then draw a plan or build a model of the house. Students might then present their models at an alternative energy night held at the school or at a local alternative energy fair or meeting. Project-based learning can be highly effective because it encourages reflection and self-direction and provides a great way to integrate the curriculum.

Self-paced learning is learning that moves forward at the pace set by the student him- or herself. This can take many forms. Students may be given initial objectives and then textbooks, worksheets, or other learning materials and told to proceed through them at their own pace and work toward mastery of the given objectives. Self-paced learning can also be in a digital format where students complete online lessons at their own pace. Some programs are even calibrated to advance students to new material only when the requisite material has been mastered. Self-paced learning can be quite effective for students who are self-directed learners as they may be able to proceed through the curriculum more quickly than they might otherwise if they had to wait for the pacing of the class as a whole. This disadvantage is, of course, that not all students will retain motivation to persevere in their studies, particularly when certain concepts are challenging. Other students may also need more support and explanation than the curriculum itself is able to provide.

In some cases, self-directed learning is the backbone of an entire school or program. Many schools that use an emergent curriculum, Montessori, or project-based learning philosophy emphasize self-direction in almost every aspect of the school day. In an **emergent curriculum**, the interests of the student guide the daily activities. Often, teachers serve more as facilitators who provide learning experiences that students can undertake independently or collaboratively with other students to enable them to further explore these interests. This might involve, for example, a sixth-grade student expressing an interest in airplanes. The teacher might then help the student devise a research plan to find out more about the history of the airplane and give a presentation to the class, thus learning language and social studies skills. Perhaps the student might be encouraged to research aerodynamics and the physics behind flight and then construct a model plane to learn science concepts. The key is that the student is helping to set the course of the curriculum itself.

> **HELPFUL HINT**
>
> Most classrooms do have some time devoted to independent learning. It is important to provide time for independent work, particularly when students are receiving instructional interventions. Students will gain confidence as they experience accomplishing many tasks on their own.

In a **Montessori** classroom environment, students are often placed in an environment full of different activities and learning materials. Students are then able to make choices about what materials they wish to use and how they wish to meet learning objectives. Montessori classrooms tend to heavily emphasize self-directed learning through student choice. The underlying idea is that the innate curiosity and desire to learn new things will drive the ambition of students.

Seminal to independent learning is student motivation and goal-setting. Goal-setting can be formal or informal, but research shows that it is a crucial part of getting students to become self-directed learners. Students who are **self-directed learners** are able to understand their own learning needs, set learning goals, and then formulate and implement a plan for how to meet those goals. Of course, many students will need teacher assistance in this process. One way to provide students with a framework to achieve learning goals is a **learning contract**. A learning contract typically has four parts:

1. the goals or objectives
2. the strategies and resources the student will use to meet the goals
3. the way the goals will be assessed
4. the time frame for completion

As students undertake the fulfillment of their learning contract, they should be self-reflective as to whether they are on track to meet objectives within the time frame and what strategies and resources they are finding the most effective to meet these goals.

Beyond formal learning contracts, teachers can still assist students to set goals prior to almost any learning task or assignment. For example, a student with a specific learning disability who is receiving assignment modifications on a writing assignment might be asked to set incremental goals. Perhaps in week 1, the student is only asked to write three sentences, but then in week 4, the student sets a goal to

> **STUDY TIPS**
>
> Use the mnemonic "Good students always try" (GSAT) to remember the four parts of a learning contract: goals, strategies, assessment, time.

write four sentences; in week 6 the goal is stretched to six sentences and so on. This is a great way for all students to be encouraged to become more self-directed learners. Research also suggests that many students with IEPs can and should be active participants in developing and self-monitoring progress toward these goals. In this way, students understand how they learn and what learning strategies they should use to meet each goal. This self-reflective goal-setting and progress-monitoring can also empower students to seek out the accommodations or modifications they need to meet these goals.

SAMPLE QUESTIONS

5) Mr. Howe is helping Robbie, his fifth-grade math student, develop a learning contract. So far, the contract states that Robbie will use educational software, worksheets, and oral drills to increase his fluency with multiplication facts up to 12 × 12. What part or parts of the learning contract are missing?

   A. objectives and resources to meet goals

   B. resources to meet goals and assessment

   C. assessment and time frame

   D. time frame and goals

6) One of Lana's goals is to take the SAT and achieve a sufficient score so that she does not need to take developmental (remedial) courses in college. She asks her twelfth-grade English teacher to recommend or assign some additional grammar exercises since Lana knows that grammar is her weakness and that it is tested on the SAT. What would be a reasonable statement to make about Lana?

   A. She is a self-directed learner.

   B. She has a learning contract already established.

   C. She attends a school that employs an emergent curriculum.

   D. She could benefit from more direct instruction from her teacher.

EXPERIENTIAL LEARNING

Though perhaps first proposed by Aristotle around BCE 350 in his work *Nichomachean Ethics*, the modern incantation of experiential learning was spearheaded by David Kolb in the 1970s. In this framework, learners learn by doing and then reflect on the doing. The experiential learning model has four components: concrete experience, reflective observation, abstract conceptualization, and active experimentation.

During the **concrete experience** stage, students have an actual experience. Perhaps a second-grade class in an urban area takes a field trip to a farm where they are given the opportunity to milk a cow. Next, during **reflective observation**, students think back on the experience. The teacher might ask guiding questions such as "Was milking the cow easy or hard?" "What did it feel like?" "How did the cow react?" "How much milk came out?"

During the **abstract conceptualization** stage, students begin to understand what they have experienced in terms of broader concepts. They might, for example, think about dairy cows in the context of how they help humans as a science construct or they might think about the role of farms in the production of foods like milk as a social studies construct. They would then engage in **active experimentation** where they are able to actually put what they have learned into a real-world context. Students might, for example, be asked to track how much milk their family consumes each week or month and think about how important this single product is to their household.

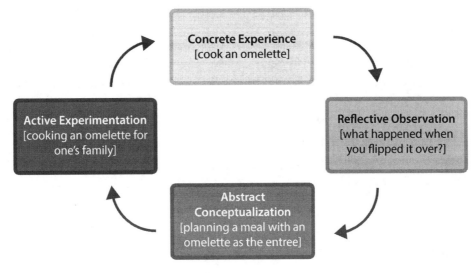

Figure 4.2. Experiential Learning

Experiential learning is often used synonymously with hands-on learning or learning by doing. However, for learning to be truly experiential, students must reflect upon their experiences. This means that any type of hands-on activity must be followed up with a teacher-guided reflection period. For example, a kindergarten class that went to the zoo on a field trip could be asked to reflect on new animals they saw that they had not seen before and perhaps draw a picture of one. A high school home and consumer economics class could be asked to write down two challenges that they encountered while completing a baking assignment and how they overcame them. An elementary school class doing role plays to develop conflict-resolution skills could be asked how they felt during the role-play scenarios and how they might have acted differently.

Often the end goal of experiential learning is to help students make connections between their education and the real world. Vocational education programs housed within schools and internship programs are excellent examples of experiential learning. However, educators must be sure that students are reflecting upon their learning in the field. Life skills education programs are also prime examples of experiential learning. These programs often offer opportunities for students to immediately apply what they have learned in a real-world context.

SAMPLE QUESTIONS

7) A special education teacher with a self-contained life skills class gives her students a lesson on using the microwave. One of her students does not cover the dish and the microwave becomes very dirty. She asks the student the following question: "Why did that happen?" What phase of the experiential learning process is she engaging the student in?

A.   concrete experience

B.   reflective observation

C.   abstract conceptualization

D.   active experimentation

8)   **A physical education teacher takes his fourth-grade class to a bowling alley. Which question would best help students abstractly conceptualize what they have learned?**

A.   How many spares or strikes did you get?

B.   Was bowling easy or difficult for you?

C.   Was bowling more difficult than other sports we have played?

D.   When do you think you might be able to use the skills you learned today?

INTERACTIVE LEARNING

Interactive learning merely describes a learning framework in which students are active versus passive participants in the learning process. Interactive learning often involves the learner interacting with others, either in person or through a technology platform.

One time-tested interactive learning strategy is **think-pair-share**. During this activity, students first think on their own about a question or topic posed by the teacher. They then share their ideas with a partner, often a student in the seat next to them. Then, ideas are shared with the class at large. This is an excellent way to start a classroom **discussion**, which some students might feel shy about participating in without first sharing their ideas in a seemingly safer space. Discussions, of course, can give rise to disparity of opinion, and this is another opportunity for interactive learning. Outside of formal debates, teachers can use online polling/survey applications to have students instantaneously (and anonymously) weigh in on an issue. Students can also be asked to move to one side of the room if they agree with a statement or the other side of the room if they disagree.

There are any number of interactive learning activities that can take place in pairs or small groups. Students can turn to their neighbors to brainstorm the best way to solve a math problem. Students can interview each other at the beginning of the year to learn more about classmates and develop communication skills.

One newer strategy that has taken hold in many schools is the **interactive notebook**. While this strategy does not involve interaction with people, it does allow for

DID YOU KNOW?

Participation in sports can be a great interactive way for children with learning and attention exceptionalities to develop socially. However, they may need support from adults in learning the rules and following directions, accepting feedback, and showing empathy for other players.

students to interact with learning material in a new way. While there are many different ways to set up interactive notebooks, most employ an input-output organization. On the right-hand side of the notebook are teacher-directed materials and lessons—the input. This might be vocabulary and definitions, example problems, notes, graphic organizers, steps in a process, mini-lessons, and so on. On the left-hand side of the notebook are student output/reflection notes. These are created in response to the material on the right-hand side and might include drawings, mnemonics, questions, opinions, summaries, and other reflections showing connections being made with the input.

Of course, technology makes interaction possible even if people are not in the same place. Many programs and applications allow for interaction and collaboration among students even if they are not in the same physical location. From chatting with or writing to students in other countries to peer-reviewing essays, there are numerous applications that allow students to work together.

SAMPLE QUESTIONS

9) **A high school algebra teacher begins using interactive notebooks with her students. What types of notes might be found on the left-hand output side of the notebook?**

   A. definitions and steps in the problem-solving process

   B. lecture notes

   C. questions students have about a given problem

   D. graphic organizers

10) **An eighth-grade social studies teacher wants to understand how his students feel about a controversial topic. Which format would be the best way to get this information?**

   A. asking for a show of hands

   B. having students who agree/disagree move to one side of the room

   C. calling on more verbal students first and less verbal students second

   D. taking an anonymous online poll

UNIVERSAL DESIGN FOR LEARNING

Under the Individuals with Disabilities Education Act (IDEA), all students must be given access to the general curriculum. Of course, not all students will be able to access the curriculum in the same way or be assessed in the same way. This is where the Universal Design for Learning (UDL) comes in. It allows *all* students in a given classroom, from academically gifted students to students with profound impairments, to be able to learn from the same lesson plan. It also enables classrooms and students to meet guidelines set forth under IDEA.

The **Universal Design for Learning** defines three principles: multiple means of representation, multiple means of expression, and multiple means of engagement. **Multiple means of representation** refers to the "what" of learning, or the actual lesson content and how it is presented. Multiple means of representation refers to the way that the same content can be presented to different learners with different needs in different ways. For example, worksheets or textbooks in braille would be one representation for visually impaired students to access written components in lessons.

Multiple means of expression refers to the "how" of learning and the multiple ways in which students express what they know. For example, a student with the diagnosed specific learning disability of dyslexia may record her answer to an essay question on an audio device instead of writing it.

QUICK REVIEW

What means of representation could be used for students who are hard of hearing?

Multiple means of engagement refers to the "why" of learning and multiple ways to motivate students and pique their interest in the topic at hand. For example, a kindergarten student fond of cars who is nervous about playing with his peers may be motivated to try more social interaction if the teacher sets up a play scenario involving another student and toy cars.

One way to use UDL in the classroom is to use **pyramid planning**. This refers to creating hierarchical goals that ensure that all students meet certain learning objectives. For example, in a fourth-grade math lesson on multiplication, the teacher may aim for some students to know and use multiple strategies for solving two-digit by two-digit multiplication. She may aim for most students to know and use two strategies for solving two-digit by two-digit multiplication. She may aim for all students to know and be able to use the standard algorithm for solving two-digit by two-digit multiplication problems.

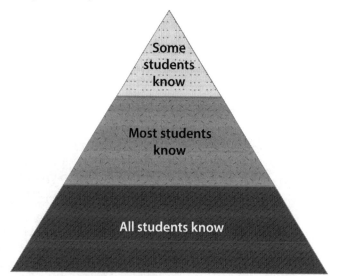

Figure 4.3. Pyramid Planning

This pyramid then serves as a framework for the teacher to devise how these objectives will be represented to students, how students will be engaged, and how students will express their learning. For example, the teacher might use a whole-class demonstration approach for some students as she works the problems on the board. She might use a tactile approach with manipulatives for other students as they use multiplication tiles. Still other students may use a tablet, touchpad, or smartboard.

Students will also require multiple means of engagement. Some students might be self-directed learners with high levels of intrinsic motivation. Others might need more ongoing feedback, encouragement, and scaffolding. When it is time to assess student learning, the teacher will also need to implement different strategies. Most students might take a standard written assessment. However, others may give directions to a scribe who will write answers for them.

The key to UDL is that teachers are ensuring that *all* students, even those with the most profound disabilities, are able to participate in classroom activities and assessments. This is required by law. Under IDEA 2004, state education agencies must use UDL principles when administering state- and district-wide assessment (multiple means of expression). IDEA also requires districts and schools to provide assistive technology for students with certain disabilities and to obtain digital versions of textbooks (multiple means of representation). Of course, UDL is also integral in ensuring students are educated in the least restrictive environment, the central principle behind IDEA.

SAMPLE QUESTION

11) **Ms. Peterson is a Spanish teacher in an inclusive seventh-grade classroom. One of her students has a receptive language disorder. What means of representation might be most effective for this student to learn conjugation of verbs in the present tense?**

    A.   repeated listening to an audio recording

    B.   choral repetition after the teacher

    C.   watching a video of native speakers

    D.   reading and writing the verb tenses

CO-TEACHING STRATEGIES

Under IDEA, students should be educated in the least restrictive environment possible, and in most cases, this is the general education classroom. **Inclusion** describes the opportunity of individuals with disabilities to learn with peers without disabilities in the general education classroom. This stands in contrast to the "**pull-out**" model where students receive individualized or small-group instruction outside of the general education classroom. However, even in the inclusive classroom, in order to provide appropriate accommodations, modifications, and specific interventions, general education teachers often rely on the help of special education teachers within the general education classroom. This practice, where special education teachers work collaboratively with general education teachers to ensure the needs of all students are met, is known as **co-teaching**. Co-teaching looks different in every classroom, and it varies based on the needs of the individual students, the number of students needing support, and the particular learning task. However, there are some general approaches to co-teaching that have become somewhat standard.

In some classrooms and for some lessons, **one teacher teaches while the other teacher observes**. This can be very helpful if clear observational criteria are set up beforehand. Perhaps the observer is tasked with determining how long certain students stay on task or maintain focus and participation. The observer might also take notes on how students approach certain problems or how long it takes them to get started on a math problem after being instructed to do so. The observer can also use **time sampling** to record tick or tally marks each time a certain student or students display certain behaviors during the instructional time. An observer can be crucial to conduct a thorough FBA to determine the antecedents or roots of a student's behavior as a first step toward planning an intervention.

Another popular model is the **one teaches and one assists or supports model**. This is a very popular model when the second educator is a paraprofessional and not a special education teacher. However, it is also used in many scenarios where a special education teacher is present and several students need specific modifications or accommodations during the lesson. As in the one teaches/one observes model, one teacher is generally at the front of the room, and the other teacher circulates to offer assistance where needed. While some of the supports might be behavioral and might follow the hierarchy of prompts, it is important when using this model that the roving teacher not be used exclusively to aid in classroom management. The primary role of the roaming educator should be instructional in nature. This model is sometimes also referred to as **push-in** services where students with special needs receive interventions and support within the context of the general education classroom.

Parallel teaching involves the class being broken into two groups and each teacher teaching the same content to his or her group. Parallel teaching is advantageous when listening to and hearing student responses is crucial (such as during oral reading or phonics instruction) and when each student needs to be given ample time to participate. Smaller groups also make some classroom activities easier from a logistical perspective, and they often ensure that each student is given more attention. Parallel teaching is typically undertaken either in a circle on the floor or in two clusters of tables or student desks. One disadvantage is that sometimes, particularly when completing oral activities, the noise from one group may be distracting to the other group, particularly if one group finishes before the other.

Station teaching is somewhat similar to parallel teaching in that the students are divided into at least two groups. However, each teacher is presenting different content, and then the students or teacher rotate to the other group. This strategy can be particularly useful when two teachers have strengths in different areas or when learning needs to be individualized more than is possible in the larger classroom. Some station teaching models break the class into even smaller groups of three or four. While two of the groups work with the two teachers, the other group or groups work on self-directed activities. In station teaching and parallel teaching, student groups are generally heterogeneous. This allows teachers to still provide accommodations and modifications as needed but ensure the principles of UDL are being adhered to.

Alternative teaching, on the other hand, involves homogeneous grouping. In alternative teaching, one teacher typically teaches a lesson to a larger group and the other works with a smaller group. This could be a way to ensure multiple means of representation or a way to provide reteaching of core concepts or specific interventions.

Team teaching is a little more challenging because it involves both teachers working together to teach the class simultaneously. In this model, both teachers are generally together at the front of the class. This approach can work well when two people are needed to demonstrate something or when principles of collaboration need to be emphasized. However, this model reduces the individual attention that each teacher can give, so it is typically not used as frequently as some of the other models.

Independent of what model is chosen for any particular lesson or classroom, the general education and special education teacher must work collaboratively to ensure that students with special needs are meeting IEP goals alongside their peers. Key to this collaboration is frequent communication and collaboration. Research suggests that many general education teachers feel overwhelmed and ill-prepared to meet their obligations to serve special needs students in their classrooms. They may lack the knowledge or experience to make their classrooms truly inclusive without significant guidance from special education professionals. Of course, special education teachers are balancing multiple priorities as well, so time for collaboration and communication is often scarce. Nevertheless, it is vitally important that general education teachers and special education teachers find time to communicate frequently about student progress. It is also seminal that these two teachers present a united front so that students see that their entire education team is working together to ensure their success.

SAMPLE QUESTIONS

12) Mr. Robles, a special education teacher, spends about half of his day providing interventions to students one-on-one in the learning resource room. The other half is spent providing learning supports to students within the general education classroom. How is his day spent?

   A.   Mr. Robles spends about half of the day in alternative teaching and half in co-teaching.

   B.   Mr. Robles spends about half of the day in pull-out instruction and half in push-in instruction.

   C.   His entire day is spent in the context of the inclusion of students in the general education classroom.

   D.   He spends half his day parallel teaching and half of his day using time sampling.

13) What is one disadvantage to the team teaching model?

   A.   Teachers are typically unable to work together to present cohesive lessons.

   B.   Students receive less individualized attention.

   C.   It can be challenging for students to follow.

   D.   It may detract from the learning of students without exceptionalities.

14) A special education co-teacher in a middle school classroom must gather data regarding a student's progress toward the IEP goal that states in part that she will remain engaged in class activities for at least a ten-minute period. Which is the best co-teaching strategy for the teacher to use to gather this data?

   A.   parallel teaching

   B.   one teach/one support

   C.   one teach/one observe

   D.   station teaching

ANSWER KEY

1) D. **Correct.** Student experimentation is not direct instruction because the teacher is not providing explicit instruction.

2) A. Incorrect. The students will get a break from the lecture, but they do not have any opportunities for learning other than direct instruction.

  B. Incorrect. Recapping the lecture might help students with retention and give them a break, but it does not necessarily follow mastery of a new concept.

  C. Incorrect. This assignment is not direct instruction.

  D. **Correct.** This assignment allows students to first master a skill through direct instruction, and then undertake a more self-directed activity to apply the newly acquired skill.

3) A. Incorrect. Direct instruction involves the teacher explicitly directing the students in their learning.

  B. Incorrect. Peer tutoring involves one student helping another student to master objectives.

  C. Incorrect. The teacher is asking students to make the catapult; she is not demonstrating how to make it.

  D. **Correct.** The teacher is having the students learn about constructing a catapult through hands-on learning without her direct involvement, so this is indirect instruction.

4) B. **Correct.** This is both an indirect teaching method and a way for students to generalize their math knowledge and apply it to real-life scenarios. The other activities would not help students generalize their math knowledge.

5) A. Incorrect. Robbie has an objective (increasing fluency up to 12 × 12) and resources to meet these objectives (software, worksheets, oral drills).

  B. Incorrect. Robbie does not have assessment, but he does have resources to meet goals.

  C. **Correct.** Robbie does not have a way to demonstrate this fluency or allow this fluency to be assessed by Mr. Howe. He also does not have a set time frame in which to complete this task.

  D. Incorrect. Robbie does not have a time frame, but he does have a clear learning goal.

6) A. **Correct.** Lana understands her learning needs, has set learning goals, and is implementing a plan in asking her teacher for resources to help her meet these goals.

7) A. Incorrect. The concrete experience stage was when the student was actually practicing using the microwave.

   B. **Correct.** The teacher is asking the student to reflect back on the experience and what caused the mess in the microwave.

   C. Incorrect. In abstract conceptualization, the student would think more broadly about the lesson. For example, he might consider what foods could be cooked in the microwave and what foods could not.

   D. Incorrect. Active experimentation would involve the student using the microwave in a real-life context.

8) A. Incorrect. This is reflective observation.

   B. Incorrect. This is reflective observation.

   C. **Correct.** This question helps students connect their experience to the broader abstraction of sports in general and how bowling fits into this framework.

   D. Incorrect. This question would guide active experimentation.

9) C. **Correct.** The output side of the notebook is for students to interact with the material, including asking questions. The other items would be on the right-hand input part of the notebook.

10) D. **Correct.** In an anonymous poll, all students can be open and honest about how they feel without fear of what others will think. The other formats could make students uncomfortable, given the nature of the topic.

11) D. **Correct.** Processing auditory information will not be a good representational strategy for a student with a receptive language disorder. Reading and writing would be better for a student with a receptive language disorder.

12) A. Incorrect. This describes a full day in the general education classroom.

    B. **Correct.** Pull-out interventions occur outside of the general education classroom and push-in interventions occur within it.

    C. Incorrect. During the pull-out time, students are not in the general education classroom.

    D. Incorrect. Parallel teaching occurs in the general education classroom. Time sampling refers to recording the frequency of student behaviors.

13) A. Incorrect. This might be true in rare cases, but the relationship between co-teachers should be one of collaboration.

    B. **Correct.** This is a disadvantage of this model and one of the reasons it is not used very frequently.

    C. Incorrect. This is not necessarily true, particularly if done skillfully.

D.   Incorrect. There is no reason to believe that team teaching is problematic for students without exceptionalities.

14)   A.   Incorrect. Parallel teaching involves the class being broken into two groups and would not be the best strategy for gathering this data.

B.   Incorrect. In this strategy, the supporting teacher should be providing academic supports, not strictly observing.

C.   **Correct.** This strategy will give the teacher ample time to observe the student's engagement in the activity for the set time period and record observations.

D.   Incorrect. In station teaching, the teacher would only see the student in question when she is at her station.

5

Assessment

MEASUREMENT CONCEPTS

Assessment refers to the process of gathering information from multiple sources to understand what students know, how they are progressing, and if any problems have arisen in students' development. Assessment of student learning is ongoing and should occur every school day.

Assessments may be conducted in multiple domains, including cognitive development, socio-emotional development, and physical development. Assessments can also be used for a variety of purposes:

- ▶ identifying developmental delays
- ▶ evaluating student mastery of learning objectives
- ▶ designing appropriate interventions
- ▶ gauging efficacy of program delivery
- ▶ determining placement of students within programs

Data gleaned from the use of assessments can then be used to make decisions. These decisions might be related to an individual student, a classroom, or even an entire school or district. Much educational research relies on assessment to yield data that can be applied broadly in other educational situations.

Assessments are ranked based on two factors: reliability and validity. **Reliability** refers to the rate at which the assessment produces the same outcome every time. One way to think about reliability is in terms of consistency across many different test takers and testing scenarios. A test can be said to have low reliability if it does not produce accurate results each time it is given.

> **STUDY TIP**
>
> Think of the concept of test reliability the same as you would a person who is reliable. A reliable person behaves as expected every time. A reliable assessment instrument does, too.

Ideally, each assessment would give the exact same results even when administered multiple times to the same student under the same conditions. Unfortunately, this is not the case. Even assessments that are thought to be reliable have measurement error. **Measurement error** refers to all the variations that impact an examinee's performance. These variations might include testing conditions (quietness of the room, behavior of the test administrator, and so on) or the emotional state of the test taker. Assessments of very young children often have significant measurement error compared to assessments of older children.

Validity is quite different from reliability and refers to whether the findings that the assessment instrument seeks to measure are accurate and backed by research and evidence. If the assessment does not measure what it is supposed to measure (achievement, personality, intelligence, or something else), then it lacks validity even if it is reliable and produces consistent results each time.

STUDY TIP

Use the roots of the words to remember quantitative and qualitative data. Quantitative data is a *quantity*. Qualitative data is the *quality* of something.

Assessment data is generally **quantitative**, or numerical, and **qualitative**, or nonnumerical. Quantitative data is often gleaned from standardized assessments such as a numerical IQ or performance in the fifteenth percentile. Qualitative data is usually obtained through interviews with parents and teachers and observational records. Both types of data should be considered in initial evaluation for special education services and in ongoing assessment of IEP outcomes.

SAMPLE QUESTION

1) Hallie is a third-grade student with dyslexia who is taking her annual state standards-based assessment with certain accommodations. She scores much lower than her teacher and parents expected, and Hallie later reveals that the room in which she was tested was very loud, and she was not able to hear all of the examiner's prompts and instructions. What can be said about this assessment?

   A.   The assessment likely had measurement error.

   B.   The assessment given was an alternate assessment.

   C.   It was most likely an assessment that lacked validity.

   D.   It could be used for initial screening for developmental delays.

STANDARDIZED ASSESSMENTS

There are numerous standardized, published assessment instruments. These instruments have standardized questions or criteria and are administered in a consistent manner. They may be administered by parents, teachers, caregivers, physicians, interventionists, or any combination of individuals familiar with the student in question. Standardized assessments are frequently administered with students in a question-and-answer form or sometimes through an observational checklist.

While opinions about the general appropriateness and efficacy of standardized testing for students with disabilities certainly vary, most professionals agree that standardized assessments only give one part of the overall picture of any given student's learning situation and level of mastery of individual objectives. Even during initial screening and assessment for exceptionalities, published assessment instruments are used alongside other methods of collecting data such as observations and parent input. Most educators agree that standardized assessment is only one way to gather data to help inform individualized planning and instruction.

NORM-REFERENCED ASSESSMENTS

Standardized assessments typically fall into two categories: norm-referenced assessment and criterion-referenced assessment. **Norm-referenced assessments** measure an individual student against a group of other test takers, typically those of the same age or grade level. Results are generally reported in a percentile ranking.

Norm-referenced tests are most often used to measure achievement, intelligence, aptitude, and personality. **Achievement tests** measure what skills a student has mastered. These often fall under categories like reading and mathematics. Achievement tests are generally multiple choice in format and require test takers to answer a standardized set of questions. Popular achievement tests include the Iowa Test of Basic Skills (ITBS), the Peabody Individual Achievement Test, the Wechsler Individual Achievement Test (WIAT-III), and the Stanford Achievement Test.

Another type of norm-referenced assessment is the **aptitude test**. Like achievement tests, aptitude tests often measure learned abilities such as mathematics and verbal reasoning. However, they also help predict the course of future learning. The SAT and ACT are two very common aptitude tests used to predict the probability of a student's success in a college environment.

Intelligence tests are another norm-referenced assessment. They are used to measure overall intellectual functioning, problem-solving skills, and aptitude for learning. The most commonly used intelligence tests are the Stanford-Binet Intelligence Scales (SB5), the Wechsler Intelligence Scale for Children (WISC-V), Woodcock Johnson III Tests of Cognitive Abilities, the Differential Ability Scales (DAS-II), and the Universal Nonverbal Intelligence Test for students with certain communication disorders. Intelligence tests can help when determining gift-

> **DID YOU KNOW?**
>
> The first exams offered by the College Board (which now produces the SAT) were administered in 1901. The sections were English, French, German, Latin, Greek, history, mathematics, chemistry, and physics. Instead of the multiple-choice format of most of today's standardized tests, they were given in essay format. Student responses were graded as very poor, poor, doubtful, good, and excellent.

edness in children and when determining the presence of an intellectual disability. Intelligence tests are also often used in tandem with achievement tests to note patterns or discrepancies in IQ and academic achievement. These discrepancies may be the result of a specific learning disability or another condition that might require special services.

Personality tests are also norm-referenced tests. These tests measure a tendency of a student to behave in a certain way. Often these tests are administered to parents and children together.

Because norm-referenced tests compare students to one another, the results have to be expressed in a format that makes this comparison possible. The most commonly used way to express this comparison is the percentile. A **percentile** is a score that shows where a student ranks in comparison to ninety-nine other students. For example, a percentile of 81 would mean that the student in question has performed equal to or outperformed eighty-one out of the other ninety-nine students who took the same test. A percentile of 14 means that the student in question only performed equal to or outperformed fourteen of the other ninety-nine test takers.

Typically, these percentiles are determined early in the development of a standardized norm-referenced assessment using an early group of test takers known as a **norming group**. Dependent upon the assessment instrument, these norming groups may be students in a particular school (school average norms) or district (a local norm group) and students with a particular diagnosed exceptionality or special learning situation (special norm group). More often, they are national norm groups. These groups are carefully selected so as to be representative of the nation as a whole. One criticism of the use of norm-referenced tests is that national norm groups are not always current and truly representative, and students might be taking a test that has not been recalibrated with a new norming group in some time.

The makers of norm-referenced tests typically base their percentiles on the idea of the **bell-shaped curve**, also sometimes called the normal curve or the normal distribution. Often tests are modified such that the results will generate a bell-shaped curve. This distribution of scores has three primary characteristics:

1. It is symmetrical from left to right.
2. The mean, median, and mode are the same score and are at the center of the symmetrical distribution.
3. The percentage within each standard deviation is known.

Not all standardized assessment instruments use percentile. There are also **grade-equivalent scores**, which provide a result in a grade level. This means that the student's performance was equal to the median performance corresponding to other students of a certain grade level. For example, if a student scores at a tenth-grade reading level, that would mean his or her score was the same as the median for all tenth graders who took the test. Some assessment instruments also use an age-equivalent score, which simply compares a student's results to the median score of other students of a certain age.

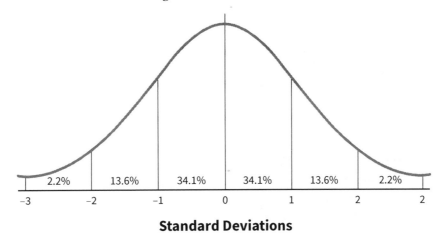

Standard Deviations

Figure 5.1. Bell-Shaped Curve (normal distribution)

SAMPLE QUESTIONS

2) Harvey scores in the 89th percentile on the Stanford Achievement Test, an annual norm-referenced test that his private elementary school gives. How can his results be interpreted?

    A. He got 89 percent of the questions correct.

    B. Eighty-nine percent of students did the same as or better than Harvey.

    C. Harvey did the same as or better than 89 percent of students.

    D. Harvey did well enough to be part of the norming group.

3) Which of the following is NOT a common criticism of norm-referenced tests?

    A. The norming group may not be of the same age and grade as the test taker.

    B. The norming group may not be a representative sample of all students.

    C. They have measurement error.

    D. They are only one part of a student's overall body of knowledge.

CRITERION–REFERENCED TESTS

In contrast to norm-referenced tests are **criterion-referenced tests**. These tests measure an individual's performance as it is related to a predetermined benchmark or criteria. These tests are generally used to measure a student's progress toward meeting certain objectives. They do not compare test takers to one another but rather compare student knowledge against the set criteria. Criterion-referenced tests include everything from annual state tests to tests created by teachers or educational publishers to assess mastery of learning objectives. One new incarnation of the criterion-referenced test that has been employed by many states is standards-referenced testing or **standards-based assessment**. These tests measure a student's performance against certain content standards as defined by each grade level and subject. They are typically scored in categories such as basic, proficient, and advanced or unsatisfactory, satisfactory, and advanced. Most annual state accountability tests such as STAAR, PARCC, and many others are standards-based, criterion-referenced tests.

> **DID YOU KNOW?**
>
> Many standards-based assessment creators rely on a framework developed by Norman Webb to ensure assessments are aligned to content standards. The criteria follow:
>
> ▸ categorical concurrence
> ▸ depth-of-knowledge consistency
> ▸ range-of-knowledge consistency
> ▸ balance of representation

SAMPLE QUESTION

4) In Texas, students take the STAAR test each year. This test is aligned to grade-level standards and state standards. Students are scored as either unsatisfactory, satisfactory, or advanced. What type of test is the STAAR test?

A. achievement test

B. standards-based assessment

C. intelligence test

D. norm-referenced test

SCREENING STUDENTS

Standardized assessment instruments are important for screening students for developmental delays and providing early interventions. Numerous such **screening instruments** such as **Bayley Scales of Infant Development (BSID-III)** and **Vineland Adaptive Behavior Scales (VABS or Vineland-3)** can help trained professionals diagnose overall functioning at a very young age. However, any standardized assessment of very young children is inherently problematic due to numerous factors, including a young child's frequent lack of cooperation with the assessment itself. Many assessment instruments that deal with socio-emotional development, such as the **Achenbach System of Empirically Based Assessment (ASEBA)**, also rely on observations and data collection from both parents and teachers. This can cause some problems in the integrity of the instrument as parents can differ from the teacher in their perceptions of a student's behavior, and teachers may even disagree among themselves.

The use of some assessment instruments is limited to physicians or psychologists, and multiple providers will be involved in a child's initial assessment upon parent request for special education services assessment. Many types of disabilities are diagnosed in part through standardized assessments. However, often several other assessment tools beyond standardized tests are given to ensure that physical disabilities or emotional disturbances are not also present or the cause of any discrepant results. Because many intellectual disabilities are the result of genetic conditions, they are most often diagnosed by physicians in early childhood. Physical disabilities such as hearing and vision problems may first appear in the general education classroom but can only be diagnosed by trained professionals.

Standardized assessment instruments will, of course, be an important part of the process of evaluation for special education services. A team of professionals, including special education teachers, will often administer these instruments based on the particular concerns of parents and general education teachers. Of course, these instruments work in conjunction with observation of students, which cannot be overemphasized as a critical component in the overall evaluation process. In fact, the Individuals with Disabilities Education Act (IDEA) specifies that no single test or criterion can be used to determine the best educational program for a student. A comprehensive assessment often includes many of the following: behavioral assessment, speech and language assessment, physical evaluation by a physician, parent interview, psychological assessment, developmental history, classroom observation, grade and test records, standardized testing, and so on. The overall assessment of students through these multiple means will guide the student's journey and will help educators make important decisions, which include:

- ▶ evaluation decisions: student progress and overall strengths/weaknesses
- ▶ diagnostic decisions: the nature of the disability
- ▶ eligibility decisions: whether the student is eligible for special education services
- ▶ IEP decisions: helping to develop the goals
- ▶ placement decisions: what classes and environments in which the student will learn best
- ▶ instructional planning decisions: what instruction will be appropriate to meet the student's needs

SAMPLE QUESTION

5) **All of the following are reasons to give multiple assessments using different instruments and assessment techniques during a student's initial evaluation for special education services EXCEPT:**

A. determining the presence of physical disabilities and emotional disturbances in addition to specific learning disabilities

B. getting perspectives from many professionals with a broad range of expertise

C. the lack of validity in using any standardized assessment instrument

D. gathering multiple perspectives on a student's past academic performance and behaviors

ACCOMMODATIONS AND ALTERNATE ASSESSMENTS

Because federal law mandates that states test all students in grades three through eight using standardized measures, this includes most students except those with very profound disabilities. The Every Student Succeeds Act (ESSA) requires that states test 99 percent of students with standard assessments. While states can appeal for a waiver to expand this pool of non-test-takers who will then take alternate assessments, these waivers are very hard to get. This means most students receiving services with an IEP or 504 plan are usually required to take the same state test that all other students take. They are given often given appropriate **accommodations** such as having extra time on the test, having the test read to them, answering orally, taking computer-based versions, and so on.

There is debate over this practice of including almost all students in statewide standardized testing. Legislation calling for this requirement points to the principles of the Universal Design for Learning (UDL), where all students should be able to learn from the same curriculum and that students with exceptionalities should be held to high standards. Some stakeholders, however, feel that standardized testing is inappropriate for some students. In some cases, accommodations, particularly those that provide students with extra time to complete the test, have been found to result in some students spending days nervously soldiering through high-stakes tests, resulting in extreme stress and needless fatigue. In other cases, when standardized tests are administered using computer-adaptive technology that adjusts the difficulty level of the questions per student response, some students with disabilities become overwhelmed at the increasing difficulty level of questions and may stop trying after realizing that they are only receiving easy questions.

In very rare cases, estimated at only 1 percent of all students, **alternate assessments** are used for annual standardized tests. This is generally only done when students will not be issued a high school diploma, since statewide standardized assessment is generally required to receive a high school diploma. Alternative assessments generally take three forms. **Alternate assessments based on alternate achievement standards** are the most common type, and they are sometimes given to students with significant cognitive disabilities who receive a waiver from state testing. These tests typically assess how far students have come toward reaching individual learning goals such as learning the alphabet or writing one's name.

QUICK REVIEW

What is the process for obtaining a waiver for standardized testing in your state? What is your state's policy on testing students with disabilities?

Another type of alternate assessment is the **alternate assessment based on modified achievement standards**. In this assessment, students are often still tested over the same material, but they may only have to answer half of the questions or may only have to choose from two multiple-choice options instead of four. While this type of alternate assessment was popular at one time, it is rapidly decreasing in use and is no longer used in most states as it does not meet many federal testing guidelines.

Last is the **alternate assessment based on grade-level achievement standards**. This allows students to show what they know about grade-level material in a different format. A student might present a research project or give a presentation instead of completing a multiple-choice standardized assessment. Like alternate assessments based on modified achievement standards, alternate assessments based on grade-level achievement standards are also very rare as they often fall outside the federal requirement that all students take state tests. Alternate assessments are altogether quite rare, and parents often have to go through an extensive process to obtain a waiver to excuse their child from annual state accountability testing.

SAMPLE QUESTION

6) **Which type of assessment asks certain special-needs test takers to answer the same test questions as all other students but to answer fewer questions or select from fewer multiple-choice options?**
   A. alternate assessments based on alternate achievement standards
   B. alternate assessment based on grade-level achievement standards
   C. alternate assessment based on modified achievement standards
   D. criterion-referenced standards-based assessment

TYPES OF ASSESSMENTS

Each classroom will use a variety of assessment techniques, and they will vary widely based on the subject, age, and developmental level of students. For example, an art teacher may use portfolio assessment as the primary means of evaluating student progress, whereas a math teacher might use more written tests. Similarly, a self-contained special education life skills teacher with five- and six-year-old students may likely rely very heavily on observation and anecdotal records versus end-of-unit summative assessments. What is important is that the assessment match the probability of extracting the needed data and also match the intended purpose for which the data is to be used.

As with other issues related to student assessment, how assessment data is used is somewhat controversial. Many experts are wary of using certain types of assessment results as the exclusive criteria from which to make large educational decisions. Multiple types of assessment, particularly frequent informal assessments, should be used to help glean the fullest overall picture of any one student.

FORMAL AND INFORMAL ASSESSMENTS

In early childhood classrooms and some self-contained special education classrooms, observation, checklists, anecdotal records, and portfolios are often used as the primary means of assessment. Most programs seek to maintain a balance between formal and informal assessment measures. **Formal assessments** are typically thought of as those in which students are given tests of some sort and then results are reported in either a percentile or percentage format. Standardized tests, chapter or unit tests, and end-of-course exams are all examples of formal assessments.

Informal assessments are ways of assessing students outside the traditional written test format. They may include observation, portfolios, projects, presentations, and oral checks among others. Informal assessment should be ongoing and should guide instruction alongside formal assessment. For example, a third-grade math teacher may use the informal assessment strategy of calling on students to answer multiplication facts as part of the ongoing informal assessment. She might then notice that many of her students are struggling with the seven times tables and focus more instruction and practice in this area. She could also, of course, give a formal written test over the multiplication tables and then target her reteaching on areas in which her students did not perform well. Both can be used to gather information and guide instruction. It should be remembered, however, that some students simply do not perform well on formal assessments or may have test anxiety. In these instances, informal assessments are often a better measure of student knowledge.

SAMPLE QUESTION

7)   Mrs. Rogers keeps a daily classroom journal in which she makes anecdotal records about each of her prekindergarten students and their progress toward socio-emotional learning goals. How can this method of assessment best be described?

   A.   as quantitative and informal

   B.   as qualitative and informal

   C.   as quantitative and formal

   D.   as qualitative and formal

FORMATIVE AND SUMMATIVE ASSESSMENTS

Assessments, either formal or informal or authentic or more traditional, can also be either formative or summative. **Formative assessment** refers to the ongoing monitoring of student progress toward learning objectives. Formative assessments are often informal assessments where teachers seek more information to streamline instruction. For example, a kindergarten teacher may give frequent formative assessments by asking each student to read words from a sight word list or consonant blend chart. This will help the teacher determine each student's progress in the journey of learning to read and provide appropriate and targeted instruction in areas where there is most need.

Formative assessments can also be more formal such as a short quiz over the day's material or a concept map or outline that students submit for grading. However, formative assessment tends to be **low-stakes assessment** or assessment that does not carry a high point value and does not significantly impact a student's course grade or chances of promotion to the next grade.

Summative assessment is designed to evaluate student learning after the end of a defined unit of study. It generally compares student knowledge to the initial learning objectives that have been addressed throughout the unit of study. It, too, may be formal or informal but may often take the form of a unit test, midterm or final exam, or a final paper or project. Summative assessments are generally **high-stakes assessments** because they carry high point values and are often critical to a student's overall grade or her or his ability to pass a course or be promoted to the next grade.

Both formative and summative assessment are important. Still, teachers should be aware of substantial research suggesting that high-stakes assessments can generate anxiety in students. Additionally, many students with diagnosed specific learning disabilities may have trouble showing what they know through traditional written summative assessments, even when given accommodations or modifications. The UDL emphasizes multiple means of expression, in which students are given multiple opportunities to show that they have met learning objectives. This may mean that not all students should be assessed in the same way at the end of a unit of study or that students should be offered different ways to demonstrate their learning.

> **STUDY TIPS**
>
> Formative assessments are used while students are *forming* their knowledge. Summative assessments are used to add up all of student learning into one lump *sum*.

A kind of middle ground between a formative and summative assessment is the **benchmark assessment**. This type of assessment is often more formal than a formative assessment, but it is not a high-stakes standardized summative assessment. Benchmark assessments are sometimes called interim assessments or predictive assessments, and they are generally used to track student progress and determine the degree to which students are on pace to perform well on future summative assessments.

Many states use benchmark assessments before the annual standards-based assessment to determine which students need interventions to help prepare for the high-stakes test. They can also be used to evaluate overall school or district goals and whether the school or district is on track to achieve those

> **DID YOU KNOW?**
>
> Some districts give benchmark tests up to ten times per year. This has led to some state lawmakers limiting the number of benchmark assessments that can be given each year in hopes of decreasing testing time and increasing instructional time. Does such a law exist in your state?

goals. In some cases, benchmark assessments are less formal. For example, a first-grade teacher using a leveled-reader program may use a benchmark assessment to determine when her students are ready to move to the program's next level. Similarly, a kindergarten teacher whose goal is to have her students know all the Dolch sight words might give students benchmark assessments over smaller sections of the list.

SAMPLE QUESTION

8) A sixth-grade general education teacher gives a daily warm-up quiz that has a low point value and covers some of the material covered the day before. What type of assessment is he giving?

A. a benchmark assessment

B. a low-stakes formative assessment

C. a low-stakes summative assessment

D. a high-stakes summative assessment

AUTHENTIC ASSESSMENTS

One important trend in student assessment is **authentic assessment**. Authentic assessment refers to an assessment measure that measures the student's ability to use knowledge in a direct, relevant, often real-world way. In an authentic math assessment, perhaps students are asked to develop a household budget or calculate what type of car they could afford based on the average annual salary of a job they are considering pursuing. This type of assessment asks students to use math skills (thus assessing that students have the skills to begin with) in order to complete another task. Authentic assessments can also offer opportunities to go much deeper than a traditional written test. While a math test might ask students to calculate sales tax on an item using a standard percentage, an authentic assessment surrounding budgeting might ask students to calculate sales tax over a year, income taxes, property taxes, and so on. This leads to a deeper understanding of the sheer volume of taxes one actually pays!

SAMPLE QUESTION

9) A tenth-grade English teacher wants to create an authentic assessment to evaluate students' skills with writing in coherent paragraphs. Which assignment would be best?

A. directing students to give a presentation to the class on something they know how to do well

B. asking students to analyze the way paragraphs are used in a newspaper article on a topic of their choice

C. assigning students a project of writing the draft of an email that they will eventually send to someone

D. having students use a graphic organizer to organize their thoughts into paragraphs before writing an essay about an assigned topic

DIAGNOSTIC ASSESSMENTS

Diagnostic assessments are typically used to determine what students already know. Many teachers give diagnostic assessments at the beginning of the school year or prior to each unit of study. This helps calibrate the intensity of instruction and can help track progress over time when diagnostic assessments are compared with summative assessments. Diagnostic assessments are particularly important when teachers are implementing pyramid planning as part of the Universal Design for Learning. If, for example, the teacher discovers through a diagnostic assessment that the majority of her first-grade students do not know all of the letter sounds, it would be unreasonable to expect all of her students to be reading sentences by the end of the first unit of study.

Diagnostic assessments can sometimes even uncover learning gaps that teachers will need to address. For example, a second-grade teacher who discovers that many of his students lack fluency with addition and subtraction facts will need to work to address this learning gap before students will be able to master addition with carrying and subtraction with borrowing. Diagnostic assessments can also be used to help develop concrete and achievable IEP goals. Meeting each individual student at his or her current learning situation is important in setting goals and targeting instruction.

SAMPLE QUESTION

10) Mrs. El-Badawi is a kindergarten teacher who wants to find out the level of phonemic awareness each of her students has at the beginning of the school year so that she can target her instruction. Which type of assessment would be best for her to use?

   A. formative assessment

   B. diagnostic assessment

   C. summative assessment

   D. play-based assessment

DYNAMIC ASSESSMENTS

Another type of assessment that has become quite popular, particularly in the field of speech-language pathology, is the **dynamic assessment**. Dynamic assessment is based on the theory of the zone of proximal development, first developed by Lev Vygotsky (see chapter 2). This idea posits that what a learner can do alone is negligible when compared to what he or she can do with the aid of a more skilled peer or adult. In a dynamic assessment, some instruction is embedded into the assessment. While there are a variety of methods for conducting a dynamic assessment, it typically involves a pretest, some type of intervention, and then a posttest. This process is often called test-teach-retest. In this way, a child's initial skills can be compared to the skills he or she displays after receiving instruction for improvement. This type of assessment can be very helpful in measuring a student's ability to learn new skills.

Proponents of this type of assessment say that it can help uncover learning potential and that it is more modifiable and responsive to the individual student. Critics of dynamic assessment point to its heavy reliance on the skill and even personality of the assessor. Assessors who make a student uncomfortable, for example, may not produce reliable or valid results.

SAMPLE QUESTION

11) Dr. Kim has Mark place number tiles on a board in a certain pattern. He then shows Mark how to place the tiles correctly on the board. Then he asks Mark to try placing the tiles again. What type of assessment is Dr. Kim administering to Mark?

   A.   dynamic assessment

   B.   benchmark assessment

   C.   criterion-referenced assessment

   D.   multi-perspective assessment

PLAY-BASED ASSESSMENT

In recent years, there has been growing controversy over testing in schools, and many types of alternative assessment methods have been used with great success to address these concerns. One area where standardized assessment instruments often fail to deliver accurate data is in early childhood. These students tend to have trouble fully understanding or cooperating with the standardized test battery and sometimes lack the concentration and emotional maturity to complete the assessment. However, early intervention is very important for future success in school, so waiting until students are older to perform assessments is unfortunately not an option.

One assessment strategy gaining in popularity for this group is the **play-based assessment**, which has become the assessment type of choice for many children through five years old. In a play-based assessment, children are assessed for a variety of skills and behaviors in a natural setting. Typically, education professionals, parents, and a peer with whom to play all participate in this type of assessment. Aside from play-based assessments, younger children are often most effectively assessed through assessment instruments that use observational checklists or developmental milestones.

Table 5.1. Common Phases in Play-Based Assessment

Unstructured facilitation	Child leads play while the facilitator plays along.
Structured facilitation	Facilitator leads the play activities.
Child-child interaction	Child plays with a typically developing peer.

Parent-child interaction	Parent and child play together.
Motor play	Facilitator guides play to observe motor skills.
Snack	Child is given a snack to observe self-help skills.

12) **A four-year-old prekindergarten student has been referred for screening based on the general education teacher's classroom observations regarding socio-emotional developmental milestones. The student is defiant during the administration of many standardized assessments that the multidisciplinary team attempts to give. Which type of assessment might be helpful to use in this case?**

   A.   peer assessment

   B.   benchmark assessment

   C.   intelligence test

   D.   play-based assessment

PEER, SELF-, AND MULTI-PERSPECTIVE ASSESSMENTS

Teachers and parents are not the only individuals who can participate in student assessment. Peers can also be very helpful in providing feedback on student learning. **Peer assessment** refers to the assessment of student work by peers. Peer assessment is widely used in higher education, particularly in large online classes where instructors are unable to give feedback on drafts of each student's work. However, if given appropriate guidance and practice, peer assessment can be used effectively in many secondary and even some elementary classrooms. While most forms of peer assessment will not result in a formal grade, they can be invaluable to aid students in revising their work before submitting it to the teacher for grading.

In a peer assessment, students are typically given a rubric or list of criteria and asked to assess another student's work based on this rubric or set of criteria. They are often asked to also offer specific feedback for improvement. This process often helps students who are unsure of how to revise or edit their work as they are given clear and actionable suggestions.

Peer assessment can also be used during collaborative learning. In this model, typically the teacher asks for feedback from other members of the group as to the level of each group member's participation. This can be particularly helpful if much of a group project happened outside of school so that the teacher can still get some idea of the particular contributions of each group member. This type of assessment is also often better when clear criteria for evaluation are set. The teacher might, for example, ask members of the group to fill out a chart showing what parts of the project each group member completed individually and which parts were completed together.

Multi-perspective assessments are also frequently used during cooperative learning activities. In this type of assessment, peers, the individual student, and teachers typically all collaborate to assess learning outcomes. This can be helpful when parts of a group project occur within the context of the classroom and others occur outside of it. In this type of assessment, the teacher may weigh input from different assessors differently when computing the total overall grade. For example, the teacher evaluation of the finished project may count for 75 percent of the grade, the peer assessment of group members may count for another 10 percent, and the student's self-assessment may count for the remaining 15 percent. Any comprehensive evaluation for special education services can also be said to be multi-perspective since a multidisciplinary team alongside a child's parents will be participating in the process.

Peer assessment and multi-perspective assessment can sometimes be used in conjunction with **self-assessment**, or a student's evaluation of his or her individual progress toward learning goals. Self-assessment is a critical part of any child's overall education. Self-assessment helps students become self-directed learners who devise and meet learning goals with little help from others. Self-assessment should be a large part of formative assessment. Students who are self-assessing can actively seek out the resources they need to meet learning objectives without waiting for teachers to realize they need them.

Self-assessment must often be explicitly taught. There are many strategies for this. Often, students are given an example of work that meets certain criteria and then asked to compare their work to this example. In other cases, students are asked to simply assess their degree of understanding of a concept. This could be anything from having students respond in journals or interactive notebooks to prompts such as "Today I learned…" or "I am still unsure about…" to students using simple symbols such as an *x*, checkmark, or happy or sad face to indicate their degree of mastery of a given concept.

Self-assessment is particularly crucial for students receiving special education services because these students must be able to monitor their level of understanding and progress to avail themselves of assistive technology when appropriate or ask for accommodations or modifications as needed. Students with individualized education plans need solid self-assessment skills because many times general education teachers consistently remind the class of progress toward grade-level objectives but may not consistently meet with students to discuss progress toward meeting IEP goals. This means these students must often take more ownership over their own learning and constantly self-assess their progress toward meeting their individual goals.

SAMPLE QUESTION

13) After a group project-based learning assignment, a high school physics teacher asks each member of the group to fill out an evaluation of their other team members. What method of assessment is he using?

A.   peer assessment

B.   multi-perspective assessment

C.   self-assessment

D.   formative assessment

Interpreting and Using Assessment Results

Using Assessments to Diagnose Disabilities

Some types of disabilities are more commonly initially diagnosed during a child's early life. These are often diagnosed by physicians or psychologists as parents or early caregivers observe atypical development and seek out professional evaluation. However, specific learning disabilities are often not apparent until elementary school when students are asked to read, write, and perform mathematical problem-solving operations.

There have been recent changes to how assessment data is used regarding learning disabilities in special education. At one time, a learning disability was defined simply as the difference between IQ and performance. In some cases, results from intelligence tests were simply compared to results from achievement tests and discrepancies were interpreted as evidence of specific learning disabilities. This is no longer a sound method for interpreting assessment results or evaluating students for special education services.

Today, a multidisciplinary team must use multiple means of assessment to gather as much data as possible. They must use the most current, valid, and reliable assessment instruments available and must be aware of cultural and linguistic biases inherent within these instruments. They should also look at functioning across multiple domains. They must use both formal and informal assessment measures and must consider perspectives from several stakeholders with multiple areas of expertise. For example, educational psychologists might be able to best interpret the results of psychoeducational test batteries, whereas parents and classroom teachers are best able to track and record the incidence of certain behaviors.

These multiple perspectives during the assessment process are crucial, and each must be respected. However, it is essential that the true nature of a student's disability be understood so that the right type of services can be provided. For example, a comprehensive evaluation may determine that a child has an intellectual disability. Parents may want a diagnosis of a learning disability as they may feel this is a better outcome. However, designing an IEP solely around a disability that does not exist or exists in conjunction with other conditions will not provide a student with the best educational outcomes.

When interpreting assessments, special education professionals must consider all components of the definition of the specific learning disability, including both inclusionary and exclusionary factors. They must also consider that some assessment data may not yield fully accurate data. For example, though many published assessment instruments are now available in multiple languages, students whose first language is not English will need to be assessed very carefully to ensure that performance is not related to problems learning English as a second or other language. Further, results from intelligence and achievement tests may not always be fully accurate as language impairments can skew these results.

Since learning disabilities are now defined as neurological conditions impacting ability to store, process, and generate information, it is crucial that they not be confused with other disabilities such as speech and language impairments or vision or hearing loss. All types of origins for a student's academic performance should be considered when evaluating assessment data.

SAMPLE QUESTION

14) Dr. Ross is one of the professionals on the multidisciplinary team conducting a comprehensive evaluation for a first-grade student. He gives a behavioral checklist to both the student's teacher and parents. Why is he likely doing this?

    A.   to compare with intelligence test results

    B.   to get a broad perspective on behavior across settings

    C.   to rule out weak motor skills development as the antecedent of the target behavior

    D.   to calibrate results; to do so, all tests must occur both in a home and school setting

RESPONSE TO INTERVENTION

Students from minority backgrounds often represent a disproportionate number of students identified as having intellectual disabilities, learning disabilities, and behavior disorders. This has led to an increased focus on ensuring that students are not overidentified as requiring special education services. One of these strategies, which is gaining traction in many states, is **response to intervention (RTI)**. Response to intervention is an approach to identifying students with special learning or behavioral needs through a process including specific criteria.

▶ High-quality evidence-based instruction ensures that poor student performance is not the result of inadequate teaching methods.

▶ Universal screening ensures that data is collected for all students and not only very high- or low-performing students.

▶ Ongoing progress monitoring ensures that assessment is being used to gauge program effectiveness.

▶ Tiered instruction allows students not excelling in the whole-group classroom to receive more targeted interventions and differentiation in a small-group setting.

▶ Parental involvement allows parents to collaborate in helping children meet academic and behavioral goals.

Through RTI, students who are not meeting learning objectives are first given interventions within the context of the general education classroom. This is known as tier 1 intervention. If students are still not meeting objectives, they receive targeted interventions to meet their learning needs in small groups. This is known as tier 2 intervention. If students are still struggling, they are given intensive interventions for a longer duration and often in a smaller group or individual setting. This is known as tier 3 intervention. If students have still not responded favorably after tier 3 intervention, they are then referred for a comprehensive evaluation for special education services. Because data is collected throughout the RTI process, it can be used as part of the comprehensive assessment. However, it cannot replace the need for the multidisciplinary comprehensive evaluation.

RTI can be helpful in the assessment of students since it does not rely on a parent or teacher referral to begin evaluating a student for special education services (after obtaining parental consent, of course). It may help to more properly identify students needing special education services since it eliminates some possibilities for underperformance such as inadequate instruction or lack of differentiation for individual student learning needs. On the other hand, it cannot be used as the sole basis for decisions regarding special education services. It is merely a method of initial screening and data collection.

QUICK REVIEW

What is your state's process for referral for evaluation for special education services? Does it use a response to intervention framework?

SAMPLE QUESTION

15) **During progress monitoring of a second-grade student during a tier 2 intervention, a teacher reaches the conclusion that the student has not yet fully mastered several high-frequency sight words. This is preventing the student from fully participating in the small-group intervention. What would be the next step?**

A. referring the student for a comprehensive evaluation for special education

B. administering a battery of standardized achievement tests

C. making a referral to the speech-language pathologist

D. targeting the student for tier 3 interventions with sight words

TURNING ASSESSMENTS INTO ACTION

When using data from ongoing assessment of student learning, special education teachers and general education teachers in the inclusive classroom must use the data for a purpose. Without action, there is no point in gathering data through assessment. This data might be used to shift instruction in a variety of ways. If a student is consistently exceeding IEP goals and daily objectives in the classroom, perhaps more rigor is warranted. If the student is consistently unable to meet these goals and objectives, perhaps the goals and objectives need to be adjusted. Further, if several students are failing to meet established criteria or objectives, perhaps a teacher's entire approach or curriculum materials need to be further evaluated.

Teachers should also assess their own instructional practices. One very popular way to accomplish this is through **action research**. Action research is a way for educators to improve instructional techniques by identifying a classroom or school-wide problem, collecting and analyzing data, and implementing a plan to address it. For example, a prekindergarten teacher might notice that many of her students are struggling to learn letter-sound correspondence with her existing instructional techniques. She might then collect data to find the root of the problem. Perhaps she then discovers that her students do not remain engaged and on task during learning center rotations, when letter-sound correspondence is taught. She might then devise a plan to increase student on-task behaviors during learning center rotations. In this way, the teacher is assessing the efficacy of her own practice and then making adjustments to benefit her students.

> **DID YOU KNOW?**
>
> Every state is reviewed annually for adherence to IDEA requirements. As of the most recent reporting year, only twenty-four states met requirements: Alabama, Connecticut, Florida, Illinois, Indiana, Iowa, Kansas, Kentucky, Massachusetts, Minnesota, Missouri, Montana, Nebraska, New Hampshire, New Jersey, North Carolina, North Dakota, Oklahoma, Pennsylvania, South Dakota, Virginia, West Virginia, Wisconsin, and Wyoming.

Assessment results are often used as demarcations of class, school, or district quality. While the underlying intentions of federal lawmakers requiring these accountability measures are good in that states should be accountable for providing quality educational experiences for their students, much debate exists over the overall usefulness of this assessment data. Standardized test scores are no longer the only measurements of the overall quality of a school or district. Progress from year to year, teacher tenure and education, diversity measures, and access to special classes and diploma programs are now just some of the other data collected and analyzed.

Additionally, the scope and breadth of special educational services provided at a particular school or district, such as number of special education teachers or interventionists and the types of services provided by school personnel (such as speech or occupational therapy), are also often used as demarcations of overall program quality, particularly by parents of special needs students.

SAMPLE QUESTION

16) A middle school math teacher wants to assess her instruction to determine which teaching methods are most effective in helping students learn to convert improper fractions to mixed numbers. What method might be helpful?

A.   achievement testing

B.   formative assessment

C.   action research

D.   response to intervention

ANSWER KEY

1) **A.   Correct.** Measurement error refers to the factors, such as test conditions, that impact the test results.

   B.   Incorrect. This was the annual state standards-based assessment. It was not an alternate assessment.

   C.   Incorrect. Measurement errors are part of every assessment, and the presence of measurement error does not mean the assessment lacked validity.

   D.   Incorrect. Hallie is in third grade, so this screening should have already occurred. Also, a standards-based assessment is not the best instrument to screen for developmental delays.

2) A.   Incorrect. Percentile refers to how well one student performed in relation to others.

   B.   Incorrect. The reverse is true.

   C.   Correct. Harvey's score was equal to or better than 89 percent of students to whom he is being compared.

   D.   Incorrect. The norming group is the initial group of test takers that is used to formulate the percentile.

3) **A.   Correct.** This is not a criticism of norm-referenced tests because this is by definition how a norming group is constructed. The other choices are all common criticisms of norm-referenced tests.

4) A.   Incorrect. An achievement test compares test takers to each other and is a norm-referenced test.

   B.   Correct. Most annual state accountability tests are standards-based assessments that are criterion referenced based on state standards.

   C.   Incorrect. Intelligence tests measure IQ.

   D.   Incorrect. Standards-based assessments are criterion-referenced tests.

5) A.   Incorrect. This is a definite reason to give multiple assessments.

   B.   Incorrect. This is a definite reason to give multiple assessments.

   C.   Correct. Published assessment instruments in widespread use are backed by research, so they are valid instruments.

   D.   Incorrect. This is a definite reason to give multiple assessments.

6) A.   Incorrect. Alternate assessments based on alternate achievement standards assess students on individual learning goals.

B.   Incorrect. In an alternate assessment based on grade-level achievement standards, students can show their knowledge through some means other than a standardized test.

C.   **Correct.** In an alternate assessment based on modified achievement standards, the assessment itself is modified.

D.   Incorrect. Alternate assessments are offered as an alternative to criterion-referenced standards-based assessment.

7) A.   Incorrect. The assessment uses notes and not numbers, so it is qualitative.

B.   **Correct.** Anecdotal records are informal assessments that do not use numbers, so they are qualitative.

C.   Incorrect. Anecdotal records are informal assessments that do not use numbers, so they are qualitative.

D.   Incorrect. While the anecdotal records are qualitative, they are an informal method of assessment.

8) A.   Incorrect. A benchmark assessment is generally the middle ground between a formative assessment and a summative assessment. This does not define a daily warm-up quiz, which is a low-stakes formative assessment.

B.   **Correct.** A daily warm-up quiz is a low-stakes formative assessment as it is designed to be an ongoing monitoring of student learning and has a low point value.

C.   Incorrect. While the daily warm-up quiz is a low-stakes assessment, it is formative, not summative.

D.   Incorrect. A daily warm-up quiz has low point value and is assessing ongoing learning, so it is a low-stakes formative assessment.

9) A.   Incorrect. This is authentic assessment, but it does not address the teacher's intended point of evaluation because the students do not write paragraphs.

B.   Incorrect. This assignment is also authentic assessment, but it does not address students actually writing in paragraphs.

C.   **Correct.** This assignment is authentic assessment because students will actually send the email to someone, so the assessment has a real-world application. It also allows the teacher to assess the student's use of paragraphs.

D.   Incorrect. This assignment would help students organize their writing beforehand, but it is more of an organizational strategy than an assessment.

10) A.   Incorrect. Mrs. El-Badawi is not trying to monitor her students' ongoing learning but rather assess what they already know.

B.   **Correct.** This will aid Mrs. El-Badawi in determining her students' existing knowledge of phonemic awareness.

C.   Incorrect. Mrs. El-Badawi is not giving an assessment at the end of a unit of study.

D.   Incorrect. While a play-based assessment might be useful for this age group, it will not give information on phonemic awareness.

11) **A.   Correct.** A dynamic assessment occurs when there is a test-teach-retest format.

B.   Incorrect. Benchmark assessments are used to track student progress toward objectives.

C.   Incorrect. A criterion-referenced assessment involves students meeting a particular objective criterion. One cannot tell from the example that this is a criterion-referenced test.

D.   Incorrect. It seems that Dr. Kim is the only assessor.

12) A.   Incorrect. Prekindergartners are not able to assess each other.

B.   Incorrect. The student does not necessarily need to be assessed for meeting incremental learning goals.

C.   Incorrect. Intelligence tests can be quite unreliable in students of this age, and this is not the general education teacher's concern.

D.   **Correct.** A play-based assessment will allow the student to be assessed in a more natural environment and will help assess socio-emotional learning as she plays with a peer. It will also address the problems incurred during the attempts at using other assessment instruments.

13) **A.   Correct.** Students assessing other students is peer assessment.

B.   Incorrect. While peer assessment is part of multi-perspective assessment, multi-perspective assessment also involves self-assessment and teacher assessment.

C.   Incorrect. Students are assessing each other, not themselves.

D.   Incorrect. The assessment is happening at the end of a long project (per the definition of project-based learning), so it is a summative assessment.

14) A.   Incorrect. Behavioral checklists would likely not be used for direct comparison with intelligence tests.

B.   **Correct.** Behavior at home and school can vary, and input from all individuals should be considered.

C.   Incorrect. A behavioral checklist is not aimed at motor skills assessment.

D.   Incorrect. This is not necessarily true. Many assessments are given in only a single setting.

15) A.   Incorrect. This only occurs in the RTI framework after tier 3 interventions.

B.   Incorrect. Administering such tests would not be helpful as the teacher seems to have already identified the learning issue.

C.   Incorrect. A referral to a speech-language pathologist does not seem warranted based solely upon the student's lack of proficiency with sight word memorization.

D.   Correct. In the RTI framework, if students are not making sufficient progress in tier 2 interventions, they are then given more intensive tier 3 interventions.

16) A.   Incorrect. Achievement testing is not helpful in this very specific case since the teacher wishes to understand one facet of instruction.

B.   Incorrect. The teacher might use formative assessment to understand student learning, but not her own teaching.

C.   Correct. Action research is one way for teachers to assess their own instructional practices and improve them.

D.   Incorrect. Response to intervention (RTI) describes a way to ensure that all students are appropriately screened for learning and behavioral issues.

6

Reading Instruction

LANGUAGE AND READING DEVELOPMENT

LANGUAGE DEVELOPMENT

Language development describes how humans develop the ability to understand and create words and sentences to communicate. Many experts believe that children have an innate ability to acquire **oral language** from their environment. Even before babies can speak when they are in the **pre-speech stage**, they cry in reaction to environmental stimuli or to communicate their needs. At around eight weeks, babies begin **cooing**, or creating various vowel sounds such as *ah* and *oh*. They also begin to recognize basic variants in the speech patterns of those around them, for instance contrasting sounds when they are exposed to new languages. This awareness, cooing, and crying quickly turn into **babbling**, the first stage of language development. This stage generally lasts from six months to around twelve months. In this stage, infants make a variety of sounds but may begin to focus on sounds for which they receive positive reinforcement. For example, babbles such as *baba* and *yaya* tend to garner praise and excitement from parents, so these may be repeated until the coveted *mama* or *dada* is produced.

> **DID YOU KNOW?**
>
> Ninety-five percent of all babbling by babies throughout the world is composed of only twelve consonants: *p, b, t, d, k, g, m, n, s, h, w, j.*

At around one year old, but varying from child to child, children start using first words, generally nouns. During this single-word stage, or **holophrastic stage**, these solitary words are usually used to express entire ideas. For example, "Toy!" may mean "Give me the toy." After a few months, this shifts to two-word utterances such as "Mommy go" or "David bad." The **two-word stage** may last through early toddlerhood but generally gives rise to the **telegraphic phase** of oral language development at around age two and a half. In this stage, speech patterns become more advanced, though sometimes prepositions, articles, and other short words are missing. Telegraphic speech includes phrases such as "See plane go!" and "There go teacher." This stage persists until children are mostly fluent in the home language, generally at age three or four. In this **later multiword stage**, comprehension of the commands and requests of others increases as does the child's ability to understand terms to describe objects. While most children go through these typical stages of language development, the pace may vary considerably from child to child.

It is important to make the distinction between what a child understands is being said, known as **receptive language**, and what a child can say, known as **expressive language**. If a child is not meeting typical communication milestones for both receptive and expressive language, the child should be referred to a speech-language pathologist (SLP). That professional may recommend speech therapy if a speech or language delay is diagnosed.

Students with diagnosed hearing loss may have problems in the development of both receptive and expressive language. They may find it challenging to develop vocabulary and perceive subtle speech sounds and word endings. However, research suggests that identifying and providing services to these children early can have a tremendous impact. Many studies have found that children with hearing loss may be able to develop language skills, either spoken or signed, at the same rate as children without hearing loss.

For other students, hearing is a challenge not from a physical impairment but from a processing disorder. Children with an auditory processing disorder, sometimes called central auditory processing disorder, have trouble processing or distinguishing between certain sounds even though these sounds have been "heard" by the structures of the ear. These students might struggle with listening skills and may have trouble remembering oral directions, understanding jokes or figurative language, and avoiding distractions from background noise. These students often benefit from visual and haptic (touch) stimuli and may need frequent checks from teachers to ensure they understand information presented orally.

Supporting a young child's oral language development is crucial in any classroom setting for students with and without exceptionalities. Teachers can help build vocabulary through conversation, songs, and reading aloud to students. Songs and developmentally appropriate books can help reinforce new vocabulary for young students through cadence and repetition. A teacher narrating his or her own actions ("Now, I am getting the lunch ready") and introducing students to new vocabulary ("This is a drum") through pictures or objects paired with language can help young students as they look to adults for exposure to new words and phrases. Above all, educators must ensure their classrooms are rich in conversation and questions. The more adults speak to and ask open-ended questions of students, the greater students' opportunities to grow in oral language skills.

Teachers at all levels should make appropriate accommodations and modifications for students with speech and communication disabilities. These might include using visuals alongside auditory directions, allowing for longer response times, and modifying oral assignments. Students without oral language abilities might benefit from various assistive communication devices, which teachers should become proficient in using to maximize interaction with and development of all students.

SAMPLE QUESTIONS

1) **A young child who screams "Truck! Truck!" when he sees a fire truck drive by is likely in which stage of language development?**

   A.   babbling

   B.   holophrastic

   C.   telegraphic

   D.   later multiword

2) **Zoey is a sixth grader with auditory processing disorder in Mrs. Barnes's reading class. One of the goals of her IEP is that she follow directions the first time they are given. Mrs. Barnes wants to assist Zoey in meeting this goal. What is one strategy that she might use?**

   A.   repeating oral directions at least twice

   B.   speaking loudly and clearly as she gives directions to the class

   C.   allowing extra time for students to follow oral directions before they are repeated

   D.   writing directions on the board in addition to speaking them aloud

READING DEVELOPMENT

Children learn to read in stages, though the length of each stage may vary considerably. The first stage is the development of **print awareness**. Print awareness involves a basic understanding of the nature of reading: that we read from left to right and top to bottom, and that we are reading words on a page. Very young children without solid print awareness may believe that meaning is gleaned from pictures on a page rather than words. Some younger children may understand that books convey meaning but may not quite know how. Teachers may see these children modeling reading a book upside down.

Key to print awareness are many **concepts of print**. These are the many underlying principles that must be mastered before learning to read. They include things such as knowledge and identification of a word, letter, and sentence; knowledge of the many uses of print; and knowledge of the overarching structure of a book or story (title, beginning, middle, end). Kindergarten students should be able to follow words from left to right and top to bottom and understand that a story read aloud is the representation of the words in print that are separated by spaces.

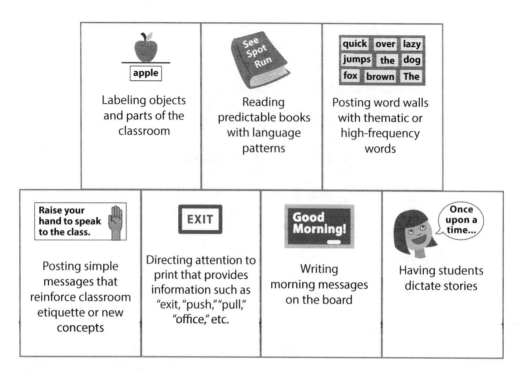

Figure 6.1. Concepts of Print Classroom Strategies

Many students have some print awareness through **environmental print**, or the words printed throughout their everyday environment. Environmental print includes product names, street signs, business names, menus at restaurants, and any other print that students encounter in the normal course of their lives. Teachers can use common environmental print such as the names and logos of popular children's products, stores, and restaurants to encourage pre-readers to "read" these names. Teachers should also consider using environmental print in the classroom in each of the home languages of their students. For example, a teacher may label the door in English, Spanish, Chinese, and Vietnamese. This builds confidence and familiarity and reinforces the idea that these words in languages other than English also have meaning. These strategies will help kindergarten students meet standards for print concepts such as understanding that words are separated by spaces and that letters may be either capital or lowercase.

When working with young students, teachers should have students point to words on a page and also point to words (versus pictures) themselves during storybook reading since this will reinforce concepts of print and help students develop print awareness. This will help even very young students begin to understand that while both the pictures and words on the page contribute to the overall meaning, the part being read is the words, not the pictures. Kindergarten students should be supported in understanding the purpose and role of both text and pictures in a story and how the author and illustrator work together to convey information.

Phonological awareness is the general ability to understand that within the structure of oral language, there are subparts. Development of this awareness is another crucial stage in learning to read. These subparts include individual words;

syllables, or units (typically containing a single vowel sound) within words; **onsets**, or the beginning consonant sounds of words (*sw*-im); and **rimes**, or the letters that follow (sw-*im*). Having phonological awareness is a crucial early stage in learning to read and write, and it can be fostered in the initial levels through singing songs

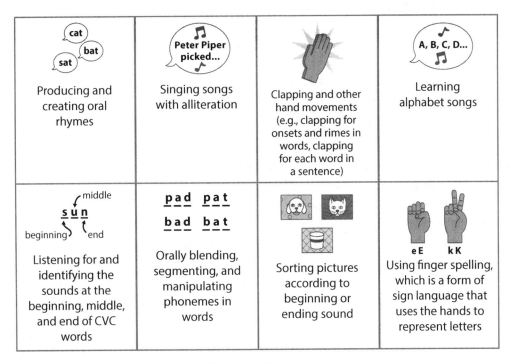

Figure 6.2. **Phonological Awareness Classroom Strategies**

and repeating rhyming words and phrases. Any speech or activities that seek to break language into component parts or that help establish an understanding of

syllables, onsets, and rimes—"Would *Son*-ya come to circle time?" "Do you want a *c*-at or a *h*-at for your birthday?"—are good choices for helping students begin to recognize the parts within language. Kindergarten students should be able to recognize and create rhyming words when prompted and should be able to blend and segment onsets and rimes in single-syllable words as part of their overall development of phonological awareness.

> **HELPFUL HINT**
>
> Remember that onsets are the first part of the word, or the first "button" readers see—the ON button. Rimes are the parts of the word that rhyme such as c-*at*, h-*at*, b-*at*, and so on.

The **alphabetic principle** presumes an understanding that words are made up of written letters that represent spoken sounds. To proceed with more advanced reading concepts, children must first have a firm grasp of letter sounds. Most experts agree that letter sounds with the greatest frequency and that allow children to begin sounding out short words quickly should be introduced first. It also may be easiest for children to master simple sounds—/t/ and /s/, for example—over more challenging or confusing sounds such as /b/, /d/, and /i/. Regardless of the way a curriculum breaks up practice with the alphabetic principle (a letter of the week or a teaching of the letters and sounds in rapid succession, etc.), teachers should recognize that repetition is key and students must be given multiple exposures to each letter and sound. By the end of kindergarten, students should be able to name the most common sound made by each consonant and both long and short vowel sounds.

DID YOU KNOW?

The alphabet song was copyrighted in 1835 but is actually an adaptation of a Mozart melody.

Phonemes are distinct units of sound and are the basic units of language. There are twenty-six letters in the alphabet, and there is some agreement among researchers that there are at least forty-four phonemes in English—some letters represent different phonemes and some phonemes are made up of more than one letter. There are eighteen consonant phonemes such as /r/ and /t/, fifteen vowel phonemes such as /Ā/ and /oi/, six *r*-controlled vowels such as /Ä/, and five digraphs such as /ch/ and /sh/. **Phonemic awareness** refers to the knowledge of and ability to use these phonemes. This awareness generally does not come naturally, and students will need explicit instruction to master these skills. It is often best to differentiate instruction and work with students in smaller groups when working on phonemic awareness because proficiency levels may vary substantially.

Various activities can aid students in developing phonemic awareness. **Phoneme blending** involves students putting given sounds together to make words. To work on phoneme blending, teachers can say sounds and ask students what word is made:

"I like /ch/ /ee/ /z/. What do I like? That's right, I like cheese."

Teachers can also ask students to simply repeat or chorally repeat the sounds in words during circle time or storybook reading:

"The car went vvvvv-rrrrr-oooo-m!"

Finally, teachers can model phoneme blending by tapping their arm as they say each part of a word and then brush their arm in one stroke as they end the word completely. Students can do this as well to make the concept more active.

Phoneme segmentation is generally the inverse of phoneme blending and involves students sounding out a word. Phoneme segmentation is important both for reading and spelling a word. More advanced phonemic awareness activities include **phoneme deletion**, in which a phoneme is removed to make a new word (e.g., ramp – /p/ = ram) and **phoneme substitution**, where one phoneme is changed to make a new

HELPFUL HINT

Phoneme *blending* involves students *blending* sounds together—like putting them in a blender—to make a word. Phoneme *segmentation* involves students "un-blending," or *segmenting*, each sound like the segments of a worm.

word (e.g., fla/t/ to fla/p/). Letter tiles are effective during small-group instruction for these activities.

Early childhood teachers should work on phonemic awareness with students in a variety of contexts. Having students manipulate language orally—"What word could I make if I took away the first letter of *cow*?"—and encouraging students in high-interest literacy activities in centers with alphabet boards, letter cards, alphabet sorters, and other manipulatives will provide multiple opportunities for students. Educators should also remember students will have varying backgrounds, skill levels, English language proficiencies, and sometimes speech and language delays and hearing loss. Some students may need modifications for certain activities; their needs should be considered when planning inclusive activities.

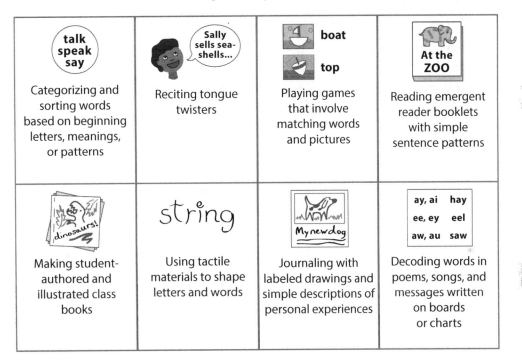

Figure 6.3. Phonics Classroom Strategies

Phonics is an age-old strategy for helping students read by connecting written language to spoken language or by correlating certain sounds with certain letters or groups of letters. Seminal to phonics instruction is a subset of the alphabetic principle—**letter-sound correspondence**. This correspondence is simply the knowledge of a phoneme associated with a given letter. Letter-sound correspondence is a foundational skill for effective phonics instruction, as most phonics strategies will require students to draw rapidly on this memory bank of letter sounds. As previously mentioned, most strategies for introducing students to the letter sounds draw on **high-frequency letter-sound correspondence**, where the most frequent and useful letter sounds are taught first. This will allow students to begin reading as soon as possible without having to wait for mastery of each letter sound.

Phonics instruction draws on the strategy of **decoding**, or the ability to pronounce the sounds of written words orally and glean meaning from them. Because of its focus on the specific sound structures of words, phonics instruction tends to involve more explicit, direct instruction and is not without critics, who believe it overemphasizes the mechanics of reading while sacrificing enjoyment. However, most classrooms today employ a combination approach that balances inquiry-based student learning, allowing students to explore high-interest literacy games and activities, with more direct instruction when necessary.

DID YOU KNOW?

Phonics instruction in the United States is thought to date from at least 1834 when *Reading Disentangled*, which included a set of flashcards, was published by British educational author Favell Lee Mortimer.

Teachers may have any number of mandated or suggested organizational structures for teaching decoding, such as centers balanced with a teacher-directed table or a mandatory computer-based phonics drill segment. Still, it is highly likely that whatever curriculum a program or school uses, it will contain some phonics component. This approach is proven to work for most students and is adaptable to a variety of student skill levels and special learning needs.

Some words are decodable, meaning they follow basic principles of phonics. These words can typically be sounded out effectively if basic structural deviations, like long vowel sounds with a word ending in –*e*, and various digraphs, where two letters make a single sound such as /th/ and /ay/, are mastered.

However, there are some words that deviate from basic sound structures and cannot be sounded out: **sight words**. They require no decoding because they are instantly recognized and read automatically. Students should be frequently exposed to sight words to facilitate memorizing them. It is recommended that some high-frequency decodable words, such as *and* and *get*, also be memorized by sight to increase student reading rate and fluency.

There are many lists of such words. The most popular is the Dolch Word List, which contains 315 words that are purported to be the most frequently used in English. Early childhood teachers might post some of these high-frequency words around the classroom for maximum exposure or encourage students to play games with sight word flashcards. Repetition will lead to mastery of these words and will help students read more quickly, fluently, and easily. By the end of kindergarten, students should be able to read several common high-frequency sight words. These words should be identified through the process of **word recognition**, or the ability to recognize a word on its own, outside of any particular context. Individual word recognition stands in contrast to **connected text**, or words that are linked together in sentences, phrases, or paragraphs.

Morphology, or the understanding of morphemes (the smallest units of meaning within words), can also aid students in both reading and writing. Morphemes can be as simple as recognizing that an *–s* on the end of a word often means that it is plural or that an *–ed* on the end of a verb frequently means it is in the past tense.

One effective way to help students learn new vocabulary is through morphology aimed at the study of roots and affixes. Many **root words** in English come from Latin or Greek. For example, the Greek root *chrono*, meaning time, makes many common words: *chronology*, *chronic*, *chronicle*, and so on. Many English words are made by adding an **affix** to a basic root word. If this affix is added at the beginning, it is known as a **prefix** (*anti–*, *un–*, etc.), and if it is added to the end of the word, it is known as a **suffix** (*–less*, *–able*, etc.). Using this decoding strategy, when students encounter a new or challenging word, they can see if any of the prefixes, suffixes, or roots seem familiar. This can help students determine meaning from likening a new word to a previously learned word. For example, a student who knows the meaning of the affix *mid–* as in *middle* and *midway* can then apply this knowledge to a history passage with the word *midcentury*. Prefixes and suffixes can also help students identify parts of speech. Words ending in *–er* and *–est*, as just one example, are generally adjectives.

Helping students practice phonics can involve a variety of strategies and activities, and these should always be developmentally appropriate for grade level and differentiated to accommodate students with varying needs and skills. Additionally, English language learners will need additional practice with phonemes that are unique to English or simply not part of their home language. Students who come from a background with a language that does not use the Latin alphabet may need more background with the alphabetic principle than native speakers. Additionally, strategies such as visual cueing to indicate certain sounds may be needed to help students who are hard of hearing master phonics.

Fluency refers to the rate, accuracy, and expression of a piece when read. Fluency is an important measure of a student's reading development; lack of fluency will hamper overall comprehension as well as enjoyment of reading. Reading **rate** is a measure of speed and is generally calculated in words per minute. **Accuracy**, or the correct decoding of words, is generally entwined with rate when measuring fluency, as reading quickly but incorrectly is not desirable.

While fluency is not limited to oral reading, it is virtually impossible to assess fluency during silent reading, and most educators rely on frequent oral reading assessments to help determine student progress. While several standard measures exist, one of the most researched is the Hasbrouck-Tindal oral reading fluency chart. This chart is designed to measure progress over the course of the school year and from grade to grade. It compares students in percentiles with their peers on a scale of words read correctly per minute. It is important to remember that all students will develop fluency on a different timeline, and assessments of fluency are most accurate when they are developmentally appropriate and when they are not presented as high-stakes testing situations.

Teachers should also be particularly attuned to the reading rate and accuracy of English language learners. Research indicates that some English language learners can read quickly and accurately while lacking comprehension. It is important to balance oral fluency checks with other methods of assessing overall comprehension, particularly for English language learners.

In addition to rate and accuracy, **prosody**, or the overall liveliness and expressiveness of reading, is also a skill to nurture in students. Prosody may involve appropriate pauses and various changes in pitch and intonation based on punctuation and the overall meaning of the piece. Developing prosody in students should involve a combination of modeling by teachers—as they read stories, passages, and even directions aloud—and giving students plenty of opportunities for oral reading practice.

Educators may find it challenging to find time for oral reading assessment in the classroom as they balance multiple priorities. However, teachers must make time to listen to all students read aloud with regularity. While examining written work and performance on independent or group practice activities may give some indication of a student's overall development, to get the fullest picture teachers must gather as much data as possible. Assessing student fluency through oral reading is key to an overall understanding of a particular student's learning situation.

Fluency is highly correlated with comprehension because students who struggle to read and decode individual words will have difficulty comprehending entire sentences and paragraphs. Additionally, students who read at a very slow rate may have trouble recalling what they have read. It is well worth the time investment to listen to students read aloud as much as possible.

Students will pass through the **stages of reading development** at different rates. Students in the *initial* or *emergent stage of reading development*, known as emergent readers, are developing the skills, knowledge, and attitudes that will help them in the conventional forms of reading and writing. These students, generally in kindergarten, are focusing on mastering concepts of print and then sounding out words. Students in the *early reading stage*, which might develop for some students in kindergarten or early first grade, may still use picture cues and other decoding strategies to make meaning. Students in the *transitional reading stage*, often first and second graders, will have a variety of decoding strategies to determine the meaning of new words but will still need scaffolding with more difficult texts and story elements. Ideally, students reach the *fluent reading stage* by third grade and can read most texts independently.

SAMPLE QUESTION

3) Michael is a kindergartner in Ms. Smith's classroom who is having tremendous success in identifying high-frequency words with flashcards and on a word chart. However, Michael is struggling in reading these same words in sentences. How should Ms. Smith focus reading instruction with Michael?

A. more practice on individual word recognition

B. more practice with connected texts

C. more practice with phonemic awareness

D. more practice in oral reading for prosody

SPECIALIZED INSTRUCTIONAL STRATEGIES

PHONICS

Students with exceptionalities are more likely to struggle with phonics, word recognition, and fluency. Phonics instruction, particularly for students with learning or intellectual disabilities, must be both explicit and systematic. **Explicit phonics instruction** refers to that which is clear and unambiguous. Explicit phonics instruction is characterized by direct instruction, modeling, and immediate feedback and correction. For example, a student who incorrectly says /d/ when presented with the word *bat* should be corrected after saying the first phoneme incorrectly. He or she may then be asked to repeat the correct sound /b/ after the teacher.

Systematic phonics instruction refers to that which has a logical sequence and in which new skills are only introduced after previously introduced skills have been mastered. This is generally characterized by a step-by-step approach where skills are broken down into component parts and then new layers are added as each previous skill has been mastered. For example, a systematic phonics program might begin with simple consonant-vowel-consonant patterns (*hat, dog, cat*) and then be gradually extended to more advanced long vowel sounds (*rope, gate*) followed by blends and digraphs (*black, bread, foil*). Generally, systematic instruction follows the pattern of direct instruction, guided practice, and then independent practice. During guided practice, the teacher should provide scaffolding to quickly reinforce correct or incorrect sounds.

> **HELPFUL HINT**
>
> Systematic instruction is also referred to as "I do, we do, you do," reflecting the pattern of instruction, guided direction, and independent work.

Additionally, small-group phonics instruction has been proven highly effective for students with exceptionalities. These groups should be formed based on skill level and composed of no more than four students. Within these small homogeneous groups, teachers can provide systematic, direct instruction using a variety of activities. These activities might include **word sorts**, where students place words (typically on small tiles or cards) into groups based on sounds, spelling, or meaning. Students in small groups can practice identifying onsets and rimes through word cards or tiles with color-coded parts. They can also use picture cues to help sound out words into onsets and rimes. Picture cues can be very effective in helping students with learning disabilities develop letter-sound correspondence. Other strategies such as chunking can be effectively taught in a small-group setting. In **chunking**, students decode words by breaking them into component parts (how/e/ver). Chunking can also be applied to sentences (I/went/to the store).

Students with intellectual and learning disabilities may also benefit from repetition, often in the form of drill with flashcards. Teachers can place unknown words or sounds into the deck at a much lower frequency than known words or sounds. This will keep students motivated and build their confidence. This practice also leads to what is sometimes referred to as **overlearning**, where a concept is practiced even beyond student mastery. Overlearning may be helpful for students with exceptionalities as they receive ample opportunities to cement newly acquired skills into their memories for immediate recall in the future. Learning to read can be a challenge for students with intellectual disabilities in particular, and it is expected that each subset of the overall task (print awareness, phonemic awareness, letter-sound correspondence, decoding, etc.) will take significantly longer. However, strategies such as direct and systematic instruction and repetition can be quite effective in working with students with intellectual disabilities as long as reasonable, incremental goals are set.

Repeated reading of familiar texts is also a proven strategy for developing fluency in students with learning disabilities. Familiar texts can also be used during **choral reading** practice, where a small group of students and the teacher read aloud together. During choral reading, students should be encouraged to follow along with their finger on the page as they read. **Echo reading**, where the teacher models oral reading (generally of a single sentence) and then has the student read after him or her, has also proven effective. This can be done individually, in small groups, or even in pairs of students where one student is a highly proficient oral reader.

When selecting texts for students, it is important to keep in mind that students may experience frustration if given difficult texts that they struggle to read. In general, for independent practice, students should be able to read with 95 percent accuracy, or no more than one error for every twenty words. This is typically referred to as a student's **independent reading level**. The **instructional reading level**, on the other hand, is more challenging for students. At this level, students can read with 90 percent accuracy. A student's **frustration reading level**, defined as that at which one reads at less than 90 percent accuracy, should generally be avoided.

It is worthwhile to remember that students with certain learning disabilities such as dyslexia and dysgraphia will likely have trouble with **phonological processing**, a three-step process involving phonological awareness, phonological memory, and the ability to rapidly recall these phonemes. These students may need ten to thirty times more practice than students without learning disabilities. Students with dyslexia may benefit from a multisensory instructional approach. In this type of instruction, students are given techniques that link learning to multiple senses. In phonics instruction,

Figure 6.4. Elkonin Box

students are generally encouraged to link sounds through visuals, sound, and touch. One effective technique for developing phonological awareness is the use of Elkonin boxes. These boxes allow students to see, hear, and touch the phonemes in a word. Students can move a marble or penny over each box as a word is broken up into its component sounds.

Monitoring student progress in phonics instruction is a critical part of the overall instructional strategy. Experts suggest that students in the lower primary grades (generally kindergarten through third grade) be screened at the beginning and middle of the year for possible reading problems. This data can be used for early intervention and prevention of future reading problems. Differentiated instruction should then be provided for all students based on current skill development. This differentiation, which generally occurs in a whole-class setting, would be a tier 1 intervention. These interventions may involve giving students practice texts at different levels of text complexity or giving certain students more time to work on vocabulary development while other students are engaged in echo reading activities with peers.

Students who fail to meet benchmarks on screenings should be targeted for tier 2 interventions in small groups that should, ideally, meet between three and five times a week for twenty to forty minutes. Tier 2 interventions should be characterized by frequent formative assessments to monitor student learning and progress. (See chapters 1 and 4 for more on tiered interventions.)

Students who do not show significant improvement after a reasonable amount of time receiving tier 2 interventions should then be referred for more intensive, daily tier 3 interventions, which might be held in smaller groups or even one-on-one. The progress of all students, even those not receiving specific, targeted intervention, should be monitored closely. One way to do this is through taking a **running record**. To do this, the teacher sits next to the student in a one-on-one setting with a copy of the text and marks student errors, miscues,

CHECK YOUR UNDERSTANDING

What are the primary differences among tier 1, 2, and 3 interventions?

and so forth with a series of checks and other symbols. This can become part of the overall **progress monitoring** that teachers may undertake to ensure that students are meeting incremental goals to ensure they are making satisfactory progress toward state standards and/or IEP goals.

SAMPLE QUESTIONS

4) Hugh is a student with a developmental delay impacting his cognitive functioning in an inclusive prekindergarten classroom. One of the goals of his IEP is that he recites at least five letter sounds on his own. Which activity would be most appropriate for his teacher to use to help Hugh meet this goal?

A.   putting letter tiles together to make CVC words

B.   having Hugh break compound words into their component parts

C.   showing Hugh the letter *b* and having him repeat the /b/ sound several times

D.   allowing Hugh to manipulate several letter magnets to make words at the literacy center

5)   **Which of the following is a multisensory approach to phonics?**

A.   Elkonin boxes

B.   chunking

C.   running records

D.   echo reading

6)   **A critical characteristic of systematic phonics instruction is that**

A.   it is clear and unambiguous.

B.   it is performed in a small-group setting.

C.   it is part of an integrated curriculum.

D.   it is taught in a logical sequence.

LITERACY

Phonics is only one part of developing overall literacy and reading skills. In addition to phonemic awareness, phonics and word recognition, and fluency, reading also includes vocabulary and comprehension. Students with reading and language-related exceptionalities will also need extra help with basic writing and understanding how to use language for communication.

Vocabulary knowledge is essential for comprehension beyond phonics because if students are unable to connect a word they have sounded out to its meaning, there is no understanding. Students with learning disabilities are particularly vulnerable to a lack of vocabulary development. This is often the result of less exposure to new words in context through reading since research shows that students who are less proficient readers spend much less time each day reading than their peers. To counter this, students with exceptionalities that might affect their reading proficiency must receive explicit vocabulary instruction. It is recommended that vocabulary instruction be targeted to important words, which are those that are necessary for the understanding of a specific text (*ecosystem* in reading a science passage, for example); useful words, which are those students will need frequently throughout their schooling; and difficult words, or words that have many meanings or are often confused.

Vocabulary can be introduced and reinforced through a variety of approaches. Students with learning disabilities especially benefit from the multisensory approach in which students use **keyword mnemonics** to associate a visual image with a new word. **Semantic mapping** (a type of graphic organizer) helps students draw connections between one vocabulary word and related words. This is a visual strategy for students to make meaning of new words. Another approach is direct instruction of new vocabulary, where students repeat new words and definitions after the teacher. Computer-aided vocabulary acquisition programs have been effective in aiding students with exceptionalities in acquiring and applying new vocabulary.

Figure 6.5. Keyword Mnemonic of "Triage"

Developing skills in reading comprehension with both narrative and expository texts is an important part of developing a student's overall literacy. However, students with learning disabilities often process information inefficiently, and this can manifest itself in weak comprehension skills. While phonics and decoding skills can be assessed on an ongoing basis, challenges in reading comprehension often do not appear until later in elementary school or even in middle school when the bulk of reading instruction shifts to exercises designed to gauge a student's overall comprehension of a text read independently. Students with learning or cognitive disabilities might be unaware of basic strategies to aid in comprehension, so these strategies must be taught explicitly. Many of these strategies will help students with **metacognition** as they "think about thinking" and constantly evaluate what they comprehend and what they do not.

In reading narrative texts, students can be supported to use the structure of the story itself to aid in organization of details. Most narratives follow the same basic **story grammar**, or main components. These include the main characters, the

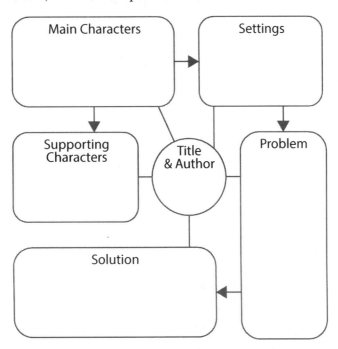

Figure 6.6. Story Map

plot or action, setting, and resolution. Students can use these elements to create visual **story maps** to help extrapolate and organize the narrative.

Reading expository texts is generally more challenging for all students, not just those with exceptionalities. This is because these texts often require more background knowledge and do not follow the same predictable, chronological structure of narratives. Research suggests that many students, particularly those with learning differences, are not given enough practice in tackling these challenging texts, putting them at a real disadvantage across multiple content areas. Students should therefore be taught how to tackle these challenging texts across multiple subject areas.

First, students must prepare for what they will read by **previewing**. (This supposes that students have been previously introduced to any new vocabulary before being exposed to it in context.) Students should preview what they will be reading, taking note of the structural elements of the text such as bolded words, headings, graphics, and so forth. They should also set a purpose for their reading. Will the text introduce new information? Review previously discussed concepts? As students read, they might organize information graphically. This will aid in students capturing key information (note taking), confirming knowledge, and making connections between ideas.

Students must also be taught **fix-up strategies**. Fix-up strategies refer to methods by which a reader can intervene on his or her own behalf when he or she realizes that there is a gap in comprehension. While highly proficient readers often use fix-up strategies as a matter of course, students with exceptionalities often need to be explicitly taught and frequently reminded of this toolkit. Fix-up strategies include rereading, summarizing, asking questions, applying background knowledge, and examining visual aids or graphics. After students have read, teachers should provide guidance in student self-monitoring of learning through targeted questioning such as "Do I understand what I have read?" "What is the main idea or summary?"

Students can also use specific graphic organizers such as the **K-W-L chart** to organize the process of comprehending expository texts. This organizer helps students identify what their prior knowledge is (what I know), set the purpose (what I want to know), and summarize/recall what was read (what I learned).

Students who continue to struggle with comprehension in the higher grades should be targeted for intervention in small groups. This instruction should be geared toward addressing underlying skill gaps such as vocabulary or even decoding. **Peer tutoring** is one popular and research-validated reading intervention in the inclusive classroom with students of varying learning needs. This strategy pairs students to reinforce key concepts.

There are several peer tutoring models; ClassWide Peer Tutoring (CWPT), where students are divided into tutoring groups with differing skill levels, is the most popular. CWPT includes many variations such as Peer-Assisted Learning

Strategies (PALS), where ability grouping is less emphasized. Peer tutoring has been found to be quite effective in getting more students one-on-one assistance and giving struggling readers more opportunities for practice and immediate feedback. It has also been found to promote self-confidence and help students develop positive social relationships with peers.

Students with challenges related to communicating orally may benefit greatly from **assistive technology**, defined as any equipment or system that aids a person with a disability. This technology might be high tech or low tech, and there are numerous examples of systems that can be used for **augmentative and alternative communication**, which are techniques to aid in the communication process of those with communication-related disorders. Students might use various low-tech aids such as a picture board to communicate through pointing or gesturing. They may also use more high-tech devices such as speech-generating devices, applications, or programs. These devices or programs can aid students in communications in the classroom.

Some students may have IEPs that specify certain types of accommodations that might also require alternative formats or technology to aid in meeting literacy standards. Students with visual impairments may need large-print text, braille materials or documents, or oral presentation of visual information. Likewise, students with hearing loss or who are deaf will need special accommodations such as sign language interpretation or assistive listening devices.

SAMPLE QUESTIONS

7) **A nonverbal student in an inclusive high school art classroom has an IEP goal to increase her communication with peers. What type of assistive technology might be most helpful for this student?**

   A. a scribe

   B. an assisted listening device

   C. a picture board

   D. a spelling and grammar checker

8) **One way that peer tutoring may promote socio-emotional learning is that it**

   A. gives students more one-on-one practice with core academic skills.

   B. allows more students to receive targeted intervention.

   C. groups students by skill level.

   D. promotes cooperation and positive social interaction.

WRITING

Even children as young as two begin to draw pictures that they use to communicate ideas—their very first written representations. This develops into scribbling, which takes on a form more similar to letters. Wavy scribbling or mock handwriting may soon appear as children are exposed to print-rich home environments and class-rooms. This emerges into forms that look like individual letters and then forms with actual letters that have some likeness to individual words strung together.

In the **transitional writing stage**, children begin writing letters with spaces in between, though real words are generally not yet being formed. Even in the transitional writing stage, however, many children can make successful attempts at copying letters and words from environmental sources. Writing a child's name or the name of a common classroom object on a card for a child to copy is a way to encourage transitional writing.

As children begin to gain knowledge of sounds, they enter a phase of invented **spelling**. They start communicating words and ideas more clearly, though many words may be represented by only a beginning and ending sound. It is vital to understand this stage as a natural part of the process of emergent writing and allow for children to express ideas and practice writing without an overemphasis on spelling errors. As children gain more and more knowledge of sounds and words, they will begin writing whole words, first with simple single-letter sound constructions such as *dog*, *hat*, and *fun*. This progresses to the correct spelling of more and more words and eventually the stringing together of words to make phrases and even short sentences.

The overall process of learning to write involves three distinct components:

▶ conceptual knowledge (understanding the purpose of writing)
▶ procedural knowledge (understanding how to form letters and words)
▶ generative knowledge (using words to communicate a meaning)

In helping young students develop conceptual knowledge of writing, teachers should focus on activities that show students the link between print and its intended purpose. Environmental print is a great resource for helping students develop this knowledge as teachers point out classroom signs and posters or those in the school building and on the playground. They can further build early conceptual knowledge by having students **draw** or **scribble** to communicate their own feelings and ideas.

Procedural knowledge involves the nuts and bolts of writing. Procedural knowledge-building activities are those that build awareness of basic letter formation, the knowledge that words are made up of letters, the knowledge that words have spaces between them, and the overall mechanics of writing. Procedural knowledge and the alphabetic principle are entwined, and the letter sounds and names should be reinforced when consciously instructing correct letter formation.

Additionally, procedural knowledge of writing will coincide with the development of fine motor skills. Fine motor skills development in the classroom cannot be overemphasized, particularly in a preschool or kindergarten setting. As in any part of emergent literacy, teachers will have students with widely divergent levels of fine motor proficiency. It is essential the classroom provides a variety of opportunities for students to build these skills through the use of manipulatives such as alphabet boards and puzzles and a variety of writing implements such as crayons, markers, and pencils.

Some students, particularly those with developmental delays, may take longer to develop fine motor skills, and teachers should make accommodations and modifications as needed. Students who continue to find fine motor skills challenging after sustained practice can be accommodated with special pencil grips, writing implements, or keyboards or other inputs.

The mechanics of writing will generally involve explicit spelling instruction, and this will likely be part of a program's overall language arts curriculum. It is important to view spelling as part of a developmental continuum and not overemphasize correct spelling too early when preschool students are still forming mock letters or letter strings. However, a standard **continuum of spelling** can be referenced to tailor spelling instruction appropriate to grade level while always keeping in mind the differing developmental levels within the classroom. Students with learning disabilities often benefit from multisensory spelling lessons that combine seeing a word, spelling it orally, and then writing it.

Explicit spelling instruction will generally begin with simple CVC patterns and progress as students learn new phonics structures. Practice with homophones (words that have the same pronunciation but a different spelling and meaning) should begin in third grade or earlier. Common homophones include *there/their/they're, to/two/too*, and so on. Students should know that software applications for detecting spelling errors often fail to pick up on spelling errors with homophones, so students should be extra vigilant when editing and revising writing containing these words.

Depending upon the goals of a student's IEP, various accommodations might be used to assist students in spelling. These may include response accommodations in the form of scribes, word processors, spelling and grammar checkers, checklists, cue cards, and word lists. Depending on the student and IEP, it might be easier for students to work on certain skills in isolation. General essay or narrative writing assignments might be modified such that spelling is not used as criteria for a student's overall assessment.

Teachers should balance more explicit spelling practice with time to allow students to practice the third part of emergent writing, generative knowledge. In this domain, students learn to write for a purpose, not just for the sake of learning the mechanics of writing. It is important to continue to develop students' conceptual and generative knowledge while teaching them to write. Having students dictate their ideas into a recorder or to a teacher can free up mental energy otherwise used on the mechanics of writing for the generation of content. This strategy can also aid students who may have low confidence in their writing ability or who are reluctant to try writing.

As students master more of the procedural knowledge of writing, they can begin generating more pieces on their own. Students generally progress from writing letter strings and word-like structures under a picture they have drawn, to writing and spelling simple words, to constructing sentences, to constructing stories. Teachers should emphasize the communicative purpose of each stage to help students construct the generative knowledge of writing.

Students with various learning disabilities may struggle with writing since they often have problems with executive functioning, which impacts their ability to organize and express information. While the term *dysgraphia* denotes a learning disability specific to difficulties in written expression, students with dyslexia and many other types of learning and cognitive disabilities may also have difficulties with writing.

Lack of initial success in writing often leads to a decrease in writing practice, so some students with learning disabilities may spend very little time practicing this essential task. To encourage writing, teachers should provide these students with explicit, significant instruction. Of paramount importance is imparting to students that writing is a process. Students must be given multiple strategies throughout this process.

The first phase in this process is planning, often called brainstorming or organizing. Students with exceptionalities often have difficulty retrieving prior knowledge to formulate a plan for a piece of writing to address a topic. They may also struggle with linking ideas into a coherent, unified piece. Instructional strategies might include semantic maps or other graphic organizers and clear **goal setting** as to purpose, organization, and audience. Students may need prompting as they are planning their writing through teacher-guided questions and goals.

After brainstorming is complete, students draft their piece and link their ideas together with an introductory statement, support, and concluding section or statement. This process of text production can be particularly challenging for students with exceptionalities as they may become fatigued with concerns in the actual production of written words: handwriting, spelling, grammar, and punctuation. Modifications for these students might include allowing more time for drafting, having students write a shorter paper, or even using a scribe or word processor for certain assignments.

Students must then go through a **revision** and **editing** process in which they strengthen their piece through the addition of more supporting details and connecting words (*because, also, then*) and proofread for capitalization, end marks, and spelling.

Teachers may assist in the revision process by providing a checklist to help students ensure they have met certain criteria. One simple revision checklist is the **COPS** mnemonic. This stands for **C**apitalization, **O**rganization, **P**unctuation, and **S**pelling and is used with success in many elementary classrooms.

Teachers may also employ peer and/or teacher feedback as part of the overall revision process. Feedback, which begins in first grade, helps reinforce the concept that the purpose of writing is ultimately to communicate ideas, so writers should account for the perceptions and suggestions of multiple readers when revising a piece. Feedback might be a helpful extension of a CWPT program, as students with learning disabilities may find it challenging to revise their writing independently.

Some students with learning disabilities may have difficulties reading their own handwriting. Computer-aided technology can ease the revision process for these students and aid in the success of peer editing and revision.

SAMPLE QUESTIONS

9) At an IEP meeting, the reading specialist, classroom teacher, and parents of a fifth-grade student determine that the student is not making adequate progress toward the standard to "write informative/explanatory texts to examine a topic and convey ideas and information clearly." After discussion, the team determines this is because the student strongly dislikes writing because of the laborious task of forming and writing letters. Which accommodation might best help this student to meet the standard?

   A. giving the student shorter assignments than the rest of the class

   B. providing targeted, small-group instruction on vocabulary development

   C. providing the student with a laptop computer on which to craft essays

   D. grading the student's essays on criteria other than spelling and overall organization

10) Which of the following is an example of a teacher aiding a student in goal setting before beginning a writing assignment?

   A. asking the student what she would like to write about

   B. directing the student to try to include at least three details about the setting

   C. having the student fill out a graphic organizer with the subheadings *First*, *Next*, and *Last*

   D. instructing the student to write for the duration of the class period

MATHEMATICS

Dyscalculia is associated with trouble writing numbers, weak number sense, frequent errors in computation, trouble in retrieving math facts, and difficulties in solving word problems. However, students with exceptionalities, even those without a specific diagnosis of dyscalculia, often struggle with math as it requires extensive memory, retrieval, and application of previously learned components.

Students with some exceptionalities might struggle with **generalizing** math skills or taking concepts learned in one context and applying them to others. Successful math instruction for students with disabilities, like successful reading instruction, must be systematic and explicit.

Explicit mathematics instruction involves very clear and specific teacher process modeling, practice and examples that are incremental and build in degree of difficulty, teacher scaffolding and feedback, and cumulative review. Teachers must also provide opportunities for drill and practice of math knowledge that will need to be instantly recalled during application alongside the development of students' overall conceptual knowledge so that they know why they are retrieving certain knowledge in a specific order of steps for application. This should be balanced with strategies to motivate students and encourage metacognition and progress monitoring.

CHECK YOUR UNDERSTANDING

What are some strategies to help students generalize math and reading skills?

Students with exceptionalities may especially struggle with word problems; these problems require conceptual, procedural, and computational knowledge. Teaching students a strategy for tackling these problems can be quite effective, particularly if the strategy involves a mnemonic displayed visually in the classroom. One such device is the **RIDE** method in which students are encouraged to **R**emember the problem, **I**dentify the needed information, **D**etermine the operations and unit, and **E**nter the correct numbers to solve. Another is **STAR**: **S**earch the word problem, **T**ranslate the words into a picture or equation, **A**nswer the problem, and **R**eview the problem.

Before tackling any new math concept, the requisite vocabulary should be assessed and pre-taught. This includes words that denote shapes or relationships (*rhombus, obtuse, tangent*) as well as words that signal the nature of word problems (*more than, in total, altogether*, etc.). Students can use keyword mnemonics or other visual association techniques to aid in solidifying this knowledge of the language of math.

Teachers can also model and encourage students to use **think aloud** procedures to help with word problems, equations, or other multi-step problems. This strategy involves articulating the problem-solving process: What do I need to do first? I think they are asking me to... I need to... Then I should... I need to multiply...and carry the three...

Think alouds not only assist students, but they can be tremendously useful in ongoing, formative math assessment. Teachers can determine at which point in the problem-solving process students are struggling and may need reteaching. They can also determine individual conceptual or computational skill gaps to target for intervention. Thinking aloud can also be used as a springboard for general strategies of metacognition in math problem-solving. Encouraging students to develop an awareness of what they

CHECK YOUR UNDERSTANDING

How would you model a think aloud for a student for the following problem? Maria has nineteen boxes containing fourteen apples each. She gave Tom two apples and Frank one apple. How many apples does Maria have left?

need further assistance with or explanation of will aid them in seeking out teacher assistance when needed.

Fluency and automaticity with the basic math operations of addition, subtraction, multiplication, and division are essential for the development of higher level math problem-solving such as algebra and geometry. Students with exceptionalities are often able to develop this fluency; they just need more practice.

It is important that students be given ample opportunities to practice these facts in an environment that is reassuring and motivating. For example, students who struggle with fine motor skills might benefit from oral practice of multiplication facts. Young students in kindergarten through second grade can be taught specific strategies, such as counting up to add and counting down to subtract, to recall math facts while they are still internalizing/memorizing them. Students in third grade and above can also be taught strategies to aid in fact retrieval, such as the commutative property (5 + 7 = 7 + 5) and the associative property [(5 + 5) + 3 = 13 and 5 + (5 + 3) = 13], to aid in fact retrieval and calculation. Digital applications may help aid teachers in individualizing the pace of this practice for the needs of each student. Depending on the individual student and IEP, timing modifications such as allowing for more time on an assignment or assessment, and assignment modifications such as allowing for the use of a calculator may be appropriate in certain cases.

As with reading, students should be formally screened at the beginning and middle of the year for potential math difficulties so that appropriate interventions can be provided. This may be done in combination with data from state-mandated standardized tests. Those students identified as needing tier 2 interventions in a small-group setting should then be provided with explicit, systematic instruction that focuses on both conceptual knowledge and the problem-solving process. At the same time, these students should build fluency with math facts. Visual representations of various mathematical concepts (charts, number lines, number trees, etc.) should also be practiced during interventions. Teachers should also emphasize strategies for solving word problems, particularly those devoted to understanding the underlying structure of the problem. Frequent progress monitoring and formative assessment alongside positive reinforcement should also be characteristics of successful tier 2 and tier 3 interventions.

Mathematics builds upon each mastered skill. Thus, student success depends on early diagnosis of difficulty and intervention as necessary. Students who have been diagnosed with certain disabilities that affect math performance can benefit from accommodations. Students with

> ### CHECK YOUR UNDERSTANDING
>
> What types of intrinsic and extrinsic motivators can be used to aid students in their study and perseverance with challenging math concepts?

trouble in computation might be aided by calculators, manipulatives, a chart of math facts, or even an abacus. Students who struggle with remembering procedures or problem organization can be aided by graphic organizers, flow charts, t-charts, or graph paper. Students with a visual impairment can be accommodated by image descriptions, tactile representations, and even proprietary math software such as Math Window.

SAMPLE QUESTIONS

11) Roderick is a first grader who is struggling to learn his addition facts. Unlike many of his classmates, he is not able to instantly recall basic addition of sums less than twenty. Which strategy would aid Roderick and help him meet state math standards for first grade?

    A.   relating counting to addition by counting up by three to add three to a given number

    B.   determining which numbers are prime and composite before adding

    C.   creating a place value chart

    D.   using an analog clock to identify the time and then adding various numbers to denote a specified time

12) Pamela is a student with an emotional disturbance in a fifth-grade inclusive classroom. She often gets extremely frustrated and acts out when she struggles to solve a word problem. She rarely seeks out appropriate help from the classroom's paraprofessional, who is trained to assist her and prevent Pamela's outbursts. Which strategy might promote inclusion while addressing Pamela's needs?

    A.   teacher modeling

    B.   cumulative assessment

    C.   think alouds

    D.   ability grouping

ANSWER KEY

1) A. Incorrect. Babbling involves using sound strings such as *baba*.

  B. Correct. In the holophrastic, or single-word, stage, children use a single word to denote an entire idea, such as "Truck!" for "I see a fire truck!"

  C. Incorrect. In the telegraphic stage, children use multiple words to express ideas, although connecting pieces such as articles and prepositions might be missing.

  D. Incorrect. In the later multiword stage, children are primarily fluent in expressing themselves in their native language.

2) A. Incorrect. This will likely not help Zoey as she struggles in processing auditory information.

  B. Incorrect. Students with auditory processing disorder often have trouble with oral directions even if they are spoken loudly and clearly.

  C. Incorrect. Allowing time for students to follow directions is important, but this will not help Zoey follow directions the first time they are given per her IEP.

  D. Correct. This will help Zoey by reinforcing directions presented orally with a visual representation she can refer to.

3) A. Incorrect. Michael is doing well with this skill per the flashcards and word chart.

  B. Correct. Michael is reading sight words in isolation well. He needs practice reading them in connected texts where these words are joined with other words in phrases or sentences.

  C. Incorrect. Phonemic awareness focuses on the ability to use sounds. Michael is working on sight words, not sounding out.

  D. Incorrect. Michael is still working on decoding and is not ready to focus on prosody or reading with expression.

4) A. Incorrect. This activity is too advanced for Hugh, and he likely needs more guidance.

  B. Incorrect. This chunking of word parts is too advanced for Hugh, and this activity does not address his IEP goal.

  C. Correct. This is explicit, direct instruction aimed at helping Hugh learn letter-sound correspondence.

  D. Incorrect. This is not explicit instruction and will likely not help Hugh directly to meet this goal.

5) **A. Correct.** Elkonin boxes allow students to make associations with sounds through sight, sound, and touch.

B.   Incorrect. Chunking involves the sense of hearing only.

C.   Incorrect. Teachers take a running record as part of monitoring a student's progress.

D.   Incorrect. Echo reading involves the sense of hearing only.

6) A.   Incorrect. This is a characteristic of explicit phonics instruction.

B.   Incorrect. This is a proven setting for systematic phonics instruction, but not the only setting in which it can be systematic.

C.   Incorrect. This is not a characteristic of systematic phonics instruction.

D.   Correct. Systematic phonics instruction is taught in a logical sequence in which skills build upon each other.

7) A.   Incorrect. A scribe would not aid a student who is unable to communicate verbally.

B.   Incorrect. An assisted listening device would likely aid a student who is hard of hearing.

C.   Correct. The student could point to the picture to communicate with others using her hand or eyes.

D.   Incorrect. A spelling and grammar checker would not help a nonverbal student communicate.

8) A.   Incorrect. This is an advantage of peer tutoring, but it is not related to socio-emotional learning.

B.   Incorrect. This is an advantage of peer tutoring, but it is not related to socio-emotional learning.

C.   Incorrect. This is a characteristic of some peer tutoring programs, but it is not related to socio-emotional learning.

D.   Correct. Peer tutoring promotes cooperation and positive social interaction among students, which contributes to socio-emotional learning.

9) A.   Incorrect. This is a modification, not an accommodation.

B.   Incorrect. This strategy is not an appropriate accommodation for the student's particular issue.

C.   Correct. This assistive device might alleviate the struggle with letter formation and aid the student to write the same essay with less effort expended on the procedural task of forming letters.

D.   Incorrect. This is a modification and will not address this particular issue.

10) A.   Incorrect. This question does not help the student develop a concrete goal to keep in mind while writing.

B.   Correct. This strategy helps develop a concrete, actionable goal that the student can work toward.

C.   Incorrect. This activity may very well help the student organize her thoughts, but it is not a part of goal setting.

D.   Incorrect. This task does not result in a specific goal for the assignment; it is merely a form of time management.

11) **A.   Correct.** This approach meets the state standard of relating counting to addition and is also an appropriate strategy to help Roderick.

B.   Incorrect. This strategy is above a first-grade level and does not address adding.

C.   Incorrect. Using a place value chart is part of the first-grade standards but does not address Roderick's issue.

D.   Incorrect. The state standards only require first graders to write time in hours and half hours using an analog clock. Furthermore, this strategy is unlikely to help Roderick develop fact recall with addition.

12) A.   Incorrect. Teacher modeling is an important instructional strategy as part of explicit math instruction, but it is not the best choice to address Pamela's needs.

B.   Incorrect. Assessing Pamela's overall knowledge is important, and cumulative assessments are part of sound math instruction. However, cumulative assessment will not address Pamela's outbursts.

C.   Correct. Having Pamela articulate what parts of the problem she understands and narrate her thought process will allow her to seek out help before she becomes upset. She will be able to identify precisely when she is stuck and needs scaffolding.

D.   Incorrect. Ability grouping is not necessarily part of creating an inclusive environment and might be detrimental to Pamela's confidence. It also does not directly address Pamela's outbursts.

7

Transition

TRANSITION PLANNING

THE TRANSITION PLANNING PROCESS

Students of all abilities require support to prepare for life after secondary school. However, students with disabilities may require more specialized support to **transition** from school to post-school life. This process can be complex and may include the student making decisions about his or her community involvement, career path, living objectives, and postsecondary education. These transition plans are not "one size fits all"—some individuals may wish to pursue postsecondary education, others may choose to join the workforce, and still others may look for a combination of both. For this reason, transition plans are flexible and allow for a wide range of goals.

The Individuals with Disabilities Education Act (IDEA), reauthorized in 2004, states that IEP meetings for students approaching the age of sixteen must involve planning and goal setting for transition. The IEP transition plan, part of the IEP's Present Levels of Performance section, must include a summary of transitional objectives and the services that will be provided. The goals and services will be summarized and planned for in the same format as academic goals on the IEP.

The transition goals and services should always revolve around student interests and aspirations. For this reason, IDEA requires that the student join the IEP team for any meetings that involve postsecondary goals and transition planning. This usually occurs when the student is between the ages of fourteen and sixteen. During these meetings—and throughout the general transition planning process—team members should encourage students to advocate for themselves. Students should be connected with

HELPFUL HINT

Transitions can, and should, be planned for before adulthood. Many students as young as fourteen years old begin work or independent living programs.

guidance counselors or faculty in other career-oriented school offices to establish their interests, create reasonable goals, and make a long-term plan.

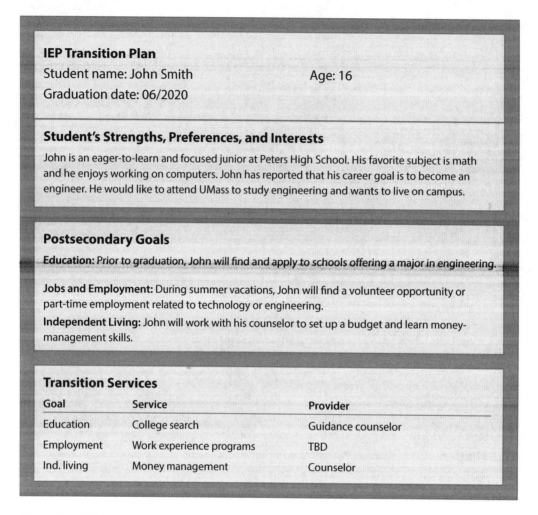

IEP Transition Plan

Student name: John Smith   Age: 16
Graduation date: 06/2020

Student's Strengths, Preferences, and Interests

John is an eager-to-learn and focused junior at Peters High School. His favorite subject is math and he enjoys working on computers. John has reported that his career goal is to become an engineer. He would like to attend UMass to study engineering and wants to live on campus.

Postsecondary Goals

Education: Prior to graduation, John will find and apply to schools offering a major in engineering.

Jobs and Employment: During summer vacations, John will find a volunteer opportunity or part-time employment related to technology or engineering.

Independent Living: John will work with his counselor to set up a budget and learn money-management skills.

Transition Services

Goal	Service	Provider
Education	College search	Guidance counselor
Employment	Work experience programs	TBD
Ind. living	Money management	Counselor

Figure 7.1. IEP Transition Plan

The transition planning process should follow the steps outlined below:

▶ **Step 1**: Administer age-appropriate transition assessments.
Educators should use age-appropriate transition assessments to determine student desires, strengths, interests, and preferences.

▶ **Step 2**: Create postsecondary goals.
Transitional goals are targeted and clearly defined objectives relating to an individual's post-school life. These goals could pertain to a chosen career, postsecondary education, and living objectives. Goals should be determined by the individual and supporting staff and should be relevant to the student's interests.

▶ **Step 3**: Determine transition services.
Transitional services describe the types of support that the team has

determined are required by the student to meet his or her goals. Services provided might include access to career counselors, participation in a work experience program, independent living goals, postsecondary education plans, and internships.

▶ **Step 4**: Coordinate with relevant programs.
In this stage of the transition planning, the IEP team should begin to partner with service providers in order to have specific plans in place once the student completes secondary schooling.

▶ **Step 5**: Write annual IEP goals.
Annual IEP goals must be based on the age-appropriate transition assessment, student-preferred goals, and predetermined services. Annual IEP transition goals must follow the *SMART* guidelines: **S**pecific, **M**easurable, **A**ttainable, **R**esults-oriented, and **T**ime-bound.

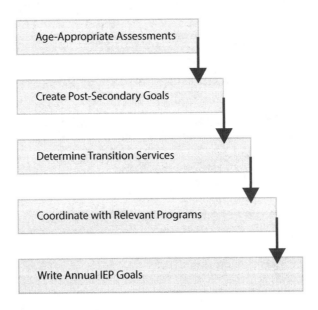

Figure 7.2. The Transition-Planning Process

1) **The transition services section of an IEP must include which of the following?**

   A.   strategies to help the student prepare for postsecondary activities

   B.   a plan for assisting the student with college applications

   C.   a list of age-appropriate assessments to determine student interests

   D.   a summary of the student's previous IEP goals

TRANSITION ASSESSMENTS

Transition assessments are designed to help individuals of all ages develop career, living, and independence goals by examining important traits and skills, such as self-care tendencies, social ability, and study habits. Each of these assessments is designed for specific ages. Typically, the number of questions and life skill areas addressed in the assessment increase as the student gets older.

A variety of well-known transition assessments are used nationally. One example is the **Casey Life Skills (CLS)** test (developed by Ansell Casey), which identifies student strengths so that the educational team can help the student plan for the future. The CLS test is an online assessment that provides rapid results students can then share with their educational team. There are four tests designed for individuals ages ten and above.

Transition Assessment Summary
Michael Smith, 14 years old

Needs: Michael needs an increase in social skill, to be taught how to resolve peer conflicts without adult supervision, and to self-regulate when upset.

Strengths: Michael makes friends easily, enjoys spending time with his peers, and is a hard worker. Michael has shown growth in his ability to self-advocate. When working, Michael is very focused and driven.

Preferences: Michael prefers hands-on activities as opposed to pen-and-paper tasks. Michael also prefers to work independently rather than on a team.

Interests: Michael is interested in video games, science experiments, and Japanese culture. Michael is interested in working with computers and graphic design.

Figure 7.3. Transition Assessment Summary

Transition assessments can be difficult for individuals with severe disabilities, but certain methods enable them to voice their preferences. One method is the **work-task preference assessment** in which an individual is asked to rank a varying number of tasks. This assessment shows the tasks that the individual prefers the most and least of a group and can inform the IEP team's choices. In addition, observations of the student and interviews with the family can be used as part of the assessment. All these age-appropriate assessments inform a summary of the student's needs, strengths, preferences, and interests.

2) Joshua is a sixteen-year-old boy with cerebral palsy. He has limited speech but can point and use gestures to make choices. What would be an effective way to administer an age-appropriate transition assessment to Joshua?

    A.   using an if-then chart

    B.   reading a traditional assessment out loud to Joshua

    C.   allowing the family to choose answers for Joshua

    D.   using a work-task preference assessment with visuals

SELF-DETERMINATION AND SELF-ADVOCACY

Person-centered planning is a process during which the IEP team and student create a plan in order to reach transitional goals. Planning is also accomplished using a **self-directed** approach in which students take the lead in the decision-making. To make informed decisions, students must learn self-advocacy and self-determination strategies early. **Self-advocacy** is the ability to represent one's own needs, wants, and interests. **Self-determination** is the ability to engage in self-determined behavior, such as setting goals and pursuing them. Self-determination skills are built through self-reflection and using experiences to inform future decisions.

Students should be encouraged to use specific strategies to build self-determination and self-advocacy skills. These strategies may include promoting:

▶ clear communication about disabilities so that the student can identify areas of strength and improvement;

▶ making choices so that students can build confidence and discover their interests;

▶ problem-solving and conflict resolution skills to enable students to reflect on a situation, determine an appropriate outcome, and make a plan to reach that outcome.

IEP rights are transferred to students (unless they are deemed incompetent) at the age of majority—usually between eighteen and twenty-one, depending on the state. At this age, individuals should be able to determine their needs and wants, understand their rights, and voice their questions and concerns to the team.

3) At which of the following ages could IEP rights be transferred to a student?

    A.   sixteen years old

    B.   fourteen years old

    C.   eighteen years old

    D.   twenty-two years old

RESOURCES FOR STUDENTS WITH DISABILITIES

Regardless of ability level, individuals with disabilities should always be pushed towards independence. There are many programs specifically designed to assist students with disabilities in reaching independence goals.

POSTSECONDARY EDUCATION

If students choose to continue their education past secondary school, it is vital that the transition team helps them prepare to advocate for themselves in college. Postsecondary institutions do not use IEP and 504 plans; instead, they work within the federal regulations in the Americans with Disabilities Act (ADA) and subpart *E* of Section 504. This difference means that students will no longer have a dedicated team to monitor their progress and suggest necessary interventions. Instead, most postsecondary institutions will have a disability services (or similarly named) office, which assists students with disabilities who require accommodations. Students will likely need to register with this office and will be assigned a contact person to oversee their accommodation requests.

DID YOU KNOW?

Students are entitled to more privacy in postsecondary institutions than they were in secondary schools. Parents cannot discuss accommodations with the school unless they have written permission from the student.

Students, their team, and their parents should research the process for requesting accommodations at prospective colleges. They should also plan to meet with college representatives before classes begin to ensure that they are receiving the appropriate accommodations. In addition, students (and possibly their parents) may wish to use the IEP to guide their conversations with the college, but the IEP itself will likely not be sufficient documentation to receive accommodations. Instead, students will be responsible for providing any documentation required by the college, including outside evaluations.

Table 7.1. Differences in Services Between Secondary and Postsecondary Education

	Secondary Education	Postsecondary Education
Which laws cover disability services?	IDEA, Section 504 of the Rehabilitation Act of 1973, ADA	Section 504 of the Rehabilitation Act of 1973, ADA
What services are provided?	special education and related services	accommodations only
Who is responsible for requesting services?	School officials identify students with disabilities and develop an IEP to ensure the student has access to the general education curriculum.	The student is responsible for providing documentation and requesting accommodations.

SAMPLE QUESTION

4) **Bilal is a junior in high school and plans to attend a state university upon graduation. Bilal has accommodations on his current IEP and his parents are concerned that these accommodations will not be provided in college. What should his parents do?**

   A. work with Bilal's team to prepare him to attend university without any accommodations

   B. encourage Bilal to reach out to the college to discuss his needs

   C. check in with the college to be sure it is following Bilal's IEP

   D. request the IEP change to a 504 so that the plan will follow Bilal to college

HOME AND COMMUNITY LIVING

If individuals have a goal of living independently, they will need a specific skill set to assist in the transition to living in their own home. These skills should be learned and practiced prior to living independently. Such skills include:

- grocery shopping
- money management
  - paying bills
  - budgeting
  - tracking spending
- self-care
  - personal hygiene
  - creating a schedule
  - managing appointments
  - engaging in social activities

Many of these skills are learned informally from teachers and guardians; however, there are specific programs in place to teach life skills for independent living. Casey Life Skills, referenced above and created by Ansell Casey, is a program that provides training and education to students during transitional periods. A case worker reviews a student's life skills assessment and identifies areas of strength and those needing improvement. Casey Life Skills provides a resource guide for caregivers that includes lesson plans for teaching skills and objectives that align with the student's needs. The Centers for Disease Control (CDC) also provides

DID YOU KNOW?

The Section 811 Supportive Housing for Persons with Disabilities Program, which is run through the US Department of Housing and Urban Development, provides rental assistance for housing that includes services for low-income adults with disabilities. These funds are available through state agencies.

students and their team access to resources on healthy living, independent living, and emotional self-care.

Besides living at home or independently, individuals with disabilities can live in communities that provide independent living supports. Communities may take the form of dormitory-like facilities, apartment-based communities, or group homes. These facilities provide a range of supports.

▶ **Supervised group housing** provides a high level of support, with onsite staff who assist with skills like medication management, meals, and running errands.

▶ **Partially supervised group housing** provides independence combined with staff (onsite during business hours) who can provide some assistance as needed.

▶ **Supportive housing** provides a high level of independence with offsite staff who are available for problems or emergencies.

SAMPLE QUESTION

5) Patricia is a twenty-one-year-old adult with Down syndrome. While she is able to follow a schedule, cook meals for herself, and work full-time, she struggles to budget money. Patricia would like to live alone, but her parents are concerned that she needs more support. Which of the following would be the best living situation for Patricia?

A. live independently

B. live at home with her parents

C. live in partially supervised group housing

D. live in a supervised group home

EMPLOYMENT

Employment can always begin as volunteer work. Volunteer work allows individuals to sample a variety of fields and fine-tune their interests. Once an individual has chosen a field, he or she can pursue a job hunt. Programs such as Ticket to Work and work experience programs assist individuals with disabilities in finding employment.

Ticket to Work is a program designed for individuals with disabilities ranging from eighteen to sixty-four years old who receive Social Security Disability Insurance (SSDI) or Supplemental Security Income (SSI) payments to connect with potential employers. The program helps these individuals with career guidance, training, self-advocacy skills, and job placement. The program is free of charge for participants. Ticket to Work encourages independence for individuals with disabilities and decreases their reliance on SSDI or SSI payments and benefits.

Community-based work experience programs are internships that serve as a stepping stone to employment. During a work experience program, participants will work to improve skills and abilities. Many times, these programs partner with companies that will hire individuals once on-the-job training is complete. **On-the-job training** is instruction, typically one-to-one, that teaches skills required for a specific job at the workplace. This differs from traditional training and education, which takes place outside of the work environment.

SAMPLE QUESTION

6) **Ticket to Work is a program that**
  - A. connects individuals with disabilities with potential employers.
  - B. helps fund tuition for students with disabilities.
  - C. matches people with disabilities with available jobs in the federal government.
  - D. provides internships, which serve as a stepping-stone to employment.

PROGRAMS FOR CAREER DEVELOPMENT

There are many programs in place to assist individuals with disabilities in reaching their transitional goals. One of these is the **Workforce Innovation and Opportunity Act (WIOA)**, a system in which potential employers, educational programs, and training is made accessible to individuals who are seeking employment, including those with disabilities.

Programs like these were developed as a response to the **Carl D. Perkins Career and Technical Education Act of 2006**, which made it mandatory for states to develop **Career Technical Education (CTE)** programs of study that intertwine academics with trade training. These programs, formerly known as vocational education programs, lead to a cumulative degree or certificate. CTE programs are available for nearly every trade imaginable, including culinary, interior design, and health services. The range of programs allow students to choose a focus that relates to their interests and long-term goals. The programs can begin in high school or after secondary school completion. CTE programs are relatable to the skills and opportunities that employers are seeking in candidates, making their participants even more marketable after program completion. CTE programs are held to the same learning standards as public schools and may also be required to meet CTE-specific standards.

SAMPLE QUESTION

7) **Which of the following is an example of a CTE program?**
  - A. a one-hour cooking class
  - B. a four-year college program in English
  - C. a two-year culinary program resulting in a certificate
  - D. a volunteer position with a local soup kitchen

The Office of Special Education and Rehabilitative Services

The **Office of Special Education and Rehabilitative Services (OSERS)** is an organization that designs programs to educate and rehabilitate individuals with disabilities. The organization consists of two sub-groups: the **Office of Special Education Programs (OSEP)** and the **Rehabilitation Services Administration (RSA)**. OSEP services individuals with disabilities from birth through twenty-one years old and provides grants, funding, and leadership to ensure the best education programs possible for children with disabilities. OSEP also provides information through parent centers for parents of children with functional needs.

RSA's mission is to assist state and local organizations in providing services such as vocational rehabilitation for individuals with disabilities. **Vocational rehabilitation (VR)** is a process that assists individuals with disabilities in gaining employment in order to increase independence and self-sustainability. VR consists of goal setting, career counseling, and case management. Processes like VR increase independence in individuals with disabilities.

SAMPLE QUESTION

8)   **Which of the following is NOT a duty of OSERS?**

   A.   providing students with grants in order to access education programs

   B.   providing information for parents through parent centers

   C.   providing support to assist individuals with disabilities in gaining employment

   D.   providing students with vocational training leading to a cumulative degree

ANSWER KEY

1) **A.** **Correct.** The transition services section of an IEP includes services the team has determined are required to help a student reach his or her goals.

   B. Incorrect. While transition services may pertain to college, college plans are not a required element of the transition service section.

   C. Incorrect. Age-appropriate assessments are used to determine interest in postsecondary activities; they are not discussed in the transition services section.

   D. Incorrect. The transition services section of the IEP focuses only on transition.

2) A. Incorrect. An if-then chart is used as a behavior management strategy.

   B. Incorrect. If Joshua has trouble communicating verbally, a read-aloud accommodation on an assessment does not assist him in answering appropriately.

   C. Incorrect. It is inappropriate to have family choose answers for Joshua, as he is able to point and communicate using gestures.

   D. **Correct.** A work-task preference assessment would allow Joshua to independently rank his choices of most- to least-desired tasks.

3) A. Incorrect. At the age of sixteen, a transition plan must be developed, but rights are not transferred.

   B. Incorrect. Transitional planning may begin at age fourteen, but rights are not transferred.

   C. **Correct.** Depending on the state, a student reaches the age of majority at age eighteen, at which point the IEP rights are transferred from parent to student.

   D. Incorrect. IEPs follow a student until the age of twenty-two, but this is not the age at which rights are transferred in any state. Unless deemed incompetent, students receive IEP rights by age twenty-one at the latest.

4) A. Incorrect. While IEP and 504 plans do not follow students to college, colleges are required to accommodate students with disabilities.

   B. **Correct.** Bilal's parents cannot discuss his accommodations with the college. They will need to encourage Bilal to self-advocate and reach out to his college's disabilities services office.

   C. Incorrect. Colleges do not follow IEP plans, and Bilal's parents would need his permission to discuss his accommodations with the college.

   D. Incorrect. Colleges do not follow IEP or 504 plans, and the two are not interchangeable.

5)   A.   Incorrect. Because Patricia has not shown the ability to manage money, which could lead to unhealthy living, she should improve these skills prior to living independently.

   B.   Incorrect. Patricia demonstrates some independent living skills and should be pushed towards independence.

   C.   Correct. Patricia should choose a partially supervised facility that will offer her some independence but will also provide the particular support she needs.

   D.   Incorrect. While Patricia does lack budgeting skills, she is capable of living in a more independent situation than that provided by a supervised group home.

6)   **A.   Correct.** Ticket to Work is a government-run program that connects individuals with disabilities who receive SSI or SSDI payments to potential employers.

   B.   Incorrect. Ticket to Work is not involved in funding for tuition.

   C.   Incorrect. Ticket to Work partners with multiple companies and organizations, not just government offices.

   D.   Incorrect. A work experience program is an internship serving as a stepping-stone to employment.

7)   A.   Incorrect. A one-time cooking class does not lead to a degree or certificate; it is therefore not considered a CTE program.

   B.   Incorrect. There is no trade aspect to an English degree; it is therefore not considered a CTE program.

   C.   Correct. A two-year trade program that results in a certificate is considered a CTE program.

   D.   Incorrect. While a volunteer position is a step toward employment, there is no certificate or cumulative degree; therefore it is not considered a CTE program.

8)   A.   Incorrect. OSERS does provide grants for students.

   B.   Incorrect. OSERS does provide information for parents.

   C.   Incorrect. OSERS does provide support in gaining employment for individuals with disabilities.

   D.   Correct. Training and providing students with vocational training leading to a cumulative degree is the objective of a CTE program.

Professional Responsibilities

ROLES AND RESPONSIBILITIES

Special education refers to a range of services and supports provided to students with exceptionalities that allow them to access education and make adequate academic progress. Special education services may include accommodations, modifications, specialized instruction, assistive technology support, and related services. **Special education teachers** are the educators responsible for providing specialized instruction and managing other special education supports according to each student's individualized education program (IEP).

Special education teachers play a central role in ensuring that students with exceptionalities have their individual needs met. Because every student with a disability has unique needs, special education teachers must fill a variety of roles to serve their students. One important role is collaborating with families and a team of professionals to develop an IEP for each student.

In order to recommend appropriate supports for students, special educators must have strong background knowledge in child development, specific disabilities, and grade-level curriculum expectations. They also must have strong communication skills and be able to maintain student confidentiality laws set forth by the Family Educational Rights and Privacy Act (FERPA) and the Individuals with Disabilities Education Act (IDEA). Confidentiality laws require that special education files must be secured and accessible only to school officials with legitimate educational interest (e.g., teachers, counselors, administrators).

Another important responsibility is the delivery of specialized instruction. Special education teachers are responsible for providing interventions in areas of need (often reading, math, writing, or socio-emotional skills) to aid students with disabilities in making progress at the same pace as their peers (even though their learning objectives may be different). They need strong background knowledge in each academic area and an understanding of research-based interventions to maximize student learning. To support all areas of student development, special educators need experience in both social skill and adaptive behavior interventions as well as academic interventions. Special educators work with general education teachers to provide direct and indirect instruction in the classroom. They ensure students receive specified accommodations and modifications, adapting the general education curriculum as necessary.

Special education teachers must be fluent in data collection and analysis. They need to have knowledge of a variety of assessment and evaluation tools, and they need to be able to interpret evaluation results to make service recommendations.

> **QUICK REVIEW**
>
> What might a day in the life of a special education teacher look like?

Once an intervention is implemented and a goal is set, special educators are responsible for collecting data on progress to verify that the intervention is effective. They must be organized and conscientious record-keepers, responsible for documenting progress toward goals and reporting that progress to parents during conferences and annual IEP meetings. Finally, they must participate in professional development opportunities to stay current on best practices in special education and maintain appropriate credentials.

SAMPLE QUESTIONS

1) **What are educators typically responsible for managing services and supports for students with disabilities in the classroom setting called?**

   A.   general education teachers

   B.   school psychologists

   C.   school counselors

   D.   special education teachers

2) **Which of the following is NOT a responsibility of a special education teacher?**

   A.   administering psychological tests

   B.   tracking student progress

   C.   collaborating with families

   D.   planning behavioral interventions

FEDERAL LEGISLATION AND REQUIREMENTS

FEDERAL LEGISLATION

Today's special education landscape has been shaped by federal legislation over the last fifty years. Prior to federal legislation mandating school access, many individuals with disabilities were institutionalized rather than given opportunities for education. In institutions, systemic neglect and abuse was common. In the 1960s, alongside other civil rights movements, the disability rights movement raised public awareness of the treatment of individuals with disabilities. The federal government responded with legislation supporting educational opportunities for people with disabilities. In 1965, Congress enacted the **Elementary and Secondary Education Act (ESEA)**, which seeks to improve student academic achievement through supplementary educational services as well as increased educational research and training. It also provides financial assistance to schools servicing a high percentage of students from low-income families (Title I funding). ESEA was the first legislation to provide states with direct financial assistance to support the education of students with disabilities.

> **DID YOU KNOW?**
>
> In 1970, only one in five children with disabilities attended US schools. In fact, many states at that time had laws excluding students with certain disabilities from school.

A major civil rights victory for individuals with disabilities came with the **Rehabilitation Act of 1973**, which ensures all students with disabilities a right to public education. **Section 504 of the Rehabilitation Act** prohibits programs which receive federal financial assistance from discriminating on the basis of disability. As federally funded institutions, public schools are required to ensure that students with disabilities receive a comparable education to students without disabilities. If a student with a disability does not qualify for services under IDEA, they may still receive support through a *504 plan*. Under Section 504, students with disabilities may receive related services, accommodations, and modifications to ensure equal access to education.

The most comprehensive civil rights legislation for individuals with disabilities to date is the 1990 **Americans with Disabilities Act (ADA)**. The ADA prohibits discrimination on the basis of disability in the workplace and in all public places (e.g., restaurants, parks, schools, businesses). The passage of the ADA has led to increased community access, accessibility of public transportation, and more equal employment opportunities for individuals with disabilities. As a comprehensive civil rights law, the ADA provides another layer of legal protection for the right of students with disabilities to have equal access to public education.

The first legislation targeting educational rights was the 1975 **Education for All Handicapped Children Act (EHA, also referred to as P.L. 94-142)**. P.L. 94-142 expands educational rights for students with disabilities. The legislation ensures that students with disabilities can access any accommodations, modifications, related services, and specially designed instruction needed to make adequate educational progress in a public school setting. Congress reauthorized EHA as the **Individuals with Disabilities Education Act (IDEA)** in 1990 and again with amendments in 1997 and 2004. Part B of IDEA provides for school-aged services for students between the ages of three and twenty-one, while Part C provides for early intervention services for students from birth to three years old.

Since its original authorization, IDEA has operated under six foundational principles:

▶ **Free Appropriate Public Education (FAPE):** FAPE maintains that students with disabilities have a right to an education at no additional cost to parents. (Parents of students with disabilities are still responsible for school fees which apply to all students.) The education is required to meet the student's unique educational needs in a public school setting.

▶ **Appropriate and Nondiscriminatory Evaluation:** Evaluations must be completed by a team of trained professionals (e.g., teachers, school psychologists) and should include information from parents. Evaluations should address all areas of concern, and materials must be sound and nondiscriminatory. Evaluations must be conducted in a timely manner, and re-evaluations must occur a minimum of every three years.

▶ **Individualized Education Program (IEP):** An IEP is a legal document developed by the IEP team (parents, general educators, special educators, administrators, related service providers) which reports present levels of performance, annual goals and objectives, accommodations, modifications, related services, and specially designed instruction in order to make adequate educational progress. See page 12, *Individualized Education Program*, for details.

▶ **Least Restrictive Environment (LRE):** Students with disabilities must be provided supports with nondisabled peers to the maximum extent appropriate for them to make educational progress. This includes **access to the general curriculum**, which ensures students with disabilities have access to the same curriculum as their nondisabled peers. LRE emphasizes placement in the general education classroom with supplemental aides and services as much as possible.

▶ **Parent (and student) Participation**: Parents must have a shared role in all special education decisions, including IEP reviews, evaluation, and placement decisions.

▶ **Procedural Safeguards**: Parents must receive written notice of procedural safeguards, parent and student rights, meetings, and all educational decisions. Parents have access to all student educational records. Parents may take due process measures in the event of a disagreement between the parent and a school district.

QUICK REVIEW

What impact did IDEA have on the education of students with disabilities? Can you give an example of each of the six principles?

The most recent authorization of IDEA is the **2004 Individuals with Disabilities Education Improvement Act**. IDEA 2004 expands procedures for identifying students with learning disabilities to include identification through response to intervention. IDEA 2004 also includes several changes to align with the 2001 **No Child Left Behind (NCLB)** legislation. The main purpose of NCLB is to improve the academic performance of all students through increased accountability for results, emphasizing research-based instruction and ensuring such instruction is delivered by **highly qualified teachers (HQT)**.

Title I of NCLB provided schools with high percentages of students from low-income families with increased funding to support additional academic assistance for students who were struggling. NCLB required teachers of Title I programs and teachers of core academic subjects to be highly qualified in the subject area they teach by meeting content knowledge and teaching skill requirements. The legislation increased school accountability for students' performance by requiring that all (including students with disabilities, with accommodations if needed) participate in standardized assessments over rigorous state academic standards. Title I funds were contingent upon participation in and performance on the required state assessments. In alignment with new requirements under NCLB, IDEA 2004 increases requirements for HQT in the area of special education and further emphasizes the access of students with disabilities to the general education curriculum (including general education assessments).

In 2015, Congress passed the **Every Student Succeeds Act (ESSA)** to replace NCLB, effective starting the 2017 – 2018 school year. ESSA rolls back many of the federal education requirements, giving power back to the states. Under ESSA, states are required to create accountability plans, track state-set accountability goals, and incorporate accountability systems (e.g., state assessments, English language proficiency, postsecondary readiness, and school safety). ESSA removes the federal HQT requirement of NCLB. However, each state must set expectations for ensuring highly qualified teachers are providing instruction. Moreover, ESSA maintains the state assessment requirements of NCLB and Title I funding for schools.

Table 8.1. IEP versus Section 504 Plan

	IEP	Section 504 Plan
Law	Individuals with Disabilities Education Act (IDEA)	Section 504 of the Rehabilitation Act of 1973
Department	Department of Education	Office of Civil Rights
Eligibility	a disability as defined in IDEA that impacts educational performance	a disability that impacts a major life function
Included	specialized education services, accommodations, modifications, related services	accommodations, modifications, related services
Age	0 to 21 years	no age limits
Location	schools through grade 12	school through grade 12, college, work

SAMPLE QUESTIONS

3) **Which provision of IDEA stipulates that parents must receive written notification of educational placement decisions?**
    A.   parent participation
    B.   procedural safeguards
    C.   individualized education program
    D.   appropriate evaluation

4) **Which of the following was the first legislation to provide students with disabilities the right to a public education?**
    A.   Individuals with Disabilities Education Act (IDEA)
    B.   Education for All Handicapped Children Act (EHA)
    C.   Elementary and Secondary Education Act (ESEA)
    D.   Section 504 of the Rehabilitation Act

IMPORTANT COURT CASES

Supreme Court decisions have been equally important in ensuring rights for individuals with disabilities. Time and again, families have challenged the court to guarantee that students with disabilities receive opportunities equal to those of their nondisabled peers. Cases argued in the US court systems have ensured that current laws are fully implemented and have even spurred new legislation.

Brown v. Topeka Board of Education (1954) resulted in a landmark civil rights decision which establishes that segregation on the basis of race is illegal. Further, the decision strikes down the idea that facilities can be "separate but equal." Though the ruling is based on racial segregation, the *Brown* decision that separate facilities are "inherently unequal" holds implications for children with disabilities educated in separate facilities from their nondisabled peers. The *Brown* ruling increases educational opportunities for historically marginalized populations. It prompted investigations into the current state of education which laid the foundation for ESEA in 1965.

The *Diana v. State Board of Education of California* (1970) case focused on appropriate evaluation procedures for students whose primary language is not English. Diana, a student who primarily spoke Spanish, was placed in an "educable mentally retarded program" based on the results of an IQ test given in English. The plaintiffs in the case argued that the IQ tests were culturally biased and resulted in discrimination against non-English speaking students. The court ruled that evaluations should be based on tests given to students in their native language. The ruling contributed to the inclusion of nondiscriminatory evaluation guidelines in P.L. 94-142.

In 1971, the Pennsylvania Association for Retarded Children (PARC) sued the Commonwealth of Pennsylvania over a law which allowed schools to deny children who had not "attained the mental age of five years" entry into public education. The plaintiffs argued the laws violated the *Brown* ruling and their rights under the Fourteenth Amendment to the Constitution. The case ended in a consent agreement which deemed the laws at the time were unconstitutional and required the state to provide education for all exceptional students. The ***PARC v. Pennsylvania*** agreement provides some of the framework for FAPE requirements in IDEA.

Plaintiffs representing African American school children in California challenged the use of IQ tests for placement into "educable mentally retarded" ("EMR") programs in ***Larry P. v. Riles*** (1972). The plaintiffs presented evidence that IQ tests resulted in African American students being placed in alternate programs at a disproportionate rate and were therefore discriminatory. While African American students made up only 10 percent of the Californian population at the time, they represented 25 percent of the population in the "EMR" program. The court ruled that the IQ tests were racially discriminatory and could not be the sole determinant to place students in alternate educational programs.

The intent of the FAPE requirement of IDEA was challenged in the 1982 case of ***Board of Education of the Hendrick Hudson Central School District v. Rowley (Hudson v. Rowley)***. Amy Rowley was a kindergarten student in the Hudson School District who was deaf and making educational progress consistent with her peers in the general education setting through the use of a frequency modulation (FM) hearing aid, daily intervention with a tutor for people who are deaf, and speech therapy. At her annual IEP meeting, Amy's parents requested a sign language interpreter, arguing that Amy was making progress but not meeting her potential without the interpreter. After court decisions and appeals won by both sides, the case was seen by the Supreme Court. The Supreme Court ruled in favor of the school district, explaining that FAPE requires schools to provide access to education and student growth, but schools are not required to demonstrate that they have maximized each student's potential.

> **DID YOU KNOW?**
>
> The Rowley decision is considered one of the most significant special education decisions because it was the only occasion the Supreme Court ruled on the requirement of schools to provide FAPE to students until the *Endrew F. v. Douglas County School District* (2017) case. Since the ruling, it has been cited by over 3,280 other cases.

The case of ***Irving Independent School District v. Tatro*** (1984) challenged whether catheterization is required as a related service. Amber Tatro was an eight-year-old with spina bifida who required catheterization every three hours in order to prevent kidney damage. The school refused to provide Amber with catheterization as part of her IEP, stating that it was a medical service rather than a related service. The Supreme Court ruled that catheterization was required for Amber to receive FAPE and qualified as a related service because a physician is not required to administer the procedure.

The Supreme Court's decision in **Honig v. Doe** (1988) established new disciplinary requirements for schools when dealing with students with disabilities. The issue in the case was whether a school could exclude or expel a student for actions arising from the student's disability. The court ruled that a student may not be removed for behavior resulting from their disability without due process rights provided for in IDEA. The Court established the "ten-day rule" which requires a "manifestation determination" review once a child has been suspended from school for ten days in a school year. The purpose of the manifestation review is to determine whether the behavior is a manifestation of the student's disability.

The case of **Cedar Rapids Community School District v. Garret F.** (1999) once again brought the issue of the provision of health services in school to the Supreme Court. Garret F. was a student who required one-on-one physical assistance in order to attend school. The school district argued that it was not obligated to provide the service because it was medical service which was too much of a financial burden. Citing its previous *Tatro* (1984) decision, the Court ruled in favor of the plaintiff stating the services needed were not "medical services" because they did not require a physician. Furthermore, the court ruled that the district must fund the related service in order to guarantee that Garret had access to FAPE.

When the appropriateness of an IEP is in dispute, is it the responsibility of the school district to prove the effectiveness of the IEP? This question of burden of proof is addressed by the Supreme Court in **Schaffer v. Weast** (2005). The court determined that when an IEP is questioned, the burden of proof is owned by the complaining party. In short, if parents question the appropriateness of an IEP, it is the responsibility of the parents to prove that the IEP services are ineffective.

When parents and school districts cannot come to an agreement on services, parents must often turn to the court system to advance their case. The case of **Arlington Central School District v. Pearl and Theodore Murphy** (2006) addressed the issue of whether school districts must reimburse parents' expert legal fees in instances where parents prevail over districts in court decisions. The court ruled that while IDEA does provide reimbursement for reasonable attorney's fee, school districts are not required to pay expert fees.

In 2007, Jeff and Sandee Winkelman filed suit in order to provide their son with paid placement in a private school. The appeals court dismissed the suit due to the Winkelmans filing without a lawyer. In the case of **Winkelman v. Parma City School District** (2007), the Winkelmans then argued that they had the right to act on behalf of their child under IDEA. The Supreme Court ruled that parents had the right to represent their child in special education cases before the federal court without a lawyer present.

The 2017 case of **Endrew F. v. Douglas County School District** challenged the intent of FAPE in IDEA, especially as concerns what is considered an appropriate education. In the public school setting, Endrew, a student with autism, exhibited behaviors including screaming, running away, and climbing. In fourth grade, his parents decided to place him in a school specializing in educating students with autism. With more supports at the new school, Endrew made significant behavioral and academic progress. Endrew's parents sued the Douglas County School District for reimbursement for his private school tuition, arguing that because the public school was not able meet his educational needs, it should pay his private school tuition under IDEA. The school district argued that Endrew was making adequate (if not maximized) progress in public school. The court ruled unanimously in favor of Endrew, stating that appropriate progress for most children would allow them to be integrated into the classroom and advance from grade to grade.

SAMPLE QUESTIONS

5) **Which Supreme Court case helped lead to the Elementary and Secondary Education Act (ESEA) by spurring investigations into the current state of education?**

   A. *Endrew F. v. Douglas County*

   B. *Brown v. Topeka Board of Education*

   C. *Irving v. Tatro*

   D. *Arlington School District v. Pearl and Theodore Murphy*

6) **Court cases such as *Diana v. State Board of Education of California* and *Larry P. v. Riles* mandate**

   A. that related services be provided.

   B. nondiscriminatory evaluation.

   C. access to the general education curriculum.

   D. testing accommodations.

DETERMINATION OF ELIGIBILITY

School districts are responsible for determining if students are eligible for special education services under IDEA. Districts must follow a multi-step process for identifying which students may benefit from special education services and conduct a multifaceted evaluation to determine if identified students qualify for supports.

1. **Recognition**: The recognition phase of determining eligibility consists of identifying students who appear to be struggling academically or behaviorally. Many schools use a **response to intervention (RTI)** process to recognize struggling students. **Tier 1** of the RTI process involves research-based, differentiated instruction for all learners in a general education setting. As part of tier 1, schools conduct **universal screenings** to assess the academic and behavioral performances of all students. Students who do not meet pre-set benchmarks are identified as "at risk." The RTI process is discussed in depth in chapter 4.

2.   **Pre-referral**: Many schools have **student assistance teams** (also called student support teams, teacher assistance teams, intervention assistance teams, and so forth) that contribute to recommendations about appropriate supports for at-risk students. Student assistance teams may include the general education teacher, an administrator, the student's parents, special education teachers, school counselors, school psychologists, and any other personnel who work with the student.

Student assistance teams (which should include a student's parents) work together to determine if a student may benefit from additional services in **tier 2** of the RTI process. Tier 2 services are interventions provided in addition to tier 1 instruction. Tier 2 interventions are usually done in small groups three to five times a week. They may include pre-teaching or reteaching of material or may be supplemental interventions to the core curriculum. Student performance in tier 2 is frequently progress-monitored (usually weekly) to assess if students are making adequate growth with the supports provided. After six to eight weeks of progress monitoring is collected, student assistance teams determine if interventions are effective.

If students are not progressing in tier 2, they may be considered for more intensive interventions as part of **tier 3**. At tier 3 of the RTI process, students receive intensive, individualized interventions. Often, students who require tier 3 interventions are referred by the student assistance team for comprehensive evaluation.

Table 8.2. Tiers of the RTI Process

	Assessment	Instruction
Tier 1	▸ Benchmark assessments: fall, winter, spring ▸ Core program assessments ▸ Screening	▸ Low risk ▸ Regular education ▸ Benchmark in core program ▸ Regular classroom instruction ▸ Extra support/enrichment in small groups ▸ Research-based supplemental programs
Tier 2	▸ Benchmark assessments: fall, winter, spring ▸ Core program assessments ▸ Progress monitoring (regularly) ▸ Diagnostic assessments	▸ Some risk ▸ Regular education ▸ Below benchmark in core program ▸ Regular classroom instruction ▸ Pre-teaching/reteaching in small groups ▸ Research-based supplemental programs

	Assessment	Instruction
Tier 3	▸ Benchmark assessments: fall, winter, spring ▸ Core program assessments ▸ Progress monitoring (frequently) ▸ Diagnostic assessments	▸ At risk ▸ Regular and/or special education ▸ Unsuccessful in core program ▸ Small-group instruction ▸ Intensive support in core ▸ Research-based remedial/replacement programs

3. **Referral**: A referral for a comprehensive special education evaluation may be made by school personnel, parents, or other adult guardians. Schools must have evidence to support that interventions within the general education environment (such as through the RTI process) are not adequate for appropriate educational progress before initiating a referral. IDEA allows parents to initiate a referral for eligibility for special education services at any time. Once a referral is made, written **parent consent** is needed, meaning parents must agree to have their child undergo a comprehensive evaluation. Usually, written consent is obtained in a face-to-face meeting with parents where an evaluation plan is created based on potential areas of need. Schools have sixty days to complete the evaluation once a referral is made.

4. **Evaluation**: Evaluations are conducted by a **multidisciplinary evaluation team** (eligibility team). Multidisciplinary teams often include school psychologists, special educators, general educators, and parents. They may also include related service providers, such as physical therapists, occupational therapists, and speech language pathologists. Depending on the nature of the disability, medical records may also be collected as part of the evaluation. The evaluation must include a comprehensive battery of technically sound assessments as well as informal observations and background information. Areas of assessment may include adaptive behavior, cognition, communication, academic achievement, motor skills, socio-emotional behavior, and health. Vision and hearing screenings must also be done as part of the assessment process. All assessments must be administered in a student's primary language. Assessments should be chosen based on their likelihood to provide accurate information about the child's development and may not be biased in regard to language, race, culture, or disability.

5. **Eligibility**: Assessments, observations, and background information are collected into

DID YOU KNOW?

Research suggests a gender bias in special education placement. Even after controlling for academic and behavioral performance, boys are twice as likely as girls to qualify for special education services.

an **eligibility report** (evaluation team report). Once evaluations are complete, the multidisciplinary team meets to review the report and determine if a student is eligible for special education services. A student is eligible for special education services if the evaluation demonstrates the child has a disability and an educational need that requires specially designed instruction as a result of that disability. School districts must also show that the educational need is not a result of lack of appropriate instruction or a biased assessment process. For example, if a student is an English language learner, the report must demonstrate that the student received research-based instruction and intervention for English language learners and the assessments adequately assessed ability with cultural bias.

The multidisciplinary team, with parents as equal participants, must determine if the student meets eligibility requirements based on the information in the eligibility report. Students may qualify for services under the fourteen disability categories described in IDEA. If the team determines that the student meets eligibility requirements, the school district has thirty days to meet with parents about an IEP.

SAMPLE QUESTIONS

7) **Courtney is a second-grade student who is half a year behind her peers in reading. She participates in a small group reading intervention three days a week to try to catch up to grade-level expectations. Which tier of the RTI process is Courtney most likely in?**

   A. tier 1

   B. tier 2

   C. tier 3

   D. She is a special education student and not part of RTI.

8) **Elijah's parents wrote to the school principal requesting that he be evaluated for special education services. Should the school district move forward with a formal evaluation?**

   A. No; the school does not have enough intervention information.

   B. Yes; the school has thirty days to complete an evaluation.

   C. No; Elijah's parents must write to the special education director.

   D. Yes; the school has sixty days to complete an evaluation.

INDIVIDUALIZED EDUCATION PROGRAM

Once a student qualifies for special education services, the next step is the development of an **individualized education program (IEP)**. Briefly addressed earlier in this chapter, an IEP is a legal contract between the parents and school district which presents a plan of services and goals to ensure that a student with a disability makes growth in their current educational environment. The individual education plan is developed by a team of professionals and parents.

The IEP team MUST include

- the parent or legal guardian of the student;
- one general education teacher;
- one special education teacher;
- a representative of the school (often a school administrator);
- an individual who can interpret evaluations;
- the student (when appropriate).

The IEP team MAY include

- related services providers (e.g., physical or occupational therapists, speech-language pathologists, audiologists, and so forth);
- representatives from community agencies;
- other family members;
- a parent advocate.

The team is responsible for writing a **legally defensible IEP**, meaning that the IEP will stand up in court as providing the student with FAPE. Legally defensible IEPs are composed of several main components.

IEPs must include dates of initiation and duration of services and goals. The IEP must be reviewed at least once each year, although progress toward goals is reported more frequently. Each IEP contains a student profile. The profile contains background information as well as the preferences, interests, needs, and strengths of the student. A student profile should also report classroom and formal assessments and a statement of educational need based on the disability.

IEPs include goal pages. Goal pages indicate the student's present level of performance and set goals for growth. A student should have at least one **measurable annual goal** for each area of need identified through the evaluation process. For each goal, a statement of the present level of academic or functional performance must be provided. The present level of performance indicates the student's current level of achievement in the areas for which goals will be set. Legally defensible IEPs must include goals which are measurable. Each goal contains benchmarks or objectives that must be achieved for the goal to be met. *Objectives* are subskills that must be mastered to achieve larger goals; *benchmarks* are incremental steps increasing degree of mastery from baseline until the expectation stated in the goal. To be measurable, goals must answer the following questions:

- Who? (e.g., the student)
- Will do what? (What behavior or skill will the student demonstrate? It must be observable.)
- To what level or degree? (indicates expectation for mastery)

▶ Under what condition? (What setting, prompting level, or materials will trigger the behavior?)

▶ In what length of time? (What is the time frame for the goal to be mastered?)

▶ How will progress be measured? (e.g., assessment method for goal)

For students aged sixteen or older, the IEP must include a **transition plan**, or a plan for students to obtain long-term goals once they graduate. Transition plans include goals for postsecondary education or training, employment, and independent living (if necessary). The IEP must determine a plan of services to be provided to achieve transition goals. Some examples of possible transition services include special instruction, community experiences, career or college counseling, help with daily living skills, or job explorations. Student interests should guide the transition plan, with students taking a leadership role in developing the plan.

IEPs must include a clear description of services which will be provided to the student to ensure he or she makes adequate educational growth. For each area of need, a student should receive specially designed instruction. A clear statement of specially designed instruction includes

▶ the type of instruction to be provided;

▶ the setting in which it will be delivered;

▶ the service provider who will deliver the instruction;

▶ the amount of time the instruction will be provided.

The IEP must also provide a list of accommodations and modifications which will be provided to the student. **Accommodations** are changes in how information is presented or assessed that do not change what the student is expected to master. Some examples of accommodations include extra time to complete assignments, breaks during instruction, specialized keyboards, a quiet workspace, or visual supports. **Modifications** make fundamental changes to the curriculum. Modifications may include shortening assignments, providing texts at a lower reading level, or using alternate assessments which are less rigorous than the standard exam.

Most states require written educational plans for students who are eligible for gifted education. However, requirements for gifted testing, eligibility, and planning vary from state to state. Some states use **educational plans (EPs)** for students who are eligible for gifted education. Similar to an IEP, an EP identifies the specific needs of a student and describes the services which will be put in place to ensure those needs are met. EP participant requirements mirror those of IEPs. EPs also include a student profile, measurable goals, and a description of specially designed instruction. Unlike IEPs, most states do not require EPs to be reviewed annually, and students on an EP do not qualify for standardized testing accommodations.

Throughout the evaluation and IEP process, procedural safeguards for parents must be protected. **Procedural safeguards** are guarantees for parents and students for participation in the IEP process, access to student educational information, and options for solving disagreements. As part of their procedural safeguards, parents should receive written invitations to all meetings. They should also receive in writing any educational decision which will affect their child's educational placement or program (called a prior written notice). Parents have access at any time to their child's educational records. When parents and school districts are unable to come to an agreement, parents may exercise their due process rights to settle disagreements through arbitration. Prior to an evaluation or IEP, parents should be given a copy of their procedural safeguards in writing.

SAMPLE QUESTIONS

9) Mr. Peralta wrote an annual IEP for his twelve-year-old student, Mark. In the IEP, he included a student profile, service dates, measurable goals and benchmarks, specially designed instruction, and accommodations. Which of the following components is missing for Mark's IEP to be legally defensible?

   A.   transition plan

   B.   related services

   C.   present level of performance

   D.   strengths and interests

10) Who are the required members of an IEP team?

   A.   parent, general education teacher, special education teacher, and an individual who can interpret evaluations

   B.   parent, school psychologist, special education teacher, school representative, and an individual who can interpret evaluations

   C.   parent, general education teacher, school psychologist, school representative, and an individual who can interpret evaluations

   D.   parent, general education teacher, special education teacher, school representative, and an individual who can interpret evaluations

SPECIAL EDUCATION IN PRIVATE SCHOOLS

Most laws that govern the rights to education of students with disabilities, such as IDEA, apply only to publicly funded institutions (public schools). Therefore, students with disabilities who attend private schools are not guaranteed the same services a child might receive in a public school. However, public schools maintain some responsibility for ensuring a student who lives within the school district receives services, even if the student attends a private school.

The IDEA **Child Find** mandate requires public school districts to identify and evaluate any student within the district who may have a disability. The Child Find mandate applies to students who attend private school and to students who are home-schooled. Therefore, if the parents or school of a student suspects a disability, the public school where the child would attend is responsible for conducting a full evaluation to determine if the child is eligible for special education.

In most cases, a child eligible for special education who attends private school receives services under an **instructional school plan (ISP)**. ISPs are created through collaboration between the private school and the public school district. Like IEPs, ISPs require measurable annual goals and supports, such as direct instruction and therapy. However unlike IEPs, ISPs require school districts to provide only equitable services to students in a private school setting. **Equitable services** (such as speech therapy, physical therapy, or reading intervention) for a private school setting may be less frequent and intense than those that a student would receive in a public school setting. Students with disabilities in a private school setting should receive full accommodations under Section 504 of the Rehabilitation Act.

Some private schools specialize in working with students with disabilities. For example, parents may want their child to attend a school for children with autism or learning disabilities. In some cases, if the school district and the parents agree that a private school placement is optimal for a student's needs, the school district may cover the cost of the private school. If a public school district refers a student to a private school, the public school district is responsible for the student receiving all services mandated by IDEA. If a parent and school district disagree over where a child should attend school, parents may exercise due process rights to try to mandate that the public school provide funding or services in the private school setting.

SAMPLE QUESTION

11) **Which federal mandate requires public schools to evaluate a student who may have a disability?**

    A.   equitable services

    B.   due process

    C.   Section 504

    D.   Child Find

COLLABORATION

Special education is a team effort. IDEA requires educational decisions to be made by a team of professionals in collaboration with the student and his or her family. Ensuring that the unique needs of an individual with a disability are met requires constant collaboration and communication between everyone on the student's team. As case managers, special education teachers are often responsible for facilitating the communication and collaboration among the various members of a student's educational team.

Collaboration means that all team members are working together toward mutual goals. When everyone on a student's team is working together toward a common goal, services are most effective. However, collaboration requires work. In true collaboration, everyone shares responsibility, resources, and accountability for implementation and results. Stakeholders must give up territoriality and be willing to work with others. Collaboration means consistently improving communication and ensuring all team members are valued contributors.

Effective collaboration has many benefits. Student performance is maximized, students may have greater access to their LRE, and expertise and resources are shared to the benefit of all. Proper collaboration leads to improved respect and understanding among team members. Still, collaboration has its challenges. Planning and style are common obstacles. People within the team may need to overcome personality conflicts or differences in teaching styles. Everyone must be willing to communicate honestly without fear of judgment or criticism. Each team member must trust that everyone is working toward the best interest of the student.

FAMILY–SCHOOL COLLABORATION

Within a special education team, collaboration encompasses many stakeholders, and parents are especially important stakeholders in a student's education. Research has consistently shown that students achieve better when parents are actively involved in their education, and collaboration between teachers and parents is one of the main principles of IDEA.

An important component of an effective parent-teacher collaborative relationship is open communication. **Open communication** allows parents and teachers to work together to make the best decisions for students' academic progress. Parents often have unique knowledge of their child's medical and educational history—knowledge that is essential in making appropriate service decisions for students. Especially when students are younger, communication with parents often begins prior to the beginning of the school year. Many schools have "meet the teacher" nights when parents, students, and teachers can build an understanding of expectations before school starts.

Special education teachers may find it helpful to schedule a more private meeting with parents of students with disabilities. At an early meeting, parents and teachers can work together to make sure all needed supports are in place before the student arrives at school. A student's health needs, motivators and interests, and any behavior plans or concerns should be discussed. Teachers should listen to parent contributions and concerns for the upcoming school year.

During the meeting, parents and teachers should establish expectations for how school and home will work together toward student learning. For example, are there behavior plans or homework expectations that will need to be completed each day once a child arrives home? Teachers should identify the best methods and times to contact and meet parents; likewise, they should share with parents easy ways to contact them with questions or concerns. A plan for ongoing, two-way communication should be established between home and school settings. Some common communication strategies include

▶   home-school communication notebooks;

▶   daily behavioral checklists;

▶   emails sent home;

▶   daily messages through school-wide software.

Throughout the school year, teachers and families should work together to implement goals and evaluate the effectiveness of the current educational plan.

Family-school collaboration must be built on a relationship of trust and understanding. To build the relationship, many barriers must often be overcome. Families and professionals both may experience some uneasiness entering into the relationship. Parents may have anxiety about advocating for their child or fear that their child will not be able to get the support he or she needs. Teachers can help ease parents' concerns by offering training sessions or providing them with information about available local and online resources supporting parents of students with disabilities. Some parents may be more willing to take an active role in their child's education. Even when a family is hesitant, it is the responsibility of the special educator to plan opportunities for parent involvement.

Professionals may worry that they will not be able to meet the demands of the family. Professionals can show understanding of parents' requests, even when unable to fulfill them, and help parents identify options and support collaborative problem-solving. Either partner may feel that the responsibility for student growth is not shared equally. For an equal partnership, school professionals need to respect parents' expertise and values for their child. Parents, likewise, need to honor the important role school professionals play in their child's development and respect their specialized training and experiences. Both parties must be willing to communicate with the other, and professionals must make it a priority to protect confidentiality for both family and child.

Building a trustful relationship may be especially difficult when there are cultural, socio-economic, or language barriers. It is important for professionals to gain an understanding of a student's racial, cultural, and socio-economic background and to respect it. Teachers need to build personal relationships with the family to understand these unique values rather than make assumptions based on the student's background. If necessary, an interpreter may be used to foster communication. Understanding comes through giving families the opportunity to share their personal experiences and cultural values, and basing interactions with the family according to their individual preference.

Figure 8.1. Keys for Successful Family-School Collaboration

SAMPLE QUESTION

12) Mrs. Violet is a teacher for elementary students with multiple disabilities. She always meets with the families of her students prior to the start of school. What is one important reason for Mrs. Violet to meet with families right away?

A.   to gain access to a student's IEP

B.   to gain access to a student's most recent evaluation

C.   to ensure that supports are in place for a student's physical and emotional needs

D.   to assess whether any skills may have been lost over the summer

COLLABORATING WITH OTHER PROFESSIONALS

Parents and special education teachers often play a central role in planning the appropriate services for a student to make educational progress. However, the education of a student with a disability also often involves a team of professionals working together to meet the best needs of the child.

Students with disabilities should be integrated as much as possible with peers who are not disabled. Almost all students with disabilities are responsible for mastering general education standards. Therefore, **general education teachers** are often responsible for the majority of instruction for students with disabilities. Collaboration between special education teachers and general education teachers is important to ensure that all of a student's individual needs are met in the general education setting. One model of collaboration between special education and general education teachers is co-teaching. In **co-teaching**, general education and special education teachers work together to plan and deliver instruction in integrated classrooms.

Even when not co-teaching, special education and general education teachers work together to meet the needs of all students. Shared planning, or teaming time, strengthens the ability of teachers to effectively collaborate. Special education teachers need to be familiar with the standards and curriculum in each classroom they service. Special education teachers should work with general education teachers before the beginning of the school year to ensure that general education teachers understand the accommodations and services for each student with disabilities in their classroom. Throughout the school year, special education teachers should provide support for differentiation of instruction and assessment, the adaptation of classroom materials, pre-teaching concepts, accommodations, or the delivery of interventions.

Paraprofessionals also play an important role in providing supports for students with disabilities. Paraprofessionals work closely with special education teachers to provide accommodations, implement behavior plans, and sometimes provide instruction. They are often instrumental in ensuring supports and services for a student are provided throughout the school day. Consistently provided accommodations and interventions delivered with fidelity are extremely important for students with disabilities to make educational progress. Paraprofessionals are often responsible for delivering those services.

The special education teacher must provide corrective feedback when necessary to ensure that paraprofessionals are effectively supporting students. Special education teachers need to clearly communicate expectations to paraprofessionals. They often set paraprofessionals' schedules and determine which specific students they will be working with. Special education teachers may also be responsible for planning interventions and activities and training paraprofessionals to effectively deliver those interventions. Regular meetings with written expectations and agreements between general education teachers, special education teachers, and paraprofessionals are important to ensure that services are being delivered consistently across providers.

School psychologists often take a leading role in the evaluation and identification process. School psychologists administer psychological tests to students, discuss developmental history with parents, and obtain social-emotional information from teachers and parents. They advise evaluation team members on potential educational supports based on the results of the evaluation. School psychologists can also serve as valuable resources to work with parents, teachers, and students to develop and implement interventions for the social-emotional needs of students.

School counselors serve a variety of roles within the school setting, which varies by academic level. At all levels, school counselors support students' social and emotional development through individual or group counseling. They listen to students' concerns and help develop problem-solving skills. They may help build school/parent relationships and can be a resource for other mental health services. School counselors may facilitate drug prevention programs. At the secondary level, school counselors may help with scheduling. They support student transitions into adult life through job interest inventories, transition planning, college applications, job attainment skills, and scholarship applications. School counselors and special education teachers often work together to build social skills and support successful transitions to adult life for students.

Another professional who works with family relationships and students' social-emotional well-being is the **school social worker**. School social workers provide social work services within the school setting. They act as a liaison between community resources, families, and schools. School social workers may perform home visits to help support home/school collaboration. They often work together with special education teachers to provide social-emotional interventions with students and to coordinate supports with community resources and families.

Speech/language pathologists (SLPs) provide therapy to students with speech and language difficulties. SLPs may provide therapy in a pull-out or inclusive setting. Speech disorders may include articulation errors, disfluency, or problems with voice resonance. Language disorders include difficulty with receptive language (e.g., understanding others) and expressive language (e.g., communicating ideas). Special educators can collaborate with SLPs to practice targeted speech sounds or to integrate curricular targets into language therapy. For students who are nonverbal, SLPs and special education teachers may work together to implement augmentative and alternative communication (AAC) systems for students.

> **STUDY TIP**
>
> When you think of <u>receptive</u> communication, picture *receiving* information from another person. When you think of <u>expressive</u> communication, picture *expressing* your ideas to someone else.

School nurses provide direct health care services to students. An important role of school nurses is to promote a healthy school environment through education, verification of immunizations, infectious disease reporting, and mandated health screening programs. They assess students who have health complaints and contact parents when necessary. School nurses administer medications and perform daily care for students. They work with other members of IEP and 504 teams to develop individualized health care plans for students with special health needs.

Occupational therapists provide support for students who have difficulty completing activities necessary in daily life. Occupational therapists may work with students on fine motor skills like handwriting and typing. They address daily living needs such as self-feeding, shoe tying, and clothing fasteners. Occupational therapists also address sensory needs that may be interfering with learning or other daily living activities. Occupational therapists or occupational therapy assistants often perform weekly therapy with students and consult with special education or general education teachers. It is often the responsibility of the special education teacher to ensure that the accommodations and interventions recommended by the occupational therapist are implemented throughout the school week.

QUICK REVIEW

What are some keys for successful collaboration between special education teachers and other educational team members?

Physical therapists work in the school setting with students who need gross motor and functional mobility support in order to access the school environment. They perform direct therapy with students and work with other school professionals to provide adaptations as needed to provide access. They also work as a liaison between schools, medical personnel, and medical equipment vendors. Physical therapists train school personnel on necessary therapies, appropriate lifting and positioning, and how to adapt environments. Special education teachers and physical therapists work together to ensure functional mobility interventions and supports are consistently provided to students.

Educational interpreters help students who are deaf or hard of hearing access educational environments by providing communication support. They are responsible for accurately relaying classroom instruction to the student. Educational interpreters facilitate communication between educators, students, and families.

SAMPLE QUESTIONS

13) Jamal is a third-grade student. Every day before recess and before going home, he asks for adult help to zip up his coat; sometimes he needs help buttoning his pants after using the restroom. Which professional could Jamal's teacher consult for strategies to help Jamal with fasteners?

   A. school psychologist
   B. school social worker
   C. occupational therapist
   D. physical therapist

14) Which professional would most likely collaborate with a special education teacher to provide a résumé-writing workshop for students?

   A. school counselor
   B. school psychologist
   C. occupational therapist
   D. educational interpreter

BIAS ISSUES

Within the school system, the attitudes of teachers and students toward a student with a disability impact functioning. Unfortunately, **bias** continues to be an issue in the school setting. **Bias** is a belief that favors one group over another. Bias is problematic in that people may not be aware of their biased attitudes or actions and deny their biased actions affect others.

One difficulty with bias is that people often might not recognize it or be conscious of their biased attitudes and therefore don't feel it affects the way they interact with others. **Systemic bias** occurs when everyday practices (e.g., hiring practices, curriculum or testing in the case of school) result in the advancement of one group over another. Bias may be based on culture, socio-economic status, race, or ability.

Some bias occurs based on a student's ethnicity or race. An **ethnic group** is a group of people who share cultural similarities. **Culture** refers to language, arts, music, heritage, foods, and other similarities within a social group. While ethnicity primarily relates to common experiences, **race** is based on the appearance of a person (especially skin color). Other traits associated with race may include hair and eye color and bone structure.

Teachers may hold bias—including unconscious bias—toward ethnic and racial groups as well as students affected by poverty. For example, some teachers are biased toward students who are African American or poor and therefore hold lower behavioral and academic expectations of them. African American students and students from low-income families are also suspended more frequently than their peers. On the other hand, teachers may have higher expectations for students with an East Asian or South Asian background.

Systemic bias occurs within the school system when minority groups, such as African Americans, have less access to high quality education. Another example of systemic bias is a lack of high quality, culturally relevant instructional materials for certain minority groups. Schools can combat bias through professional development to help teachers recognize their own bias. A culture of respect for and education about diversity is also important in reducing bias in schools.

Bias may lead to **disproportionality**, or unequal representation, of ethnic or racial groups in special education. Disproportionality often is determined using a **standard risk ratio** which compares the risk of one group to the risk of all other groups combined (e.g., risk percentage of African Americans versus risk percentage of all other groups combined). Using a risk-ratio measurement, some ethnic or racial groups are much more likely to be placed in special education. Black students are nearly twice as likely as white students to be labeled as cognitively disabled or having an emotional or behavioral disorder. Other groups, such as Asian students, are under-represented in special education programs when compared with the general population.

Research indicates that many students and teachers still possess negative bias toward students with disabilities. Teachers may view students with disabilities as inferior to other students or prefer working with students without disabilities. Some teachers feel students with disabilities cannot learn, are always behavior problems, or will increase their workload. Similarly, many students report preferring to play or work with students without disabilities. Attitudes toward individuals with disabilities affect access to the general education system, leading to low expectations and less inclusion for students with disabilities. Negative attitudes toward people with disabilities have been linked to discrimination toward those individuals. Students with disabilities may internalize the negative attitudes and actions of others, leading to low self-esteem and difficulty with social relationships and education.

QUICK REVIEW

Which biases might affect you as a teacher? What can you do to address these?

The impact of negative attitudes on the functioning of students with disabilities can have long-lasting adverse consequences. Therefore, it is important for teachers and school systems to be aware of such behavior and to work to promote positive attitudes toward students with disabilities. Research has shown that negative attitudes toward students are often linked to feelings of inadequacy in staff supporting students with disabilities. Therefore, it is important that personnel working with those students have adequate training and supports to feel prepared to provide services.

Training to increase knowledge and understanding of students with disabilities can improve attitudes of adults and peers. Teachers should be supported in accommodating and differentiating learning to emphasize the strengths of all learners. They should also be trained in strategies to promote social interactions between individuals with disabilities and their peers, such as modeling appropriate ways to interact. Student attitudes can be improved through cooperative learning groups, collaborative problem solving (e.g., classroom meetings), and peer tutoring. Finally, everyone benefits from a school environment that promotes tolerance for all differences, celebrates diversity, and uses positive behavioral supports.

SAMPLE QUESTIONS

15) When Ms. Johnson gets a new group of kindergartners in her classroom, she believes she will have more behavior problems from students who live in the government-subsidized housing in town. Ms. Johnson's attitudes toward those students is an example of what?

A. bias

B. discrimination

C. hatred

D. harassment

16) Which of the following BEST describes when biased instruction and assessment lead to unequal representation of certain groups in special education?

    A.   discrimination

    B.   disproportionality

    C.   unbiased evaluation

    D.   systemic bias

IMPACT OF FAMILY SYSTEMS OF INDIVIDUALS WITH DISABILITIES

Family systems play a significant role in the development of individuals with disabilities. Conversely, having a child with a disability can have significant impacts on family systems. Most often, families are the constant throughout a student's life. As a special education professional, it is important to recognize that the social and economic reality of each family is unique and understand the impact disability may have within a family system.

ECONOMIC AND SOCIAL CONSIDERATIONS

Economic hardship is more frequent in families with children who have disabilities. In fact, children with disabilities are twice as likely to experience poverty. Financial difficulties are even more common for families who are racial minorities, single-parent households, or have more than one family member with a disability. The impact of financial hardship on families with members with disabilities is two-fold. First, poverty is a major predictor of child health and well-being. Simply put, living with financial hardship may significantly impact the functioning of a child, especially one with a disability. Second, having a child with a disability can lead to many additional expenses for a family. Some additional expenses that arise with a disability may include adaptive equipment, assistive devices, medication expenses, additional insurance cost, and paying for therapies. The increased financial hardship may increase stress within the family system.

Work instability and difficulty finding child care can add to the financial stress already experienced by families. Many children with disabilities have specific medical needs that make it nearly impossible to find an affordable childcare situation beyond family members. As a result, many parents of children with disabilities may have to leave their job or reduce hours in order to make sure their child receives appropriate care. For parents who are able to work, job flexibility is necessary to handle medical or mental health emergencies. Two-parent families of children with disabilities are more likely to include a parent who does not work outside of the home, another parent with reduced work hours, and may be more likely to rely on some public assistance.

Allocation of time is an important consideration for the family of a child with a disability. Children with disabilities may require more time and resources than nondisabled siblings. Siblings may have mixed feelings about their brother or sister with a disability due to the time and care required for their sibling. Parents may have less opportunity for social outings due to childcare concerns and more difficulty going on community outings. Time demands often become physical demands when parents are required to schedule multiple therapies and medical services as well as provide around-the-clock care for their children. Although having a child with a disability may lead to increased stressors on a family, research indicates that social support can work as a sufficient buffer in helping families cope. Many families of students with disabilities may receive social support through extended family, religious organizations, disability groups, and community organizations.

FAMILY MENTAL HEALTH AND RELATIONSHIPS

Having a child with a disability can have mental health implications for all family members. Children with disabilities, siblings, and parents may experience bouts of depression. Studies indicate that having a child with a disability increases the likelihood that parents will divorce or live apart. Some parents of children with disabilities experience guilt or low self-esteem linked to a child's disability. If a disability has a hereditary component, they may feel guilt that they "gave" the child the disability. Parents may feel bad that they didn't catch the disability "early enough" or feel like they cannot give their child the support he or she needs. Some parents might even experience the blame of others for "causing" the disability.

Although unwarranted, feelings of blame and guilt are likely common because the causes of many disabilities remain unknown. When working with a family, a special educator should never blame parents for anything related to their child's disability. Instead, the educator should help families highlight their strengths and help the parents build new skills to support their child's development.

There are also many positive effects of having a family member with a disability. Families with children with disabilities have reported stronger family cohesion. Because of the importance of social support, having a child with a disability may lead to engagement with community or disability groups. Many siblings of children with disabilities are more nurturing and tolerant individuals. Families of children with disabilities demonstrate resilience in persevering through challenges. Furthermore, they demonstrate more openness in accepting the differences of others.

Family relationships can have an enabling or disabling effect on the nature of a disability. If families lack the social support to handle stressors, they will likely negatively impact the growth of their family member with a disability. Some families promote dependency or accept limitations without seeking opportunities for growth. Situations such as abuse and neglect of children also increase the likelihood of a disability. Furthermore, children with disabilities are at increased risk for abuse and neglect. It is the legal obligation of all school staff members to report signs of abuse or neglect.

Most of the time, however, families play a central role in supporting a person with a disability. Family resiliency, cohesion, and open-mindedness can contribute to the maximization of student potential. A caring, resilient environment promotes student self-esteem and student growth. Families, including extended families, often provide support services for individuals with disabilities. An extended family can help provide child care, transportation, and economic support. Extended family can provide emotional support for the person with a disability as well as their parents and siblings. As a special educator working with a family, it is important to provide part of that social support by being understanding of family needs and valuing the contributions they can make.

SAMPLE QUESTIONS

17) **Which of the following is NOT a frequent stressor for families of students with disabilities?**

A.   medical costs

B.   unequal allocation of time between siblings

C.   increased social obligations

D.   lack of child care

18) **What is one probable explanation for the feelings of guilt experienced by parents of children with disabilities?**

A.   The cause of the disability is often unexplained.

B.   The parents were abusive.

C.   The parents were neglectful.

D.   They lack social support.

ENVIRONMENTAL AND SOCIAL INFLUENCES ON INDIVIDUALS WITH DISABILITIES

Contemporary models of disability view it not as a characteristic of a person, but rather a concept of how an individual is able to function within an environment based on societal standards. Consequently, environment often affects the degree of disability experienced by a person. Societal attitudes, accommodations provided, and access to technology play a large role in how a person might experience a disability. Students with very similar skill sets may function differently based on whether their environment is positive and enabling or negative and disabling.

The physical environment around a student can affect degrees of disability. Many enabling environments follow the principle of **universal design**, meaning they are ergonomically designed to be accessible for everyone. An enabling environment provides accessibility to all locations and objects a person may need. Location accessibility supports might include curb cuts, wide doors and aisles, chair lifts, Braille, or auditory descriptions. An enabling environment allows individuals easy access to everyday objects and assistive technology tools. For example, a communication device must always be available to a person who needs it. Sinks, shelves, cabinets, and tables should be at a height which allows for easy access to the materials kept within. Finally, an enabling environment should provide appropriate levels of sensory stimulation. Volume, light, or fragrances may need to be limited for individuals with sensory sensitivities. Conversely, individuals who are visually impaired or hard of hearing may need additional auditory, tactile, or visual cues to support interactions within the environment (e.g., bumps to signal a curb cut to the street and beeping to indicate when it is safe to cross).

When the physical environment is not equipped with appropriate supports, the effect a disability has on functioning is multiplied. Rough terrain, poor weather, steps with no ramps, narrow passageways, inaccessible objects, or over/under stimulation can contribute to a disability resulting in a person being unable to adequately function within the physical environment.

DID YOU KNOW?

The Universal Design for Learning (UDL) was inspired by the architectural concept of universal design. Universal design in the environment means designing areas for easy, equitable, and flexible usage (e.g., curb cuts, automatic doors). UDL relates the same principles for education through lessons which provide multiple means of engagement, representation, and expression to meet the needs of all.

Furthermore, poverty can hinder access to services which could help to mitigate aversive effects related to the impairment. Individuals experiencing poverty may have less access to medical care, both for preventative and treatment purposes. They also may have less access to transportation services, therapies, or assistive technologies which can lessen the impact of the disability. People with disabilities who experience poverty may have more difficulty improving their situation through gainful employment. Disability compensation programs (such as workers' compensation) provide health insurance while many jobs available to people with disabilities may not. The risk of losing health insurance benefits may make it difficult for people with a disability to change their financial situation through employment.

The economic status of the community in which the individual lives can also impact the degree to which a person with disabilities is enabled. Financially well-off communities are more likely to provide environmental and service supports to individuals with disabilities within their community. A community that is doing well is more likely to have newer buildings which are universally designed. Community-provided services such as early intervention, high quality schools, or employment training can help maximize the potential functioning of people with disabilities. Furthermore, a community which is doing well financially will have more job opportunities for individuals with disabilities. Children with disabilities who live in low-income communities may have less access to services than similar children in a community with more resources. The effects of poverty are com-pounded when the child has one or more parent with a disability who also struggles to access services and employment opportunities within the community.

Culture affects the degree to which a disability may impact a person. A person's culture may affect whether an illness leads to a disability. Some cultures participate in more preventative medical treatment or seek health care more frequently or quickly when feeling ill. As a result, those illnesses are more likely to be prevented or cured and less likely to result in disability. Cultural perception of disability also plays a large role in the impact it will have on a person. Some cultures may believe that a disability is the result of witchcraft or a personal transgression. If blame is placed on the person with a disability, supports and services may be less available. Other times, what one culture considers a disability may not be considered as such by others. For example, deafness is not considered a disability within the Deaf community. Often, how a functional limitation is viewed within a culture determines whether that functional limitation is considered a disability.

As much as 14 percent of the population may be affected by some type of disability. The prevalence of disability has a major impact in society. In fact, disability management may cost as much as $3.5 billion each year. Physical, educational, community, and social supports can help lessen the long-term financial costs of a disability. With such a huge economic impact, it is important that as a society we are maximizing supports to ensure individuals with disabilities reach their full potential.

SAMPLE QUESTIONS

19) **Physical environments which are designed to support access for all follow which architectural principle?**

    A.   Universal Design for Learning (UDL)

    B.   Americans with Disabilities Act (ADA)

    C.   Individuals with Disabilities Education Act (IDEA)

    D.   universal design

20) **Which of the following community characteristics is most likely to have an enabling effect on people with disabilities?**

    A.   low-income neighborhood

    B.   early intervention programs

    C.   limited job market

    D.   lack of social support

Answer Key

1) A. Incorrect. General education teachers are responsible for academic instruction in the general education classroom.

   B. Incorrect. School psychologists work with teachers and families to evaluate students, determine eligibility for accommodations, and consult on appropriate supports.

   C. Incorrect. School counselors support the socio-emotional well-being of students.

   D. Correct. Special education teachers work with a team of professionals to provide supports to students with disabilities.

2) **A. Correct.** Psychological testing is done by the school psychologist.

   B. Incorrect. Special education teachers track student progress.

   C. Incorrect. Collaborating with families is a responsibility of the special education teacher.

   D. Incorrect. Special education teachers are responsible for planning behavioral interventions.

3) A. Incorrect. Parent participation requires that parents play a role in decision-making but does not stipulate written notification.

   B. Correct. Procedural safeguards require parents to receive written notification for all meeting dates and educational decisions.

   C. Incorrect. The IEP is the annual written plan laying out supports for students to make educational progress.

   D. Incorrect. Appropriate evaluation refers to the process of evaluating students for qualification of services.

4) A. Incorrect. The Individuals with Disabilities Education Act (IDEA) was first passed in 1990.

   B. Incorrect. The Education for All Handicapped Children Act (EHA, P.L. 94-142) was first passed in 1975.

   C. Incorrect. The Elementary and Secondary Education Act (ESEA) was passed in 1965 but did not guarantee students with disabilities the right to a public education.

   D. Correct. Section 504 of the Rehabilitation Act was passed in 1973 and was the first legislation to guarantee students with disabilities the right to a public education.

5) A. Incorrect. *Endrew F. v. Douglas County* established expectations for FAPE under IDEA.

    B.   **Correct.** *Brown v. Board of Education* prompted an investigation into whether separate school facilities were equal, uncovering needs which Congress tried to address through ESEA.

    C.   Incorrect. *Irving v. Tatro* recognized the provision of catheterization as a related service.

    D.   Incorrect. *Arlington v. Pearl and Theodore Murphy* addressed whether parents had the right to be reimbursed for expert fees.

6)   A.   Incorrect. Related services are not addressed in either case.

    B.   **Correct.** *Diana v. State Board of Education of California* established the requirement for students to be tested in their native language, while *Larry P. v. Riles* resulted in a ruling that IQ tests are culturally biased.

    C.   Incorrect. Although nondiscriminatory evaluation may affect access to the general education curriculum, that was not the primary focus of either case.

    D.   Incorrect. Accommodations may be necessary as part of a nondiscriminatory evaluation process but were not related to the ruling in either case.

7)   A.   Incorrect. Tier 1 instruction is provided to all students.

    B.   **Correct.** A small group intervention three days a week is an appropriate tier 2 support.

    C.   Incorrect. Tier 3 supports are intensive and individualized. A tier 3 support would occur more frequently than three times a week and may be in an individualized setting.

    D.   Incorrect. The RTI process applies to all students, even students already identified as qualifying for special education services.

8)   A.   Incorrect. Parents may request an evaluation under IDEA.

    B.   Incorrect. The school has sixty days to complete an evaluation once a referral is made.

    C.   Incorrect. Parents do not have to contact the special education director to request an evaluation.

    D.   **Correct.** Parents may request an evaluation under IDEA, and the school has sixty days to complete an evaluation once a request is made.

9)   A.   Incorrect. Transition plans are not required until a student is sixteen.

    B.   Incorrect. Not all IEPs include related services.

    C.   **Correct.** The IEP must have a present level of performance for each area of need in order to track progress based on that baseline level.

    D.   Incorrect. Strengths and interests should be included in the student profile, which was listed.

10)   A.   Incorrect. IEP teams must have a school representative.

B.   Incorrect. The school psychologist is not a required team member, though he or she may be included as someone who can interpret evaluations. The general education teacher is missing.

C.   Incorrect. The school psychologist is not a required team member, though he or she may be included as someone who can interpret evaluations. The special education teacher is missing.

D.   Correct. IEP teams must include the parent or guardian, general education teacher, special education teacher, school representative, and an individual who can interpret evaluations.

11) A.   Incorrect. Equitable services are those which a public school district may provide to a student in a private school setting to improve educational progress.

B.   Incorrect. Under IDEA, due process is a legal right of parents when in disagreement with services provided to their child.

C.   Incorrect. Section 504 requires that students with disabilities receive related services, accommodations, and modifications to ensure equal access to education.

D.   Correct. Child Find is a mandate within IDEA that requires school districts to evaluate students who may have a disability.

12) A.   Incorrect. Teachers generally have access to an IEP through school records.

B.   Incorrect. Teachers generally have access to a student's most recent evaluation through school records.

C.   Correct. Many students with multiple disabilities will need a specific plan in place to meet physical and behavioral needs on the first day of school. Needs may change over the summer, so it is important that a teacher is ready to support all needs before the student returns to school.

D.   Incorrect. Assessment of skills may take place once school begins.

13) A.   Incorrect. School psychologists primarily consult on academic and social-emotional needs.

B.   Incorrect. School social workers support social-emotional needs and work as family, school, and community resource liaisons.

C.   Correct. Occupational therapists help support daily living skills, including the fine motor skills needed to fasten clothing.

D.   Incorrect. Physical therapists support gross motor and functional mobility needs.

14) **A.   Correct.** School counselors often work with students on college and job-readiness skills.

B.   Incorrect. School psychologists lead evaluations and consult on academic and social-emotional needs but do not regularly instruct students on job-readiness skills.

C.   Incorrect. Occupational therapists help support daily living skills, including the fine motor skills needed to fasten clothing.

D.   Incorrect. Educational interpreters facilitate communication between educators, students, and families.

15) A.   **Correct.** Bias is the belief of inequality between groups, which often leads to prejudiced action. It may be an unconsciously held belief.

B.   Incorrect. Discrimination is the act of treating a person or group of people unfairly.

C.   Incorrect. Hatred is a negative emotion; bias may be positive or negative.

D.   Incorrect. Harassment is a negative action toward another rather than a belief.

16) A.   Incorrect. Discrimination—the act of treating a person or group unfairly—may play a role in biased instruction and assessment, but it does not describe unequal representation of groups.

B.   **Correct.** Disproportionality is when groups are unequally represented in special education compared to general populations.

C.   Incorrect. Unbiased evaluation helps prevent disproportionality.

D.   Incorrect. Systemic bias explains the processes which lead to the disproportionality, which is the result of those processes.

17) A.   Incorrect. Care for children with disabilities can include large medical and therapy costs.

B.   Incorrect. Many parents worry about the extra time necessary to meet the needs of a student with a disability and the effects it has on other children.

C.   **Correct.** Many families of children with disabilities have less opportunity for social outings.

D.   Incorrect. Child care appropriate for children with functional needs is costly.

18) A.   **Correct.** Unknown cause of the disability may lead to parental feelings of guilt.

B.   Incorrect. Abuse is a contributor to disability in only a small percentage of instances.

C.   Incorrect. Neglect is a contributor to disability in only a small percentage of instances.

D.   Incorrect. Some families report increased cohesion and social support through extended family, religious organizations, disability groups, and community organizations.

19) A.   Incorrect. Universal Design for Learning (UDL) is an educational model for differentiation of instruction.

      B.   Incorrect. While the Americans with Disabilities Act (ADA) has many accessibility requirements, it is not an architectural principle.

      C.   Incorrect. The Individuals with Disabilities Education Act (IDEA) is legislation that provides services for students with disabilities in education.

      D.   **Correct.** The principle of universal design promotes designing spaces in a way that is easily accessible and benefits everyone.

20) A.   Incorrect. Low-income neighborhoods often have less access to community supports.

      B.   **Correct.** Early intervention programs help improve long-term outcomes for individuals with disabilities.

      C.   Incorrect. A limited job market makes it difficult for individuals with disabilities or their family members to find jobs with benefits.

      D.   Incorrect. A lack of social support will make it more difficult for families to overcome some of the stresses associated with disability.

Practice Test

MODULE ONE

Read the question, and then choose the most correct answer.

1

Under IDEA, are parents allowed to act on behalf of their child in court without a lawyer present?

A. Yes, as established by the case of *Arlington Central v. Murphy* (2006).

B. No, as established by the case of *Arlington Central v. Murphy* (2006).

C. Yes, as established by the case of *Winkelman v. Parma City School District* (2007).

D. No, as established by the case of *Winkelman v. Parma City School District* (2007).

2

A school principal is selecting educational intervention software for students at his school who struggle in math. He asks the sales rep about how the software helps students make connections between what they are learning in the software program and how this will help them with their other classwork. Which theory best backs up his question?

A. attribution theory

B. needs theory

C. self-determination theory

D. psychosocial theory

3

Which of the following criteria is necessary in order for a student to qualify as having a learning disability?

A. The team must determine the student has impaired cognitive ability based on an IQ score.

B. The evaluation must include a medical diagnosis.

C. The team must demonstrate that achievement delays are not a result of inadequate instruction.

D. The team must demonstrate that economic factors result in achievement delays.

4

Which of the following is NOT a procedural safeguard provided to parents under IDEA?

A. final say in placement decisions

B. written notice for all meetings and changes in placement

C. access to educational records

D. due process rights

5

Occupational therapy, physical therapy, and speech language therapy are examples of what?

A. mandatory services

B. accommodations

C. modifications

D. related services

6

What level of cognitive functioning is generally considered to indicate an intellectual disability?

A. an IQ score that is one standard deviation above the mean, or higher than 115

B. an IQ score that is equal to the mean, or 100

C. an IQ score that is one standard deviation below the mean, or lower than 85

D. an IQ score that is two standard deviations below the mean, or lower than 70

7

The SAT and ACT are all of the following EXCEPT

A. aptitude tests.

B. norm-referenced assessments.

C. scored based on a norming group.

D. benchmark assessments.

8

Which of the following would be cause for concern regarding atypical socio-emotional development of a kindergartner?

A.   a strong preference for solitary play

B.   needing to be accepted by peers

C.   a desire to play make-believe

D.   crying when falling on the playground

9

Ms. Atoya has a student in her class who is deaf-blind. What strategy might Ms. Atoya use to announce her presence to the student and alert him or her to changes in activity?

A.   touch cues

B.   American Sign Language (ASL)

C.   visual schedule

D.   auditory cues

10

Mr. Miller, a sixth-grade teacher, has a student in his class who is blind. Which professional would be most qualified to recommend accommodations Mr. Miller can use to support this student's learning?

A.   orientation and mobility specialist

B.   audiologist

C.   special education teacher

D.   teacher of the visually impaired (TVI)

11

A norm-referenced assessment that examines results among students with auditory impairments uses a

A.   school average norm.

B.   local norm group.

C.   special norm group.

D.   national norm group.

12

Which assessment tool is best for determining a child's obtainment of developmental milestones throughout the year?

A.   checklist

B.   time sampling

C.   anecdotal records

D.   observational records

13

Liam is a student with an autism spectrum disorder. He speaks clearly and correctly uses complex words and sentence structures, but he has difficulty initiating and sustaining conversations with others. In which area of speech or language does Liam most likely have a deficit?

A.   pragmatics

B.   semantics

C.   phonology

D.   morphology

14

A tenth-grade history teacher proposes the following assignment to her class: "Think about a topic we have or have not studied this year that you want to know more about. Write a research question; then gather sources to answer your research question in a five-page paper." Which instructional method best describes this assignment?

A.   project-based learning

B.   inquiry-based learning

C.   self-paced learning

D.   reflective observation

15

A special education teacher observing an inclusive third-grade classroom uses time-sampling to track the incidences of aggressive behavior exhibited by one of the students. What type of data is she collecting?

A.   anonymous

B.   multidisciplinary

C.   qualitative

D.   quantitative

16

A sixth-grade student is new to a school and receiving special education services for a diagnosed disability. While receiving push-in services in the general education classroom, the student engages in a behavior that is a violation of the school's code of conduct and requires suspension per the student handbook. What is the next step for the school to take?

A.   expelling the student from school

B.   suspending special education services indefinitely

C.   making changes to the IEP

D.   holding a manifestation meeting

17

Mr. Rankin's eighth-grade Science, Technology, Engineering, and Math (STEM) class completes one large project each grading period. This project involves significant planning and research and is in response to a societal problem. Which instructional methodology is Mr. Rankin using?

A.   self-paced learning

B.   experiential learning

C.   project-based learning

D.   inquiry-based learning

18

Who should generally undertake the diagnosis of physical delays or disabilities?

A.   a physician

B.   an educational psychologist

C.   an educational diagnostician

D.   a speech and language pathologist

19

Positive behavior interventions and supports (PBIS) often uses which theoretical framework as part of its programming?

A.   constructivist ideas about learners forming knowledge from their environment

B.   Bruner's stages of cognitive development

C.   extrinsic motivation based on behaviorist ideas of response to praise and consequences

D.   intrinsic motivation based on Bloom's ideas about mastery learning

20

Mrs. Martinez wants her students to learn to do laundry. She decides that she will first teach sorting clothes, then measuring detergent, then the use of the washing machine, then dryer use, and then a lesson on folding clothes. What method is she using to organize learning objectives?

A.   hierarchy of needs

B.   running record

C.   task analysis

D.   concept mapping

21

A general education teacher in an inclusive third-grade classroom wants to use an informal method of assessment to determine her students' mastery of the concept of division as the inverse of multiplication. Which activity would be best?

A. a timed multiplication test

B. exploratory centers where students can multiply and divide with manipulatives

C. asking students if they have any questions after a lecture on multiplication and division

D. having students think of a multiplication problem that relates to the problem $12 \div 3$

22

Mrs. Van Hook's fourth-grade students have an objective to be reading orally at a set rate of words per minute by the end of the year. Mrs. Van Hook decides to give them an oral assessment at midyear to determine their progress. What type of assessment is she giving?

A. benchmark assessment

B. achievement test

C. high-stakes assessment

D. summative assessment

23

When is the best time to contact parents of students with disabilities with whom a teacher has not yet previously worked?

A. a couple weeks into the school year

B. prior to the start of school

C. at parent-teacher conferences

D. when the IEP is due

24

Which of the following describes atypical physical development for a five-year-old?

A. inability to recognize high-frequency sight words

B. inability to feed him- or herself

C. favoring the right hand over the left hand

D. becoming tired quickly when writing long assignments

25

Amaya is a high school junior who was recently in a motor vehicle accident. Prior to the accident, she was a strong student with no educational difficulties. Since the accident, Amaya struggles with emotional regulation and has extreme outbursts when angry or frustrated. Amaya is falling behind in all her classes because she is unable to focus and frequently fails to complete assignments. Under which disability category might Amaya qualify for special education services?

A.   other health impairment

B.   emotional disorder

C.   traumatic brain injury (TBI)

D.   specific learning disability

26

Which of the following questions is related to evaluation decisions that may be made after initial comprehensive evaluation for special education services?

A.   What type of disabilities does this student have?

B.   What IEP goals are most appropriate?

C.   What learning environment is best suited to the needs of the student?

D.   What are the student's greatest strengths?

27

Collin is a fourth-grade student who has received research-based interventions in math for over a year in addition to his core math instruction. He performs on grade level in all other academic areas but continues to fall behind his peers in math. Under which category might Collin qualify for special education services?

A.   specific learning disability

B.   intellectual disability

C.   speech or language impairment

D.   other health impairment

28

A kindergarten teacher is using a reading assessment instrument of her own design in her classroom. Her district is requiring her to switch to a standardized, published instrument. What is the best reason for the switch?

A.   The teacher-created assessment does not yet have validity.

B.   Assessments from educational publishers are always better than teacher-created materials.

C.   The teacher-created assessment will have significant measurement error.

D.   The assessment the teacher is using is likely not criterion-referenced.

29

At the end of a unit on tennis skills, a physical education teacher observes eleventh-grade students playing tennis to assess their knowledge of the rules of play and their use of the forehand and backhand. What type of assessment is the teacher using?

A. formative

B. benchmark

C. authentic

D. play-based

30

What must a multidisciplinary team determine in order to qualify a student for special education services?

A. that the student has a disability

B. that the student is performing at a level below his or her peers

C. that the student needs specially designed instruction

D. that the student has a disability which negatively impacts educational progress

31

Which of the following is indicative of typical socio-emotional development for a four-year-old prekindergartner?

A. dressing up as a wizard and "casting a spell"

B. a large collection of comic books

C. having a person he or she considers to be a "best friend"

D. mainly parallel play

32

Under which disability category do the largest percentage of students receive special education services?

A. other health impairment (OHI)

B. speech or language impairment

C. specific learning disability

D. autism

33

Which type of tests compare students to one another?

A. norm-referenced tests

B. criterion-referenced tests

C. achievement tests

D. standards-based assessments

34

An educational psychologist learns that her new school's version of the Stanford-Binet Intelligence Scales is out-of-date. What is the best reason for her to request that the school purchase the newest version?

A.   The older version will have at least a ten-point IQ variance.

B.   The new version will have more validity.

C.   The new version will yield qualitative data.

D.   The older version will not express results in comparison to others.

35

Which of the following is reflective of Bruner's iconic stage of cognitive development?

A.   A child points to a horse in a field and says "horse."

B.   A child counts out three Cheerios as he counts "one, two, three."

C.   A child is shown a picture of plants and flowers in bloom and says "spring."

D.   A child understands the abstract concept of generosity without any concrete representation.

36

A child with a visual impairment may struggle to understand that actions have consequences. What is this cognitive concept called?

A.   object permanence

B.   classification

C.   causation

D.   conservation

37

In the Supreme Court case of *Hudson v. Rowley* (1982), the parents of Amy Rowley filed suit to force the school to provide Amy with a sign language interpreter. Which side did the court rule in favor of?

A.   The court ruled in favor of the parents, stating that a sign language interpreter was necessary for Amy to be provided with free appropriate public education (FAPE).

B.   The court ruled in favor of the parents, stating that a sign language interpreter was necessary for Amy to access her LRE.

C.   The court ruled in favor of the school district, stating that Amy's potential was maximized without a sign language interpreter.

D.   The court ruled in favor of the school district, stating that Amy was making adequate educational process and FAPE did not necessitate schools to maximize student potential.

38

Which term best describes the range of services and supports provided to educate students with disabilities?

A. LRE

B. procedural safeguards

C. special education

D. general education

39

A behavior intervention plan (BIP) is designed to address which of the following?

A. the most common disruptive behavior

B. a primary disability

C. a target behavior

D. positive behavior

40

Mrs. Martinez notices that one of her prekindergarten students, Joely, has tremendous difficulty playing with the developmentally appropriate classroom toys. Joely seems unable to figure out how to best use them. Within which domain might Joely be developing atypically?

A. socio-emotional

B. cognitive

C. affective

D. psychomotor

41

Which disorder is characterized by periods of mania during which a person feels extremely happy with excessive energy followed by periods of depression?

A. social anxiety disorder

B. schizophrenia

C. major depression

D. bipolar disorder

MODULE TWO

Read the question, and then choose the most correct answer.

1

Which of the following is the most effective classroom management strategy?

A. using rewards and consequences

B. reacting quickly to undesirable behavior

C. using a hierarchy of prompts

D. preventing negative behaviors

2

A prekindergarten teacher notices her students have become very interested in ladybugs that they see one day on the playground. She decides to plan more activities to allow students to explore their interests in bugs. What type of curriculum planning is the teacher using?

A. integrated curriculum

B. project-based curriculum

C. multi-media curriculum

D. emergent curriculum

3

Mrs. Rogers is a Pre–K-3 teacher at a half-day program. Which of the following should she expect when her students are dropped off each morning?

A. They will have trouble separating from their parents for most of the school year.

B. They will have no recognition of school as a familiar place even after significant time has passed.

C. They will need to be reintroduced both to her and the other students each morning as their ability to remember is limited.

D. Most will separate easily from their parents as the year progresses.

4

Which of the following is NOT an alternative to traditional out-of-school suspensions?

A. mindfulness detentions

B. Saturday school

C. emergency removal

D. youth court

5

Progress monitoring during response to intervention should occur

A.   during tier 2 interventions.

B.   during tier 3 interventions.

C.   during tier 1, 2, and 3 interventions.

D.   upon the initial diagnostic assessment.

6

Within which phase of the experiential learning model would taking a field trip fit?

A.   concrete experience

B.   reflective observation

C.   abstract conceptualization

D.   active experimentation

7

During which grade level is direct instruction typically the least effective approach?

A.   high school

B.   middle school

C.   elementary school

D.   preschool

8

Mark, a high school student, and his family are considering enrolling him in an online school where he will work through lessons at his own pace. What type of instructional methodology does this school use?

A.   competency-based instruction

B.   inquiry-based learning

C.   student-directed learning

D.   self-paced learning

9

Which of the following best describes an inclusion setting?

A.   Students work with special education teachers in a resource room.

B.   Students receive services within the general education classroom alongside peers.

C.   Students with functional needs are served in a self-contained separate classroom.

D.   Students with functional needs are included in school-wide activities, such as recess and lunchtime.

10

Dominica is a fourth-grade student in Mr. White's class who just moved to the United States and speaks no English. Mr. White notices that Dominica very seldom speaks though she does appear to be listening and participating in activities when she can. What conclusion can Mr. White draw about Dominica?

A. She is developing atypically in the language domain.

B. She should be screened for a possible intellectual disability.

C. She is going through a silent period during new language acquisition.

D. She needs further encouragement to develop socially and emotionally in order to interact with others.

11

Who would be most likely to deliver specialized instruction in the area of reading to special education students?

A. occupational therapist

B. school psychologist

C. physical therapist

D. special education teacher

12

Mr. Freytag teaches in a self-contained special education classroom with several students with diagnosed emotional disturbances. What is the most important consideration he should account for when organizing classroom supplies?

A. the degree of student mobility to access supplies

B. keeping sharp objects out of the learning environment

C. desk groupings for collaborative learning opportunities

D. encouragement of teacher-student interaction

13

The general education teacher and special education teacher in an inclusive sixth-grade classroom work together to demonstrate how to work with a partner to review key vocabulary for the upcoming social studies test. What can be said about these teachers?

A. They are using parallel teaching and indirect instruction.

B. They are using parallel teaching and direct instruction.

C. They are using team teaching and indirect instruction.

D. They are using team teaching and direct instruction.

14

Which of the following statements about Response to Intervention (RTI) is NOT true?

A.   It is a way to provide universal screening to all students.

B.   It provides for tiered levels of interventions.

C.   It seeks to rule out ineffective teaching as the root of learning issues.

D.   It is a means to determine if a learning disability is present.

15

Which is an example of prior knowledge that a fifth-grade student would need before beginning a unit on making inferences?

A.   an understanding of why people need to make inferences while reading

B.   the ability to spell the word *inference*

C.   an ability to comprehend the literal meaning of the text

D.   basic understanding of phonemes

16

An elementary teacher gives her students three examples of changes: crushing a soda can, slicing a pizza, and baking cookies. She then asks students to determine which are examples of physical changes and which are not. Which instructional method is the teacher using?

A.   direct instruction

B.   examples and non-examples

C.   demonstration

D.   problem-solving

17

Mr. Alvarez is an elementary special education teacher for students with emotional disturbances. Most of his students are integrated into a general education classroom with paraprofessional support. Upon entering the integrated classroom, Mr. Alvarez notices that the general education teacher and paraprofessional are not following the student's behavior plan. What should Mr. Alvarez do to address the situation?

A.   report the situation to his principal

B.   meet with the general education teacher and paraprofessional to review the plan

C.   remove the student from the general education classroom

D.   write an email to the general education teacher to describe what is wrong

18

An elementary school has a dedicated room where students being served by special education services can go to play in a small ball pit, use clay, swing, and even participate in yoga. Which term is best used to describe this room?

A. sensory room

B. playscape

C. indoor physical education platform

D. occupational therapy room

19

Which of the following is characteristic of most Montessori-based classroom environments?

A. a balance of direct instruction and indirect instruction

B. students being given a choice among learning materials

C. homogeneous ability grouping

D. the presence of a special education co-teacher

20

Miss Green has a goal for her third- grade class that they will become self-directed learners by the end of the school year. Which of the following describes a student behavior that would indicate the goal has been met?

A. Students are able to self-regulate their behavior during school assemblies.

B. Students are able to self-assess their own level of understanding of material.

C. Students understand the daily classroom routines without being prompted.

D. Students keep their desks neat and orderly and always have the needed supplies.

21

A fifth-grade social studies teacher is working on a unit regarding supply and demand. She wants to use an integrated approach where students also work to develop reading comprehension skills. Which activity would best meet her goals?

A. asking students to create a product and then create a false scarcity to see what happens

B. having students read and analyze case studies about particular product shortages

C. asking students to define research questions and then independently research the global supply of a certain resource

D. having students brainstorm solutions for the global problem of inequitable distribution of food resources

22

Greg is a student with hemophilia who is in Miss Bishop's kindergarten classroom. What action might Miss Bishop take to promote understanding of the student's health needs by other students in the classroom?

A. give students a book to read about hemophilia

B. send home a letter to all parents about the needs of a student with hemophilia

C. collaborate with Greg's parents to have a class meeting about hemophilia

D. start a social skills group for Greg and a few peers

23

A fourth-grade teacher breaks her students into groups and gives each group a new type of math problem they have never seen before. She asks each group to think of a strategy to use and then solve the problem. What is one possible disadvantage of this approach?

A. Students may not have the necessary motivation to try the new problem.

B. Students may select and use a method which gives them the wrong answer.

C. Students within the group will have different levels of understanding.

D. The teacher will not be able to observe the students' thought processes.

24

Which instructional strategy would be best when introducing a seventh-grade science class to lab safety?

A. discussion

B. indirect instruction

C. demonstration

D. inquiry-based learning

25

A kindergarten class has a spelling center where students use letter magnets to spell out the names of different objects based on a picture card. Johnny has just correctly spelled *dog* with the magnets correctly placed under the picture of the dog. The teacher comes by and says to Johnny, "Let's read this word together: /d/ /o/ /g/. What word did I sound out?" Which of the following concepts is the teacher trying to help Johnny develop?

A. onset and rime

B. phoneme segmentation

C. phoneme blending

D. phoneme deletion

26

Ms. Salter, a reading interventionist, is working one-on-one with one of her first-grade students, Sasha, who needs practice with high-frequency sight words. Sasha is prone to outbursts and frustration, particularly when she feels like she is not performing up to Ms. Salter's expectations. How might Ms. Salter best structure this activity to meet Sasha's learning needs?

A.   use only flashcards of sight words that Sasha already knows to promote overlearning

B.   give Sasha clear extrinsic motivation such as offering candy if she completes the activity successfully

C.   ask Sasha to repeat each sight word multiple times to ensure mastery learning

D.   place only a few flashcards that Sasha does not know into the deck

27

Which of the following is NOT an example of environmental print?

A.   the brand name on a tube of toothpaste

B.   the school name printed on the marquis outside

C.   the words "Writing Center" affixed to the classroom writing center

D.   a page in a new storybook that is read aloud to students for the first time

28

Which reading strategy promotes comprehension by having students supply missing words that have been deleted from a passage?

A.   cloze procedure

B.   determining roots and affixes

C.   connected text

D.   phoneme substitution

29

Mr. Scott, an ESE teacher working with emergent readers, writes the following words on the board:

blimp, roar, grin

He asks his class to make a new word out of each word by removing a part of the existing word. Which of the following concepts is the teacher trying to develop in his students?

A.   the alphabetic principle

B.   phoneme deletion

C.   phoneme substitution

D.   phoneme segmentation

30

Which instructional strategy would demonstrate a haptic approach to teaching onset and rime?

A.   echo reading

B.   morphology

C.   clapping

D.   chunking

31

Lucy, a third grader, is struggling to meet state standards for spelling and has been targeted for intervention. Her teacher wants to try a strategy that will use Lucy's existing phonics knowledge to help improve her spelling. Which of the following phonics activities would help Lucy the most?

A.   phoneme substitution

B.   phoneme segmentation

C.   phoneme blending

D.   phoneme deletion

32

Which of the following concepts should be taught alongside phonics to ensure that students will be able to read quickly and fluently?

A.   print awareness

B.   sight-word recognition

C.   stroke order

D.   spelling

33

When asked what he thinks about a classmate's artwork, a toddler responds, "Mary's good art!" Which of the following phase of oral language development is the toddler likely in?

A.   babbling phase

B.   holophrastic phase

C.   two-word phase

D.   telegraphic phase

34

Which of the following is an activity that will help students develop their procedural knowledge of writing?

A.   handwriting practice

B.   drawing or scribbling to communicate an idea

C.   writing a letter to a friend to tell them about a vacation experience

D.   reading a story aloud

35

Mr. Wyatt is planning an echo reading lesson for his reading group comprised of students who need extra practice with decoding. Which of the following is a good strategy when selecting texts for students?

A. choose texts by relying mostly on qualitative factors of text complexity

B. choose texts at the independent reading level of the majority of the group

C. choose texts that are well below the grade and skill level of the students in the group

D. choose texts at the instructional reading level of the majority of the group

36

Mark, a first-grade student with a diagnosed nonverbal learning disability in an inclusive classroom, is sounding out the word *flat* during small group phonics instruction. He sounds out the word *f-l-a-t*. Which of the following is true about Mark?

A. He is lacking basic knowledge of the alphabetic principle.

B. He needs more practice with affixes.

C. He sounded out each letter individually versus the onset and rime.

D. He has a strong knowledge of consonant blends.

37

Bridgett is beginning second grade in an inclusive classroom, and her IEP specifies that she strive to develop phonemic awareness and become proficient at sounding out CVC words by the end of the year. What can be said about Bridgett?

A. Her IEP should be revised to reflect grade-level expectations.

B. She is an emergent reader.

C. She is a transitional reader.

D. She is a fluent reader.

38

A teacher notices that Eva, one of her kindergarten students, is trying to read the following sentence:

The ball sits.

Eva can sound out the words *ball* and *sits* but is struggling with the word *the*. Which of the following targeted practices should be used with Eva?

A. give her more practice with challenging digraphs like *th*

B. give her more practice with letter-sound correspondence

C. have her practice more silent reading and less oral reading

D. give her practice with high-frequency sight words

39

Mary, a six-year-old student with an intellectual disability and few basic literacy skills, is in an ESE classroom. During the first few weeks of school she does not seem to be able to use many of the learning materials in the classroom, including the books in the literacy center. She frequently picks up a book and holds it upside down while looking at it. Mary's reading instruction should start with which of the following concepts?

A.   phonological awareness

B.   the alphabetic principle

C.   decoding

D.   print awareness

40

Danielle is a third-grade student who recently moved into the school district. Universal screenings show that Danielle is two years behind her peers in reading. Should the school district refer Danielle for evaluation for special education services?

A.   No; schools must show evidence that general education interventions have been attempted.

B.   No; parents must make the referral for evaluation.

C.   Yes; students who are several years behind may be immediately referred.

D.   Yes; all students must be able to pass state reading assessments by third grade under No Child Left Behind (NCLB).

41

Mrs. Roberts targets four of her fifth-grade students for tier 2 intervention to help them meet end-of-year math objectives that they have not met with her ongoing tier 1 interventions. Which instructional strategy would be the best framework in which to conduct these interventions?

A.   small group direct instruction

B.   experiential learning

C.   independent learning

D.   indirect instruction

Answer Key

Module One

1)

A.   Incorrect. The *Arlington Central v. Murphy* (2006) decision excused school districts from paying expert fees acquired by parents who prevailed against them in court.

B.   Incorrect. The *Arlington Central v. Murphy* (2006) decision excused school districts from paying expert fees acquired by parents who prevailed against them in court.

C.   **Correct.** The *Winkelman v. Parma City School District* (2007) decision provided parents with the right to act on behalf of their child in court.

D.   Incorrect. Parents may act on behalf of their child in court.

2)

A.   Incorrect. Attribution theory is concerned with how children ascribe causation to results.

B.   Incorrect. Needs theory is concerned with how all people have the need for achievement, affiliation, and power.

C.   **Correct.** Part of self-determination theory is that learners will be motivated if their desire to connect knowledge is met. This question speaks to the principal's desire for his students to connect their learning.

D.   Incorrect. Psychosocial theory is a theory developed by Erik Erikson consisting of eight stages through which an individual passes over a life span.

3)

A.   Incorrect. A low IQ score is not a component to qualify as having a learning disability.

B.   Incorrect. A medical diagnosis is not necessary to qualify as having a learning disability.

C.   **Correct.** In order for a student to qualify as having a learning disability, the school team must demonstrate the student received research-based intervention prior to referral.

D.   Incorrect. The team must determine that low achievement is not the result of economic factors.

4)

A.   **Correct.** Parents are an equal member of the educational team that makes placement decisions, but they do not have "final say."

B.   Incorrect. Parents must be given written notice of all meetings and placement decisions.

C.   Incorrect. Parents have access to educational records.

D.   Incorrect. Parents may exercise due process rights if they disagree with school decisions.

5)

A.   Incorrect. These services are not mandatory for all students.

B.   Incorrect. Accommodations support access without changing what a student is expected to master.

C.   Incorrect. Modifications are supports which alter learning expectations.

D.   **Correct.** Related services, such as speech therapy and occupational therapy, are supportive services to assist a child with accessing the environment.

6)

A.   Incorrect. An above-average IQ score would indicate above-average intelligence.

B.   Incorrect. An IQ score of 100 indicates average intelligence.

C.   Incorrect. An IQ which is only one standard deviation below the mean is still in the low-average range and would not indicate an intellectual disability.

D.   **Correct.** With the presence of deficits in adaptive functioning, an IQ score of 70 or below, which is two standard deviations below the mean, indicates an intellectual disability.

7)

A.   Incorrect. The SAT and ACT help predict a student's future course of learning, so they are aptitude tests.

B.   Incorrect. The SAT and ACT measure an individual against a group of other test takers.

C.   Incorrect. The SAT and ACT measure an individual against a norming group.

D.   **Correct.** Benchmark tests track student progress on learning objectives. The SAT and ACT are not benchmark tests.

8)

A.   **Correct.** By kindergarten, students should be seeking out social interactions with peers; the other choices all describe typical development.

9)

A.   **Correct.** Touch cues can be used to communicate information, such as a specific person's presence or a signal for an activity, to a student who is deaf-blind.

B.   Incorrect. A student who is deaf-blind may not have the visual acuity to utilize American Sign Language (ASL) effectively.

C.   Incorrect. Without visual cues, a visual schedule may not be the most effective strategy for a student who is deaf-blind.

D.   Incorrect. An auditory cue is likely not the best strategy for a student with hearing loss.

10)

A.   Incorrect. Orientation and mobility specialists provide training and support for students with visual impairments in navigating the environment.

B.   Incorrect. Audiologists specialize in measuring hearing impairment.

C.   Incorrect. While a special education teacher may be able to provide meaningful suggestions, this is not the most qualified professional listed since most special education teachers do not receive specialized training in working with students with visual impairments.

D.   **Correct.** A teacher of the visually impaired (TVI) is uniquely qualified to provide suggestions for learning accommodations for a student who is blind.

11)

A.   Incorrect. School average norms describe a norming group within a school.

B.   Incorrect. A local norm group is generally a district or sometimes state group.

C.   **Correct.** Special norm groups are made up of students with a particular exceptionality or special learning situation.

D.   Incorrect. National norm groups are representative of the entire nation.

12)

A.   Incorrect. A checklist will only capture the event being seen once, not the exact date and its recurrence.

B.   Incorrect. Time sampling generally involves tracking how many times a certain behavior occurs during a given time period and is often used to set up a behavioral intervention. It is not appropriate to track developmental milestones.

C.   Incorrect. While anecdotal records could be helpful to capture particular moments or events, they would not necessarily be the best mechanism with which to track growth over the course of the year.

D.   **Correct.** Observational records often involve tracking when students are attempting, practicing, and mastering a certain milestone. They include notes and dates which are helpful for monitoring progress over the year.

13)

A.   **Correct.** Pragmatics describes Liam's struggles with the appropriate use of language in social situations.

B.   Incorrect. Semantics relates to the understanding of the meaning of words, and it is stated that Liam is able to use complex words correctly.

C.   Incorrect. There is no evidence that Liam struggles with the pattern of language sounds (phonology) since he is able to correctly use complex words and sentences.

D.   Incorrect. If Liam is able to use complex words correctly, he does not struggle in word structure (morphology).

14)

A.   Incorrect. Project-based learning is generally cross-curricular, lasts a long period of time, and is shared with others.

B.   **Correct.** Students are asking a question and then answering it through research, which is inquiry-based learning.

C.   Incorrect. Presumably, this assignment has the same timeline for all students; it is not self-paced learning.

D.   Incorrect. Reflective observation is a stage in experiential learning.

15)

A.   Incorrect. Anonymous data collection would generally involve a survey or some other method in which the participants/respondents are not known.

B. Incorrect. Only one type of data is being collected. It is not across disciplines.

C. Incorrect. Qualitative data does not involve numbers or quantities.

D. **Correct.** Quantitative data involves numbers or quantities. Time-sampling yields a number of instances in which a behavior occurred.

16)

A. Incorrect. The student should not be expelled (particularly for an offense that only requires a suspension) until a manifestation meeting is held to determine if the behavior is a manifestation of the student's disability.

B. Incorrect. Special education services should not be suspended indefinitely and certainly not until the manifestation meeting has occurred.

C. Incorrect. While changes to the IEP may be necessary, this is not the initial step.

D. **Correct.** A manifestation meeting to determine if the behavior was the result of the disability or the consequence of failure to follow the IEP must be held within ten days of a decision to change the child's placement, such as a suspension.

17)

A. Incorrect. Self-paced learning involves students moving through material at their own pace.

B. Incorrect. Experiential learning involves students having authentic learning experiences and then reflecting upon them.

C. **Correct.** Long projects such as the one the STEM class is working on

are reflective of a project-based approach.

D. Incorrect. If the students were themselves formulating the research questions, the project would be inquiry-based learning, but the example does not specify.

18)

A. **Correct.** This is the most qualified person to diagnose physical developmental delays or disabilities.

B. Incorrect. This person can help with diagnoses in other domains, but not physical development.

C. Incorrect. The most qualified person is a physician.

D. Incorrect. This professional can assist with the diagnosis of language delays but not physical developmental delays or disabilities.

19)

A. Incorrect. The PBIS approach involves rewards and praise, not constructing knowledge.

B. Incorrect. Bruner's stages are concerned with cognitive learning in stages; PBIS is primarily concerned with increasing positive behaviors and reducing negative behaviors.

C. **Correct.** PBIS often gives students extrinsic motivation, primarily in the form of rewards and recognition in order to encourage positive behaviors.

D. Incorrect. PBIS uses extrinsic motivation outside of the student and is generally concerned with behavior, not mastery learning.

20)

A. Incorrect. Maslow's hierarchy of needs is a psychological theory describing human needs; it is not a method of organizing learning objectives.

B.   Incorrect. A running record is an assessment technique often used for oral reading.

C.   **Correct.** Task analysis is the process of breaking tasks into smaller steps so that students can meet objectives in increments.

D.   Incorrect. Concept mapping is a strategy of note-taking or using a graphic/visual organizer.

21)

A.   Incorrect. A timed test is a formal assessment.

B.   Incorrect. This is a learning activity, not an assessment.

C.   Incorrect. This checks for understanding in an informal way, but it does not really assess mastery of the concept.

D.   **Correct.** This is a simple, informal way to assess student understanding of this concept.

22)

A.   **Correct.** Benchmark assessments are designed to give information about how students are progressing toward meeting goals to enable success on future summative assessments.

B.   Incorrect. Achievement tests are norm-referenced. This test is not measuring students against one another.

C.   Incorrect. This is only a midyear test, so it would not make any major determinations that a high-stakes assessment would.

D.   Incorrect. An end-of-year test to see if students met this goal would be a summative assessment.

23)

A.   Incorrect. It is better to contact parents before school starts.

B.   **Correct.** Best practice is to contact parents before the start of the school year to initiate the collaboration process and ensure all supports for the student are in place.

C.   Incorrect. Parent-teacher conferences often occur a quarter into the school year; collaboration with parents should take place throughout the school year.

D.   Incorrect. Collaboration with parents should be a frequent and ongoing process, not just when the IEP is due.

24)

A.   Incorrect. This pertains to cognitive development and not physical development.

B.   **Correct.** By age three, children should be able to feed themselves.

C.   Incorrect. Hand dominance is typical at this age.

D.   Incorrect. Fatigue in writing is also typical development.

25)

A.   Incorrect. Because impairments began because of a traumatic event, traumatic brain injury (TBI) would be the appropriate disability category.

B.   Incorrect. Because Amaya's emotional dysregulation began after the accident, TBI would be the appropriate disability category.

C.   **Correct.** Because Amaya's learning issues are directly related to the accident, TBI would be the appropriate disability category.

D.   Incorrect. Because Amaya's learning issues are directly related to the accident, TBI would be the appropriate disability category.

26)

A.   Incorrect. This question is related to a diagnostic decision.

B. Incorrect. This question is related to an IEP decision.

C. Incorrect. This question is related to a placement decision.

D. Correct. This question is related to an evaluation decision by asking for a description of the student's overall strengths and weaknesses.

27)

A. Correct. Based on the information provided, Collin may qualify as a student with a specific learning disability because he has failed to make educational progress at the same rate as peers, even after being provided with research-based interventions.

B. Incorrect. With Collin performing on grade level in other academic areas, there is nothing to suggest that he has an intellectual disability.

C. Incorrect. There is no information provided that suggests the presence of a speech or language impairment.

D. Incorrect. It is unlikely that a health impairment that affects strength, vitality, or alertness would impact only math.

28)

A. Correct. For an assessment instrument to have validity it must be backed by research and evidence. While the teacher's assessment might be equally good, it does not have the same research basis as the district-required assessment.

B. Incorrect. This is not true and would be dependent on what the assessment is designed to measure.

C. Incorrect. Any assessment has measurement error.

D. Incorrect. The teacher-created assessment is likely referenced to the teacher's set criteria.

29)

A. Incorrect. This assessment is at the end of the unit, so it is a summative assessment.

B. Incorrect. This assessment is at the end of the unit, so it is a summative and not benchmark assessment.

C. Correct. The teacher is assessing as students are actually playing the game of tennis. This is an authentic assessment.

D. Incorrect. Play-based assessments are generally used in early childhood to observe overall development.

30)

A. Incorrect. The team must also demonstrate the effects the disability has on educational progress. Students with a disability that is not affecting educational progress may be serviced with a 504 plan.

B. Incorrect. The team must also confirm the student has a disability.

C. Incorrect. The team must also confirm the student has a disability.

D. Correct. The team must demonstrate that a disability exists and that specially designed instruction is needed for educational growth.

31)

A. Correct. Imaginative, make-believe play is very typical and appropriate for a four-year-old prekindergartner.

B. Incorrect. Collecting items like comic books is more typical in elementary school, especially as the child is probably not yet reading.

C. Incorrect. At age four, the child is only just beginning to fully engage in social relationships. A "best friend" is more reflective of later development.

D. Incorrect. Parallel play is more indicative of a toddler. By age four, the typically developing child should be interacting with other children.

32)

A. Incorrect. Other health impairment (OHI) is the third-largest disability category by percentage of students served.

B. Incorrect. Speech or language impairment is the second-largest disability category by percentage of students served.

C. **Correct.** Specific learning disability is the largest disability category by percentage of students served.

D. Incorrect. Autism is the fourth-largest disability category by percentage of students served.

33)

A. **Correct.** Norm-referenced tests compare a student's performance to another group of test takers.

B. Incorrect. Criterion-referenced tests compare a student's performance to a set of objective criteria.

C. Incorrect. Achievement tests are a type of norm-referenced test, but Choice A is the best answer, as it refers to the general category.

D. Incorrect. Standards-based assessments are criterion-referenced tests.

34)

A. Incorrect. This is not necessarily true.

B. **Correct.** The newest version of any assessment instrument should always be used, as it has the largest body of research and is constantly updated using new norming groups. This gives it the most validity.

C. Incorrect. Typically, an intelligence test yields an IQ, which is quantitative data.

D. Incorrect. A norm-referenced test, such as the Stanford-Binet Intelligence Scales, always expresses results in relationship to others. This

is what makes it a norm-referenced test.

35)

A. Incorrect. This would be the concrete stage as the child is identifying the actual horse.

B. Incorrect. Counting aloud in this way is characteristic of the concrete stage.

C. **Correct.** The child is learning the concept of spring through an image, and this describes the iconic stage.

D. Incorrect. Understanding abstract concepts is characteristic of the symbolic, or abstract stage.

36)

A. Incorrect. Object permanence is the understanding that objects exist even when they cannot be seen.

B. Incorrect. Classification is the ability to organize information into categories by common attributes.

C. **Correct.** Causation is the understanding that actions have consequences.

D. Incorrect. Conservation is the understanding that quantity remains the same even if other attributes, such as color or container, change.

37)

A. Incorrect. The court ruled in favor of the school district.

B. Incorrect. The court ruled in favor of the school district.

C. Incorrect. The court ruled in favor of the school district, but the opinion stated that while a sign language interpreter may benefit Amy, the school does not have to prove that it maximized student potential.

D. **Correct.** The court ruled in favor of the school district, stating that while a sign language interpreter may benefit Amy, the school does not have to prove that it maximized student potential.

38)

A.   Incorrect. LRE stands for *least restrictive environment*, the environment where services should be delivered.

B.   Incorrect. Procedural safeguards are guarantees for parents of students with disabilities.

C.   **Correct.** *Special education* describes the specialized supports available to enable students with disabilities to make adequate education progress.

D.   Incorrect. *General education* refers to the education provided to all students.

39)

A.   Incorrect. The most disruptive behaviors are not always the target behavior.

B.   Incorrect. Disabilities are not targeted through a behavior intervention plan (BIP).

C.   **Correct.** Target behaviors are addressed in a BIP.

D.   Incorrect. Positive behavior is not the focus of a BIP.

40)

A.   Incorrect. The term *socio-emotional* pertains to a student's ability to handle emotions and interaction with others.

B.   **Correct.** Joely may be developing atypically in the cognitive domain, which focuses on learning.

C.   Incorrect. The affective domain pertains to emotions and socio-emotional growth.

D.   Incorrect. The psychomotor domain is action-based and pertains to the use of physical tools or machinery.

41)

A.   Incorrect. Social anxiety disorder is primarily characterized by intense fear of social situations.

B.   Incorrect. Schizophrenia is characterized by hallucinations and delusions.

C.   Incorrect. Major depression does not include periods of mania.

D.   **Correct.** Bipolar disorder includes periods of both mania and depression.

MODULE TWO

1)

A. Incorrect. Using rewards and consequences might have some efficacy; however, preventing negative behaviors in the first place is, by far, more effective.

B. Incorrect. Again, reacting quickly to undesirable behavior might be important; however, preventing negative behaviors is the most effective.

C. Incorrect. This is a response to behaviors; it is not preventative, which is the most effective.

D. **Correct.** Preventing negative behaviors in the first place (through predictable routines, clear rules, and so forth) is the best means of classroom management.

2)

A. Incorrect. *Integrated curriculum* refers to covering multiple subjects with one activity or lesson.

B. Incorrect. The teacher has not assigned her students a project.

C. Incorrect. The curriculum is not necessarily multi-media.

D. **Correct.** The teacher is letting student interest guide the curriculum; this describes an emergent curriculum model.

3)

A. Incorrect. Three-year-olds should be comfortable at a familiar place like school. Younger children are more likely to struggle with daily separation from their parents over the course of the school year.

B. Incorrect. Three-year-olds should begin to recognize familiar places.

C. Incorrect. Three-year-olds will not necessarily have memory limitations to this degree.

D. **Correct.** Mrs. Rogers should expect her students to be somewhat nervous at first as school is new, but as time passes, they should view school as a familiar place and separate from their parents with relative ease.

4)

A. Incorrect. Mindfulness detentions typically take place after school and do not involve suspension from the school environment.

B. Incorrect. Saturday school, or having students attend school on a Saturday, is one alternative to suspension.

C. **Correct.** Emergency removal in the case of a particularly serious offense is still a method of traditional suspension because the student is removed from the school environment.

D. Incorrect. Youth court is a popular alternative to suspension that involves students participating in a judicial process with peers and then receiving a consequence for their behavior.

5)

A. Incorrect. Progress monitoring should be ongoing throughout the Response to Intervention (RTI) process.

B. Incorrect. Progress monitoring should be ongoing throughout the RTI process.

C. **Correct.** Progress monitoring should be ongoing throughout the RTI process regardless of which type of tiered intervention is in progress.

D.   Incorrect. An initial diagnostic assessment is not a fixed part of RTI, and it is a one-time assessment, not ongoing progress monitoring.

6)

A.   **Correct.** During the concrete experience phase, learners participate in the actual learning experience.

B.   Incorrect. During the reflective observation phase, students think back on the experience.

C.   Incorrect. During the abstract conceptualization phase, students begin to understand the experience in a broader context.

D.   Incorrect. During the active experimentation phase, students put what they have learned into a real-world context.

7)

A.   Incorrect. Direct instruction can be used effectively in high school.

B.   Incorrect. Direct instruction can be used effectively in middle school.

C.   Incorrect. Direct instruction can be used effectively in elementary school.

D.   **Correct.** Preschool students typically lack the attention span to sit through lessons employing direct instruction; they usually learn best with more indirect, hands-on learning methods.

8)

A.   Incorrect. All that is known about the school is that it is self-paced; one cannot infer that it employs competency-based instruction.

B.   Incorrect. The school does not necessarily have students seek out answers to their questions.

C.   Incorrect. "Student-directed learning" is a broad and somewhat non-specific term.

D.   **Correct.** This school uses a self-paced learning model where students proceed through material at their own speed.

9)

A.   Incorrect. Students work outside the general education classroom with special education teachers during pull-out services.

B.   **Correct.** In an inclusion setting, students receive services alongside peers in the general education classroom.

C.   Incorrect. In substantially separate classes, students with functional needs are served in a self-contained separate classroom.

D.   Incorrect. Students with functional needs should certainly be included in school-wide activities, but the term *inclusion setting* describes core content classes, not activities like recess or lunch.

10)

A.   Incorrect. Dominica's taciturn demeanor would be atypical only if she were a native English speaker.

B.   Incorrect. Since Dominica is participating in activities when she can, she does not seem to have an intellectual disability; furthermore, checking for one should not be the first assumption.

C.   **Correct.** Dominica is in the silent period, a natural and expected part of being immersed in a new language.

D.   Incorrect. She may need more encouragement, but this cannot be gleaned from this scenario or from her silence as it is likely from lack of English proficiency.

11)

A. Incorrect. Occupational therapists address skills for daily living.

B. Incorrect. School psychologists may recommend strategies but do not provide specialized reading instruction.

C. Incorrect. Physical therapists provide therapy for gross motor concerns.

D. Correct. Special education teachers are the primary providers of specialized instruction described in students' IEPs.

12)

A. Incorrect. Student mobility would be a consideration for students with physical disabilities.

B. Correct. It is essential to keep sharp objects out of the learning environment in case of an outburst or crisis situation to ensure the safety of all students.

C. Incorrect. Grouping desks to support collaborative learning is a factor in classroom organization, but it is not the most important one.

D. Incorrect. Student-teacher interaction is certainly a consideration, but it is not as important as student safety.

13)

A. Incorrect. Parallel teaching involves the class being broken up into two groups. Additionally, demonstration is a direct instructional technique.

B. Incorrect. Parallel teaching involves the class being broken up into two groups.

C. Incorrect. They are team teaching, but demonstration is direct instruction.

D. Correct. Team teaching involves both teachers instructing the class together. They are using demonstration which is a means of direct instruction.

14)

A. Incorrect. Response to Intervention (RTI) is a way to provide universal screening to all students.

B. Incorrect. RTI does provide for tiered levels of interventions.

C. Incorrect. RTI does seek to rule out ineffective teaching as the root of learning issues.

D. Correct. While RTI can be used to collect student data, screen, and refer for comprehensive evaluation, it cannot be used to determine the presence of a learning disability.

15)

A. Incorrect. Understanding the importance of inferences is helpful as a means of motivating the student, but it is not prior knowledge that is needed.

B. Incorrect. Being able to spell the word *inference* is not necessarily needed before a student can read a text and make an inference.

C. Correct. Before a student can make an inference, he or she needs the foundational prior knowledge of being able to understand the literal meaning of the text and what is stated explicitly.

D. Incorrect. A basic understanding of phonemes precedes learning to read entirely, which likely has occurred far earlier. This is not the best answer.

16)

A. Incorrect. The teacher is using an indirect instructional technique.

B. Correct. The teacher is using the indirect instructional technique of asking students to determine which are examples of physical changes and which is a non-example.

C. Incorrect. The teacher is not demonstrating the changes.

D.   Incorrect. The students are not solving a problem.

A.   Incorrect. It is important to talk to team members directly to foster collaboration.

B.   **Correct.** Reviewing the behavior plan can clear up any misunderstanding about it and offer the opportunity for problem-solving if there are difficulties implementing the plan in the classroom.

C.   Incorrect. Students should have access to the general education classroom as much as possible.

D.   Incorrect. A collaborative conversation is a more effective strategy to make certain all team members understand the expectations of the behavior plan.

18

A.   **Correct.** Sensory rooms are popular in many schools and allow students to take a break from the classroom in a stimulating environment.

B.   Incorrect. This is not the most accurate term for this room.

C.   Incorrect. This room would not be used for physical education but as part of special education services.

D.   Incorrect. While occupational therapists may help design or staff the room, it is called a sensory room.

19

A.   Incorrect. Montessori environments generally employ very little direct instruction.

B.   **Correct.** Allowing students to choose learning materials is a critical component of most Montessori classrooms.

C.   Incorrect. Montessori classrooms often include students of many different abilities and ages.

D.   Incorrect. Co-teaching is not specific to Montessori classrooms.

A.   Incorrect. This pertains more to meeting behavioral expectations than being self-directed learners.

B.   **Correct.** Students who are self-directed learners are able to self-assess their learning needs and adjust as needed.

C.   Incorrect. This is just good classroom management.

D.   Incorrect. This is more about students meeting classroom expectations than self-directed learning in particular.

21

A.   Incorrect. This approach does not involve reading comprehension.

B.   **Correct.** This strategy would address the teacher's goals for integrated curriculum.

C.   Incorrect. A research project is inquiry-based learning but would not necessarily address the reading comprehension goals.

D.   Incorrect. Brainstorming would be problem solving but would not directly address the reading comprehension issue.

22

A.   Incorrect. It would be ineffective to promote understanding in students at a kindergarten developmental level by providing them a book to read.

B.   Incorrect. Sending a letter home to all parents violates privacy laws if done without the permission of Greg's parents and does not ensure parents will communicate the information in the letter to their children.

C.   **Correct.** An effective strategy to promote understanding of a student's health needs is to collaborate with parents to educate other students about the condition.

D. Incorrect. A social skills group may help Greg develop relationships with a couple of peers but does not necessarily promote understanding by the entire class.

23)

A. Incorrect. One advantage of group work is that less motivated students can sometimes be motivated by peers.

B. Correct. One disadvantage of indirect instruction is that students may solve the problem incorrectly and believe this is the way to solve the problem.

C. Incorrect. Students may vary in their understanding of the material, but that is not the primary disadvantage with this approach.

D. Incorrect. This approach would actually provide a good way for the teacher to observe the thought process as students talk about ways to solve the problem.

24)

A. Incorrect. When matters of safety are involved, direct instruction techniques are best.

B. Incorrect. When matters of safety are involved, direct instruction techniques are best.

C. Correct. Demonstration allows the teacher to avoid confusion and ensure safety.

D. Incorrect. When matters of safety are involved, direct instruction techniques are best.

25)

A. Incorrect. If the teacher was using this strategy, she would have broken the word into its onset *d* and its rime *og*.

B. Incorrect. This would involve Johnny sounding out the word.

C. Correct. The teacher said the individual letter sounds and asked Johnny to blend them into a word.

D. Incorrect. In phoneme deletion, one sound would be deleted to form a new word.

26)

A. Incorrect. This will not help Sasha practice the words she does not know and needs to learn.

B. Incorrect. This type of motivation likely cannot be kept up over the long term and for all activities that Sasha finds challenging. Further, whether Sasha completes the activity "successfully" is subject to different interpretations.

C. Incorrect. This does not address Sasha's motivation and possible frustration.

D. Correct. This will help build Sasha's confidence and motivation as she sees that she knows many of the words.

27)

A. Incorrect. Environmental print is any print in a student's natural environment.

B. Incorrect. The school marquis is in a student's everyday environment.

C. Incorrect. This is in the everyday environment of the classroom.

D. Correct. This is a new exposure to print, not one found in the student's everyday environment.

28)

A. Correct. In cloze procedures, students supply words that have been deleted from a passage.

B. Incorrect. Determining roots and affixes helps students improve their vocabulary and spelling.

C. Incorrect. Connected texts are simple, multiple words connected.

D. Incorrect. Phoneme substitution involves switching sounds in words to make new words (for example, *hat*, *splat*, *rat*, and so forth).

29)

A. Incorrect. The alphabetic principle has to do with letter and sound knowledge.

B. Correct. His students will delete a sound from each word to make a new word.

C. Incorrect. Phoneme substitution would involve substituting one sound for another.

D. Incorrect. Phoneme segmentation involves sounding out words.

30)

A. Incorrect. This would be an auditory approach where the student would repeat onsets and rimes after they are read by the teacher.

B. Incorrect. Morphology would help students break words up into component pieces such as onsets and rimes, but this is not necessarily a multisensory approach.

C. Correct. Having students clap out the onset and rime of a word would bring haptics, or touch, into a lesson on onset and rime.

D. Incorrect. While chunking helps break words into component parts, it does not necessarily involve haptics.

31)

A. Incorrect. This would spell a new word entirely as Lucy substituted one sound for another.

B. **Correct.** This is the process of sounding out a word, which might help Lucy recall and write the letter that corresponds to a given sound.

C. Incorrect. This involves Lucy making a word out of given sounds, which likely would not help with third-grade spelling.

D. Incorrect. This would make a new word entirely as Lucy deletes a sound from a word.

32)

A. Incorrect. This is important but should be mastered before phonics instruction.

B. Correct. Memorizing sight words through multiple exposures will help students read more quickly and fluently.

C. Incorrect. This is related to writing, not reading.

D. Incorrect. This will not help with reading rate and fluency.

33)

A. Incorrect. This is beyond babbling.

B. Incorrect. Holophrastic speech is a single word.

C. Incorrect. The sentence has three words.

D. Correct. This sentence lacks the preposition *at* and is indicative of the telegraphic phase.

34)

A. Correct. Procedural knowledge involves how to write letters, words, and so on.

B. Incorrect. This is part of conceptual knowledge or understanding the purpose of writing.

C. Incorrect. This is about generative knowledge or being able to generate writing to accomplish a purpose.

D. Incorrect. This is a way to share or publish writing with others.

35)

A. Incorrect. Teachers should look at both qualitative and quantitative factors.

B. Incorrect. These texts would be most appropriate for more independent practice, not necessarily echo reading.

C. Incorrect. Texts should be appropriate for the skill level of the group, not well below it.

D. **Correct.** This will ensure that students can read these texts with 90 percent accuracy, a good level of proficiency for instruction such as echo reading.

36)

A. Incorrect. He knows the individual sound of each letter, so he understands the alphabetic principle.

B. Incorrect. This word does not have a prefix or suffix.

C. **Correct.** He did not sound out the word into onset *fl* and rime *at*.

D. Incorrect. He sounded the blend *fl* as two individual sounds *f-l*, so he does not seem to have a strong familiarity with it.

37)

A. Incorrect. There is no way to know based on this scenario if Bridgett's IEP should be revised. Since this plan is specific to her and since it is the beginning of the school year, we can assume that it appropriately reflects realistic goals.

B. **Correct.** Emergent readers are still developing basic skills such as phonemic awareness and letter-sound correspondence to help tackle other reading tasks ahead.

C. Incorrect. Transitional readers generally have a solid base of decoding strategies, although they may still need scaffolding with difficult texts. This does not seem to describe Bridgett.

D. Incorrect. Bridgett is not yet reading fluently; she is still building the foundations skills she needs to read fluently.

38)

A. Incorrect. *The* is a high-frequency sight word and must be memorized.

B. Incorrect. Eva has solid letter-sound correspondence, as she is able to sound out the words *ball* and *sits*.

C. Incorrect. This will not help her read the word *the*.

D. **Correct.** *The* is a high-frequency sight word and must be memorized versus sounded out.

39)

A. Incorrect. Mary is not ready for phonological awareness just yet.

B. Incorrect. Mary needs to first understand the purpose of books before she can work on letters and the sounds they make.

C. Incorrect. Mary is not ready to decode words. She must first understand concepts of print and how books are used to communicate ideas.

D. **Correct.** Mary needs to first understand the basics of reading: that we read books from left to right, top to bottom, and so on. She is not ready for instruction on the other topics.

40)

A. **Correct.** Schools must determine that a student's lack of progress is not due to lack of appropriate instruction.

B.   Incorrect. Schools may refer students for evaluation.

C.   Incorrect. Schools must have additional data to support a referral.

D.   Incorrect. Schools must not refer based on the need to pass state assessments.

41)

A.   **Correct.** Direct instruction in small groups is generally the most effective method in which to conduct tier 2 interventions.

B.   Incorrect. Experiential learning is not a recommended method for interventions.

C.   Incorrect. These students likely need significant teacher guidance to reteach concepts.

D.   Incorrect. Direct instruction in small groups is generally the most effective method in which to conduct tier 2 interventions.

Follow the link below to take your second PECT practice test:

www.cirrustestprep.com/pect-special-education-online-resources